FROM
FATHER
TO
SON

LITERARY CURRENTS IN BIBLICAL INTERPRETATION

EDITORS

Danna Nolan Fewell
Perkins School of Theology,
Southern Methodist University, Dallas TX
David M. Gunn
Columbia Theological Seminary, Decatur GA

EDITORIAL ADVISORY BOARD

Jack Dean Kingsbury
Union Theological Seminary in Virginia, Richmond VA
Peter D. Miscall
St Thomas Seminary, Denver CO
Gary A. Phillips
College of the Holy Cross, Worcester MA
Regina M. Schwartz
Department of English, Duke University, Durham NC
Mary Ann Tolbert
The Divinity School, Vanderbilt University, Nashville TN

FROM
FATHER
TO
SON

---

kinship,
conflict,
and
continuity
in
genesis

DEVORA STEINMETZ

•

WESTMINSTER/JOHN KNOX PRESS
Louisville, Kentucky

FROM FATHER TO SON:
KINSHIP, CONFLICT, AND CONTINUITY IN GENESIS

© 1991 Devora Steinmetz

First edition

Published by Westminster/John Knox Press,
Louisville, Kentucky

PRINTED IN THE UNITED STATES OF AMERICA
2 4 6 8 9 7 5 3 1

Library of Congress Cataloging-in-Publication Data

Steinmetz, Devora, 1959-
  From Father to Son : kinship, conflict, and continuity in Genesis /
Devora Steinmetz. — 1st ed.
      p.   cm. — (Literary currents in biblical interpretation)
  Includes bibliographical references and indexes.
  ISBN 0-664-25116-1

  1. Bible. O.T. Genesis—Criticism, interpretation, etc. 2. Kinship in
the Bible. 3. Fathers in the Bible. 4. Fathers and sons in literature. I.
Title. II. Series.
BS1238.K56S74 1991
222′.1106—dc20   91-4483

For David—

> I have a young conception in my brain;
> Be you my time to bring it to some shape.

—William Shakespeare
Troilus and Cressida

CONTENTS

SERIES
PREFACE

New currents in biblical interpretation are emerging. Questions about origins—authors, intentions, settings—and stages of composition are giving way to questions about the literary qualities of the Bible, the play of its language, the coherence of its final form, and the relations between text and readers.

Such literary criticism is rapidly acquiring sophistication as it learns from major developments in secular critical theory, especially in understanding the instability of language and the key role of readers in the production of meaning. Biblical critics are being called to recognize that a plurality of readings is an inevitable and legitimate consequence of the interpretive process. By the same token, interpreters are being challenged to take responsibility for the theological, social, and ethical implications of their readings.

Biblical interpretation is changing on the practical as well as the theoretical level. More readers, both inside and outside the academic guild, are discovering that the Bible in literary perspective can powerfully engage people's lives. Communities of faith where the Bible is foundational may find that literary criticism can make the Scripture accessible in a way that historical criticism seems unable to do.

Within these changes lie exciting opportunities for all who seek contemporary meaning in the ancient texts. The goal of the series is to encourage such change and such search, to breach the confines of traditional biblical criticism, and to open channels for new currents of interpretation.

—THE EDITORS

PREFACE

This book is the culmination of nine years of writing and re-flection, and I am grateful to many for their help during this time. The following provided financial support at various stages of the preparation of this work: the Associate Alumnae of Barnard College Fellowship, the Lane Cooper Fellowship and the Elliot K. V. Dobbie Fund of Columbia University, and the Maxwell Abbell Fund of the Jewish Theological Seminary of America. James Earl, Richard Sacks, George Landes, Edward Greenstein, and Ruth Fagen have contributed to this work in various ways. I thank them all for their generosity. I am indebted as well to my many teachers and students who have enriched my understanding of the biblical text and of literature in general.

An earlier version of chapters 1-4 was included in my doctoral dissertation as part of a comparative study of kinship and succession in early texts (Columbia University, 1984). That study included as well an analysis of kinship in the Old Irish *Táin Bo Cuailnge*. Comparative study highlights the degree to which a symbolic understanding of kinship reveals the self-perception and world-view of ancient cultures; the interested reader might wish to consult the original work for added perspective. The present work focuses on the book of Genesis in an attempt to demonstrate more fully the interpretive value for the biblical narrative of this approach to kinship.

A version of Chapter One appeared in *Annals of Scholarship* 3 (1985); I am grateful to the editors for permission to include a revision of this material.

This book is dedicated to my husband, David Silber, who has been for many years my teacher, colleague, and friend. His own work on biblical narrative, doubtless, has motivated many of my own thoughts, and the countless discussions between us

9

have made it impossible at times to distinguish between his ideas and mine. I am fortunate to have a partner in life with whom to share the excitement of discovery.

Finally, I would like to mention our children, Akiva, Beruria, and Abaye, who fill our days with their wonder, joy, and unquenchable desire to know.

—DEVORA STEINMETZ

May 29, 1990
Erev Shavuot, 5750
Zeman Matan Toratenu

1

CONFLICT
AND
CONTINUITY

G enesis contains the story of the beginnings of the nation of
Israel in the families of Abraham, Isaac, and Jacob. It is a
story of almost constant struggle—to survive, to retain a unique
identity, and to pass on that identity and mission to the next
generation. It is a story about the struggle to create a family
whose members can live together and share a common destiny,
a family which can be the foundation of the future nation.

The threat to survival and continuity in Genesis comes not
so much from without, but from within the patriarchal family. In
each generation, the family is threatened by the twin dangers of
conflict between members and loss of identity: either the family
members remain together and threaten to destroy one another,
or they separate and are in danger of being lost to the family's
special mission.

In order to understand the patriarchal narrative and its
place as the introduction to the history of the nation, this study
will focus on conflict and attempts at resolution of conflict within
the patriarchal family. But before moving to analyses of the
narrative, we must first try to grasp the nature of family relationships, and especially of conflict between father and son and
between brothers, in narratives such as Genesis. I shall propose
a particular symbolic understanding of kinship which I believe is
applicable to the early literature of many different societies, but
which I will develop here as a tool for understanding the book

of Genesis. First, though, I will survey a number of other approaches to kinship, particularly from the fields of psychology and anthropology, each of which has something to contribute to an understanding of family narratives, and especially of the relationship between kinship and the emergence of society.

Father-son conflict

The reference point for most inquiry into the nature and origin of family conflict, and so a sensible point at which to begin our survey, is Freud's description of the Oedipus complex. Freud's structure is triangular; while the principal characters are father and son, the mother is crucial as the motivation for rivalry. The mother is the object of the boy's sexual desire, and the father becomes an obstacle to his son's wishes. Fearing his father's power and the consequences of taking a forbidden object, the son identifies with his father rather than overthrowing him. The identification with the father, though, precedes this stage; it came about simultaneously with, or even before, the desire for the mother. But now the two drives come together, the identification with the father solving the problem caused by the desire for the mother, while the desire for the mother strengthens the primary identification with the father.

This formulation of the Oedipus complex appeared in 1923 in *The Ego and the Id*, and is probably the most familiar version.[1] But two years earlier, in *Group Psychology and the Analysis of the Ego*, Freud had suggested a somewhat different mechanism.[2] There he stresses the son's identification with his father.[3] The desire for the mother comes about independently, but the two drives eventually merge, and the identification with the father further motivates the boy to take his mother.

These two formulations of the Oedipus complex differ in the role they assign to the boy's identification with his father. In the earlier version, the identification aggravates the boy's desire for his mother; in the later version it resolves the crisis brought about by that desire. But, in both, the identification and desire are two separate drives and, most importantly, both versions stress the ambivalence of the son's identification with his father. Thus the difference between the two versions is simply a matter of emphasis. The boy's identification with his father can be a wish to be just like him or a wish to replace him. With respect to objects which his father possesses exclusively, such as the mother, the wish to be like his father is, in fact, the wish to replace him, and only through his father's power to set limits on the son does the wish to replace his father fade into the wish to be like him.[4] The boy's identification with his father, then, can be either tender or hostile, but his relationship with his mother, according to Freud, is completely affectionate.[5]

What is a father?

Freud formulated the Oedipus complex as a psychoanalytic model, but anthropologists soon adopted it and, confronted by a variety of family and social structures, began asking questions. The basic one, whether the Oedipus complex is universal or particular to a certain type of society, really depends on a definition—what is a father? What understanding of paternity and the role of fatherhood is necessary in order for the Oedipus complex to occur? Father can be understood to be a biological father, or the mother's husband, or any other man, perhaps the mother's brother, who is designated as the child's foster-father. And the role of father might be to nurture, or to exercise authority, or to transmit the familial or social heritage to the child. In the Western world these definitions of a father and his role coincided for the most part, but, in many of the non-Western societies studied by anthropologists, the roles were divided among different people, and different people could be considered a child's father, depending on the definition of fatherhood.

In the 1920s, Bronislaw Malinowski began to publish his studies of the Trobriand Islanders. The society he described is matrilineal. Boys are members of their mother's clan; they inherit the possessions of their mother's brother and learn to call their uncle's village their own.[6] Most strikingly, Malinowski found that the natives were ignorant of physiological paternity. Acknowledging no correlation between intercourse and conception, they strenuously deny any biological relationship between father and child. A woman becomes pregnant when a spirit-child is deposited on her head through the agency of another spirit, or *baloma*, and enters her womb.[7] Nevertheless, the Trobrianders are adamant about the physical similarity of son to father—so much so, in fact, that it is a great insult to tell a man that he resembles one of his maternal kinsmen, especially his brother. Even when a son looks nothing like his father, the natives affirm the resemblance and, after the father's death, friends and kinsmen will visit the son and take comfort in seeing the dead man's face in his son's.

Trobrianders offer two explanations for this similarity: the father constantly lies at the mother's side, thus molding the child's features, and he gives the young child food to eat, helping the boy to become like his father.[8] These are not merely nonbiological rationalizations of the resemblance between father and son; rather, the two explanations comprise the sociological definition of fatherhood—father is the mother's husband and the man who nurtures the son. In fact, if the mother is unmarried, the child is considered to be fatherless, a terrible misfortune because "there is no man to take it in his arms," "to nurse and hug" it.[9] Yet, while the father nurtures his child, it is the maternal uncle who exercises authority and, while the father may give his son the rights of citizenship and the use of goods during his lifetime, it is his sister's son who will inherit him after death. Likewise, the child may be taunted as a stranger in his father's village, but is welcome in his mother's brother's, and, according to the rules of exogamy, a child may marry his father's kin but not his mother's.[10]

All this led Malinowski to question the universality of the Oedipus complex. Freud's formulation, it seemed to him, was based on a certain type of social structure, a patrilineal system in which the father exercises absolute authority over his family. One could expect that, with varying degrees of paternal power and different methods of determining descent, conflicts within the family would take different forms as well.[11] Malinowski, for the most part, accepted the existence of the Oedipus complex in Western societies, in which the father is both feared and admired by his son, but he postulated a very different complex for the Trobriand society which he had studied. The role of the Western father is split in the Trobriands between the mother's

husband and her brother. The father nurtures his child, traditionally as compensation for his wife's sexual services, while the
uncle exercises authority over his nephew, is held up to the
young boy as a model, and bequeaths to the child his econom-
ic, spiritual, and social heritage.[12] Furthermore, the Trobriander boy is not separated from his mother in infancy; his childhood is free from sexual repression, as long as his interest lies
outside his maternal clan.[13] The Trobriand complex, then,
consists of an ambivalent attitude toward the mother's brother,
the boy's authority figure, and sexual desire for the sister, his
closest forbidden relative. Malinowski summarizes: "we might
say that in the Oedipus complex there is the repressed desire to
kill the father and marry the mother, while in the matrilineal
society of the Trobriands the wish is to marry the sister and to
kill the maternal uncle."[14]

Besides the identification of the characters involved in the
conflict, which soon became an issue for much debate, Malinowski's formulation differs from Freud's in two significant
ways. While Freud had taken into account the child's identification with his father as well as the father's authority over the
child, the element which he saw as bringing about the crisis in
the relationship, and which has come to characterize the Freudian approach, is the son's sexual desire for the mother. For
Malinowski, the crucial element is authority; the authority of the
Western father over his son and of the Trobriand uncle over his
nephew engenders a repressed resentment in the child.

But the elimination of sexual rivalry as the motivation for
conflict leads to a further distinction between the two formulations. Malinowski's complex still includes a repressed sexual
desire, but this element is completely divorced from the ambivalent identification with the authority figure. In fact, the taboo
which prohibits members of the mother's clan, and most strong-
ly the sister, is introduced to the boy during his infancy,[15]
years before the child learns to imitate and obey his uncle. And
the two relationships never merge, as they do for Freud, because the object of the boy's desire does not belong to his
uncle; the girl would actually be forbidden to her uncle by the
same rules of exogamy which forbid her to her brother.[16]

Repression and displacement

Malinowski's theory, then, represented far more than a shifting of the characters involved in Freud's complex. His formulation had a wholly new structure and was based on an entirely different understanding of the son's relationship with his father. In 1924, even before Malinowski had published a full length study of his findings, psychoanalysis was ready with a response to his early observations.

Ernest Jones, in a paper read before the British Psycho-Analytical Society, acknowledged the significance of Malinowski's work but analyzed the complex formed under a system of mother-right as a savage accomodation to the Oedipus complex, which patriarchal societies have learned to live with.[17] Jones suggests that the Trobrianders repress knowledge of physiological paternity in order "to deflect the hatred toward his father felt by the growing boy," a result also achieved through the institution of mother-right.[18] Instead of acknowledging the biological relationship between father and son, the Trobrianders disguise the father in the form of a further removed ancestral spirit which impregnates the mother as a *baloma*.[19] This repression frees the father to behave lovingly toward the child and allows the child to regard his father without ambivalence. But the "obsessional ambivalence of savages" remains, and the society also needs a figure on whom to displace the hostility felt toward the father.[20] The mother's brother is the most natural figure, because he is the object of the mother's incestuous desire and so, like the father, is a rival of the son.

The significance of the unconscious incestuous desire in the Trobriands, Jones continues, where it becomes the determining factor for the specific displacement of the Oedipus complex onto the mother's brother, leads to the extreme taboo between brother and sister. And, in turn, desire for the sister is really a displacement of the boy's attachment to his mother. Jones, then, agrees with Malinowski's description of the matrilineal complex as the desire "to marry the sister and to kill the maternal uncle," but he finds its origin in the repression of the "primordial" complex which involves the father, mother, and son.[21] He acknowledges the shift of characters, but retains the structure of Freud's complex as well as Freud's understanding of the nature of the boy's relationship with his father.

Conflict and culture

It is the notion of a "primordial" complex which sums up the controversy between the psychoanalytic and anthropological approaches in general. While Jones sees the psychological complex as fundamental and universal and social structures as specific adaptations to the complex, Malinowski assumes that social structures arise as a result of other causes—in the Trobriands, for example, true ignorance of physiological paternity—and that the family complex is variable and depends on the social structure within which it arises.[22]

The different approaches parallel the different aspects of the Oedipus complex which each scholar emphasizes. Jones has no qualms about the primacy of the Oedipus complex over social structure because, for him, the complex arises from an incest drive, from a mother-attachment which precedes the formation of a society.[23] But Malinowski focuses on the father-son conflict within the Oedipus complex, a conflict which arises from the father's position of authority, and for him that complex can only develop within a society which has a patriarchal structure. In fact, it is the development of human culture which first made some kind of authority necessary. The loving and nurturing role of fatherhood is natural, according to Malinowski, but culture requires that someone pass down the tribal heritage from one generation to the next and see to it that law is enforced and that order is imposed among the members of the society. In patriarchal societies this role devolved upon the father, leading to the ambivalent Oedipal relationship, but in matrilineal societies such as the Trobriander, the uncle takes on the hostile role, and the father remains a loving nurturer.[24]

Malinowski was not the first anthropologist who investigated societies which do not acknowledge physiological paternity; as early as 1903, W. E. Roth had published a report showing that the Tully River Blacks do not recognize the father's role in conception.[25] But, since Malinowski used his results to challenge the universality of the Oedipus complex, his study became the focus of continued controversy. Debate erupted with full force in the late 1960s, largely in response to Edmund Leach's contention that the natives studied by anthropologists such as Roth and Malinowski are not really ignorant of physiological paternity. Their explanations of conception and the consequent sociological nature of paternity are simply myths which emphasize the marriage bond as the block with which society is built, and these myths coexist with unarticulated recognition of biological fatherhood.[26] Leach's 1966 address provoked an attack by Melford Spiro, Leach counter-attacked, and a series of articles and notes began appearing in rapid succession, complete with accusations on all sides of ethnocentric bias, ranging from cultural snobbery to racism.[27]

Kinship as cultural myth

But, while battle raged on about what the natives really know, a quiet consensus began to form concerning how to understand what the natives say. Whether physiological paternity is unknown, repressed, or recognized came to be seen as only one part of a larger issue. Leach, through an entirely different formulation, was continuing what Jones had begun—to look at the natives' theories of conception not simply as explanations of what is not understood, but as expressions of cultural concerns, whether psychological or sociological. Similarly, H. A. Powell distinguished between "indigenous clinical knowledge" and "formal dogma," and R. M. W. Dixon identified a "basic level of belief" and a "mystic level of belief."[28] Even Phyllis Kaberry, who maintained that the natives actually are ignorant of physiological paternity, discussed the mythic significance of their conception beliefs.[29] And Spiro ultimately came to much the same conclusion that Jones had reached, that the Trobrianders' ignorance of physiological paternity is really repressed knowledge, and their conception beliefs are an attempt to deflect Oedipal hostility.[30]

While Spiro does not believe, with Jones, that the matrilineal social structure actually arose to serve the purpose of displacement,[31] he carefully examines Trobriand society and practices to determine how the natives protect themselves against the dangers of the Oedipus complex. Focusing on the "complementary" or "Laius" complex, in which the father feels hostility toward his son, as well as on the filial complex, Spiro finds that the Trobrianders separate the father and son at particularly dangerous moments. Expectant fathers are separated from their wives by the eighth month of pregnancy, and new fathers may not sleep with their wives and children for a long period after delivery. When a boy reaches puberty and, now sexually mature, poses a greater threat to his father, he leaves home and lives with his maternal uncle. Such practices, Spiro suggests, serve the same purpose as the painful initiation rites of other societies, but in a different way. Initiation rites threaten the boys and inhibit their incestuous feelings toward their mothers and aggressive ones toward their fathers, while allowing a limited expression of paternal hostility. Father-absence and child-extrusion protect the child from the hostile father and allow him to find other attachments toward which to direct his desire and hostility.[32]

For Spiro, then, Malinowski's work provides no basis for questioning the universality of the Oedipus complex. Hostility between father and son arises primarily out of competition for the mother and, as long as the boy is attached to the mother, the Freudian triangle will apply. Spiro suggests that, if a society existed in which the child did not live with his biological parents, the attachment might well be to the child's surrogate mother and the aggression toward her consort. It is the sexual relationship of the parents or substitutes, not their biological or authoritative relationship to the child, which leads to the conflict. But Malinowski's boy-sister-maternal uncle complex does not form a triangle through such a sexual relationship; it consists, rather, of two separate diadic complexes and accounts for neither the mother-attachment nor for the relationship between the respective objects of desire and aggression. The shape of the Oedipus complex, Spiro maintains, must be universal, although everything about it, even the characters, may be variable.[33] Consequences of the complex are certainly variable, and they find expression, according to Spiro, in social practices, rituals, and myths.[34]

In recent years, many scholars have come to this fruitful middle ground of 'variable universality.' Taking for granted, like Spiro, that certain very basic impulses and relationships are universal, they interest themselves in the way different cultures express these fundamentals and in the reasons for this variability. Robert A. Paul, for example, advocates "a 'generative' view of culture," in which a single, universal "deep structural level" is transformed into infinite, variable "structures" through limited, definable "symbolic operations."[35] Analysis should focus on the process of transformation in order both to explain the manifest symbols and to reveal the underlying structure. Without attempting to explain fully the nature of the Oedipus complex, Paul chooses the element of filicide for an illustration of his method. Like the son, the father is pulled in two different directions and, again like the son, the father must resolve the conflict between his two tendencies—to kill his son and to protect him.

The resolution of the conflict can only take place on the symbolic level, and Paul examines the operations by which these different manifest structures are produced in the stories of Oedipus, Isaac, and Christ. Resolution of the contradiction in the Oedipus story is achieved through a "doubling"—what Jones would call "decomposition"—of the father into a biological father, Laius, and a foster-father, Polybus. The Old Testament story allows Abraham both an attempt on his son's life and an opportunity to save his son and also introduces an animal substitute which Abraham kills in place of Isaac. The New Testament story is more elaborate because of the dual nature of Christ—man and God, son and father, for example— and requires a more complex resolution. In his early life, Jesus has two surrogate fathers: Herod, who tries to kill him, and Joseph, who protects him. At the Crucifixion, God is the father who both kills and, with the Resurrection, preserves, while Pontius Pilate complements God as a father figure who neither kills nor preserves. The story of Christ, then, combines the symbolic resolutions which the other two stories manifest separately. There is both a decomposition of the father into murderer and preserver, as in the Oedipus story, and a double enactment of murder and preservation, as in the Old Testament story, on the part of a father who is himself doubled by another, completely passive figure.[36]

Paul's model for symbolic interpretation is articulate and useful and his analysis of myths is insightful, but his conclusions are not fully satisfying. Paul distinguishes the Crucifixion from other myths by, and attributes its success to, its "formal perfection,"[37] but he does not go beyond that. His interest in the processes which generate infinite symbolic resolutions to a universal problem does not move him to examine the significance of the different transformations and symbols. His acknowledgement of "the richness, intricacy, depth, and individuality of human experience" within universal "human concerns" falls flat if the variability is merely formal. We are left wondering what the different symbolic resolutions of universal conflicts reveal about the cultures which produced them. And we are left to determine, as Paul acknowledges, the precise nature of these universal conflicts.

Violence and the loss of social distinctions

One explanation of conflict which, on the surface, seems very different from the Freudian model has been proposed by René Girard, in *Violence and the Sacred*. Freud's complex, we have seen, is triangular; conflict with the father arises through competition for the mother. In the Oedipus myth patricide is secondary to incest. But for Girard, violence is the primary force. Violence erupts when distinctions within the social or family structure are lost. The more closely two individuals resemble each other, the more each perceives the other as a threat, and the more likely they will come into conflict. Twins, therefore, are the most natural enemies, according to Girard, but any nondifferentiation will lead to violence.[38] Incest is just another manifestation of this leveling of differences. Incest is taboo, not because it leads to violent competition,[39] but because it is a part of the social crisis upon which violence feeds.[40]

Desire does have a place in Girard's model of conflict, but not a primary place. It is not "object desire," such as Freud's mother-cathexis, which leads to rivalry; rather, rivalry leads to what Girard calls "mimetic desire." One person desires an object simply because his rival, the person to whom he is closest and whom he takes as a model, desires that object.[41] Brothers so often are enemies in myth, ritual, and tragedy because little differentiates between them; once they stand in a relationship of rivalry, their desires converge on the same object, and this object becomes the focus of their violent rivalry.[42] Girard's model, then, is also triangular, but the relationship between the three elements differs from the Oedipal relationship. Girard postulates "the model, the disciple, and the object that is disputed by both because the model's desire has made the object desirable to the disciple."[43] When the model becomes also the obstacle to his disciple's desire, conflict emerges.

As Girard notes, his formulation comes very close to Freud's early description of the Oedipus complex, in *Group Psychology and the Analysis of the Ego*, in which competition with the father for the mother emerges primarily out of the son's identification with his father and consequent desire for that which is his father's. But for Freud, desire for the mother arose separately as well, as a primary object cathexis, and this drive came to be seen as the main source of the Oedipus complex. Girard traces the origin of the child's desire only to imitation of the father, not to a separate object-cathexis. And the child, although he uses the father as a model, does not perceive him as an obstacle to his desire. Only the father, seeing his child in a position to usurp what belongs to him, may sense the potential rivalry and, like Laius, take the first step toward violent conflict.[44] Ordinarily the father-son relationship is too unequal for conflict to emerge. The distinction between father and son disappears only when the entire society is submerged in a crisis of nondifferentiation. Patricide signals the breakdown of the primary unit of society, paralleling, within the family, the crime of regicide within the state. Oedipus' slaying of Laius, of course, is both patricide and regicide, and *Oedipus Rex*, like all Greek tragedy, describes the breakdown of social order through the reciprocal violence of symmetrical characters.[45]

While Malinowski saw father-son conflict as arising with the growth of human culture,[46] and Freud saw the Oedipus complex as a convergence of primal drives, Girard sees father-son conflict as symptomatic of the dissolution of society. Only when distinctions within the social order begin to break down, as they have in the past few centuries in Western society, only with the weakening of paternal authority, which brings the father nearer to his son and makes him into an obstacle for the boy's desire, can the Oedipus complex appear. In an intact patriarchal society the father would be too differentiated from his son for conflict between them to erupt.

Reviewing the Trobriand studies, Girard rejects Malinowski's view that the Trobriand complex forms between the boy and his maternal uncle. He sees this interpretation as simply a "filling out" of Freud's theory for a matrilineal society in which the uncle occupies the place of the Western father, not as a challenge to the Oedipus complex, as it has commonly been seen.

Girard rejects as well the theory of displacement of Oedipal hostility in the Trobriands from the father to the uncle, which Jones and Spiro had suggested. For Girard, conflict emerges only when the disciple's model becomes his obstacle as well, and the model only becomes an obstacle when he and the disciple "occupy the same sphere." In the Trobriands, the uncle is the boy's model, but he never becomes his nephew's rival because the two are distant; the young boy, in fact, grows up in a different village. And conflict never arises between father and son, because the child never even takes his father as a model.[47] Only brothers, who do occupy the same sphere, are likely to become rivals, and the Trobrianders guard against fraternal enmity by insisting that brothers bear no physical resemblance to each other. Resemblance between father and son, on the other hand, is emphatically asserted, because the father, in molding each child's appearance, makes him different from his brothers. The father is "the bearer of a difference," belonging to a different clan than his wife and sons, and the Trobrianders acknowledge the resemblance between father and son precisely because the father is not his son's model.[48] The extreme differentiation within Trobriand society, which, strikingly, the father represents, prevents conflict from ever arising.

The father

So far, we have encountered the Western father as authority figure (Malinowski), mother's consort (Freud and Spiro), model (Freud and Girard), and nurturer (Malinowski and Jones). But one aspect of fatherhood has been completely ignored—biological paternity.[49] In fact, all of the paternal roles which may lead to conflict can, their advocates emphasize, be assumed by figures other than the biological father. The role of model or of authority figure can be filled by the uncle, as Girard and Malinowski find in the Trobriands, and the role of mother's consort can be filled by anyone, as Spiro suggests in his hypothetical family unit. Yet biological paternity is the first criterion that we think of when we speak of fatherhood, and it is the one criterion that seems to be indispensable in the myths and literature which tell about conflict between fathers and sons. Often, in fact, the biological relationship is the only one that exists, because the son has been separated from his father in infancy.

The Oedipus story offers one example of an exclusively biological relationship, since the conflict begins with Laius' extrusion of his infant son, but the oracle before the child's birth makes an analysis of the father-son relationship and of the origin of the conflict somewhat more complicated. A clearer example can be found in the fragmentary Old High German *Hildebrandslied*. Hildebrand has left his wife and infant son for reasons having nothing to do with family relationships—he followed his lord into exile. And, as a consequence, the warrior is neither authority figure, mother's consort, model, or nurturer while his son is growing up. Nevertheless, father and son find themselves on opposing sides in a battle to the death.

This lay has generally been seen as an expression of the clash of two different loyalties, toward lord and toward kin. Yet the narrative tension does not derive from that clash at all. In fact, the moment Hildebrand learns that he faces his son, he readily slips from his arm the rings which his lord has given him and offers them to Haḋubrand in token of a truce. When his son refuses, Hildebrand lapses into a long speech which leads into the clash of weapons with which the fragment breaks off. The old warrior tells of the many years he wandered in exile, always at the forefront of battle, but always surviving, at last returning to his homeland, where his own son stands ready to slay him. Seeing no choice but to be killed by his son or to kill him, Hildebrand decides to fight Haḋubrand and, according to later sources, the son finally falls at his father's hands. The lay tells a basic story of father-son conflict.

While Haḋubrand may have ambivalent feelings toward his father, possibly implied in the young warrior's wordy reiteration that his father has died, we do not hear of them explicitly. Haḋubrand refuses to believe that the old man who faces him is his father, for his father left his wife and child long ago and, they have heard, has fallen in battle. Haḋubrand has no father. But Hildebrand has no trouble accepting that the man whom he has challenged is his son. It is the father who must decide among different courses of action, while the poem shows no hesitation on the part of the son. The dilemma is Hildebrand's exclusively; it is the father who understands the tragic fate that has befallen him no matter what he chooses to do. And the father decides to fight the man whom he recognizes as his son.

In the *Hildebrandslied*, then, only the most fundamental element of paternity, the biological link between father and son, is present. Only the father recognizes this link, and only the father responds to the relationship with ambivalence. The biological relationship is the only one common to all stories of conflict between father and son, and this relationship somehow must provide a motivation for that conflict. Furthermore, as Paul emphasized in his analysis of the Oedipus, Isaac, and Christ myths, and as Spiro and others have noted as well, it is often the father who is pulled in opposite directions with respect to his son.[50] Yet most scholars, in trying to account for this paternal ambivalence, satisfy themselves with an explanation that puts the father back into the passive role which Freud had assigned him. The "complementary Oedipus complex," for these scholars, is just that—the father's reaction to the son's ambivalent feelings toward the father.[51]

Kinship as a symbolic system

A more satisfying approach—and one that restores primacy to the father while taking into account the biological relationship with the son—is suggested by Daniel Craig's discussion of kinship as both a symbolic and substantive system.[52] For Craig, kinship answers a philosophical need, allowing people to go on living in the face of their own mortality. Kinship provides parents with a way to hand down both substance and "symbolic estate," consisting of values and social status in addition to material goods, to their children. "For those who become parents," Craig concludes, "kinship ensures the vertical transmission of their total substance, thus guaranteeing them immortality."[53] This formulation emphasizes the biological relationship between parents and children, but goes beyond it. The biological relationship, the passing on of the parents' physical substance, becomes a metaphor for the transmission of everything which belongs to the parents, both objects and ideas.

In the 1930s, Otto Rank had proposed a similarly ideological view of kinship, analyzing the Oedipus myth very differently from his older contemporary, Freud.[54] Rank traces three stages of society which are recapitulated in the ideological development of every child: the collective, the patriarchal, and the individual. In the collective stage, which moves into a matriarchal transition stage with group marriage, the child ensures the continuation of the group, both culturally and as a "collective soul-bearer."[55] Patriarchal society defines the child "as the individual successor of the personal immortality of the father," and so leads directly to the next stage, in which the child has an individual existence apart from group or father.[56] It is the tension between the patriarchal and filial principles which leads to conflict between father and son, not only because the son wants to be an individual independent of his father's authority, but because the father wants to be an individual independent of his son's succession. The individual wants to be immortal in himself, without assuming the role either of father or of son.

26

The Oedipus story, according to Rank, is not to be understood in terms of the psychology of the son but, sociologically, as "a heroic defence of the man against assuming the role of father." Laius never wanted a son, wishing instead "to be his own immortal successor," and so, when Oedipus is born, the father leaves him to die.[57] In Sophocles' play, Oedipus brings about the revelation of his deed at the end of his life, because it is then that he needs to rebel against the patriarchal ideology which allows fathers to live on only in their sons. He affirms that he has married his mother, implying the desire to make her the mother of his son, to beget himself.[58] And, striving to attain immortality through himself alone, the aged king, in *Oedipus at Colonus*, wishes that his sons might kill each other, rejecting the possibility of surviving through his offspring.[59]

Rank emphasizes that the different versions of the Oedipus myth emerge from different historical periods and that these periods correspond to stages of personal development. The different forms which the myth will take in these different historical periods reflect the perspectives of the different stages of personal development which parallel these periods: infancy, in which the child clings to his mother, corresponding to the collective/matriarchal period; childhood, in which the boy is heir to the father, corresponding to the partriarchal period; adolescence, when the youth declares his own selfhood, corresponding to the individual period; and, finally, fatherhood, when the adult is forced to accept his "racial role" in order to ensure the continuity of his existence.

Sophocles' play, for example, came at the end of the transition from group culture to patriarchy. The play begins long after Oedipus has assumed the role of husband and father and focuses on his one final attempt to renounce fatherhood and assert his individual immortality.[60] But, while Laius and Oedipus reject their sons, a father who accepts the paternal role will "naturally love his son . . . because he sees in him his direct successor and heir."[61] And, while the son may, in rebelling against the filial role which reduces him to an instrument of his father's immortality, embrace the role of father himself, he may later reject fatherhood as well, in favor of his own individuality.

Like Craig, Rank sees kinship as a system based on the concern for immortality, but Rank goes beyond that, examining the individual ego in the context of the racial ego and seeing family and society as two variable structures built on a single ideological concern.

Kinship and the continuity of self and society

My own approach to the study of family narratives shares something with each of the approaches to kinship that we have examined. Like Paul, I look to literature for mythic projections of underlying cultural concerns. But I do not see the distinctions between stories as mere formal differences masking a single solution to a psychological problem. Like Rank, I find that stories which take place between individuals and reflect the tensions which appear in different stages of personal development also take place within society and reflect the concerns of different societies.

Malinowski himself, although his work became the starting point for all subsequent attacks on the universality of the father-son conflict, suggested such a two-level approach, in finding the genesis of the father-son conflict in the birth of human culture, which necessitated a figure to transmit that culture to coming generations. Craig's notion of a "symbolic estate" fills that role with the father specifically, because it is he who hands down his substance to the son and, with it, both a material and ideological heritage. As a member of society, the father will also transmit to his son a cultural heritage. The relationship between father and son extends symbolically to include personal and social ideas as well as physiological substance and material possessions. The father-son conflict based on identification, of which Freud and Girard spoke, gains in significance, because the successful resolution of the tensions between individuals becomes the only guarantee of the survival of society and its cultural heritage.

We can well expect that the kind of resolution which takes place in each story, or whether the conflict is resolved at all, says something about the society whose mythic conception of itself the story expresses. A number of responses to the potential eruption of violence between father and son have been discussed: decomposition or displacement by Jones, differentiation by Girard, distancing by Spiro. Girard also examines violence directed at a surrogate victim, or sacrifice, and Spiro cites violent initiation rites, such as circumcision, as limited enactments of a potentially fatal conflict.

In the spectrum ranging from complete resolution to unlimited conflict, each of these solutions clearly has a different place. Sacrifice, for example, is not a resolution at all; it is simply a frantic attempt to find a substitute for the real victim against whom the violent impulse has already been let loose.[62] The mythic use of sacrifice by the father is just one step away from the mythic slaughter of the son. Distancing the father from the son, near the other end of the spectrum, does prevent violence from erupting, but only at the expense of the father's role, to transmit his heritage to his son. A myth which leaves the son without a father or the father without a son leaves no way for the society to continue from generation to generation. The two poles, of father-absence and filicide, meet in identically projecting the doom of society. As in the *Hildebrandslied*, whether the father remains in exile or returns to kill his son, his fate is the same—he is left with no one to carry on after his death.

The difficulty in finding an effective solution to the father-son conflict lies in the ambivalent nature of the relationship between the two. Fathers live on through their sons, passing down, together with physical substance, possessions, ideals, and customs. Whatever the father has accomplished will die with him if he has no son to take over. It is here that the ambivalence lies. As an extension of the father, the son ensures his immortality, yet as successor, the son usurps his place—he can continue for the father only upon the father's death.

To the father, then, the son represents both the ultimate promise and the ultimate threat, immortality and death, and the father responds both by claiming his son and by rejecting him, in being torn between nurturing and killing him. The more closely the son resembles the father, the more he seems able to continue for his father, the more likely violence will erupt. When there is no potential for violence, when father and son are distant enough to preclude danger, they are too distant for the father to live on in his son. A stable family structure will have to resolve the ambivalence inherent in the father-son relationship, allowing the father to see his son as successor without perceiving him, with violent repercussions, as usurper.

Family and cultural continuity in Genesis

The book of Genesis describes a long sequence of generations from Adam through the descendants of Jacob and, beginning with the story of Abraham, offers a narrative rich with details about a few generations in the patriarchal family. This family, of course, consists of a group of individuals, but represents at the same time the emerging nation of Israel. Indeed, I shall suggest in Chapter Five that the members of this family not only give rise to the nation but, in some sense, *are* the future nation. I shall argue too that Abraham and his family not only are the descendants of the ancestors of humankind, Adam and Noah, but that their lives are the culmination of the process of creation. For now, though, it is enough to emphasize that the patriarchal family described in chapters 12 through 50 of Genesis is to be the foundation of the nation whose history is narrated in the rest of the Bible. And, if that nation is to be built on a firm foundation, it must be the goal of the family narratives in Genesis to seek out a stable family structure, shifting kin relationships from generation to generation until a family emerges whose members are able to live together without conflict.

The structure that ultimately emerges will represent the social structure of the nation. And, if ancient literature is seen as a social construct, as an artifact left by a society struggling to define itself, then the struggle for stability within the family reflects the society's perception of its very nature, of the conflicts that threaten it, of its capacity to resolve conflict, and of the society's ultimate ability to establish itself and to survive.

In the following three chapters, I will analyze kinship structures in the narrative of the patriarchal family. While there are episodes of family conflict earlier in the book of Genesis, it is at this point in the book that family relationships begin to shape the narrative. Indeed, it is at this point that conflict between family members begins to signify something different from the universal human conflict suggested in the story of Cain and Abel. Chapter 12 begins with a command and a promise, with a mission and a blessing; it introduces a specific cultural heritage to be transmitted within a single family and to be shared among its members.

It is just such a heritage which, I have suggested, is at the core of the father-son relationship in ancient texts. If Abraham has a special mission and blessing, he will need a son to whom he may transmit this heritage. And the cultural heritage, which includes both the physical land and spiritual ideals, will be the source of conflict between brothers who seek to inherit their father's blessing. Violence threatens the family each time the blessing is about to be transmitted: violence between brothers and violence between father and son.

Violence emerges between brothers when each feels that he must be the father's successor, to the exclusion of the other. Violence also threatens the relationship between father and son, but in a far more subtle way. Paternal violence does not emerge in the book of Genesis as a conscious battle between father and son, as in many other ancient narratives. Yet, we shall note a clear pattern of potential threat to the son's life in the process of the transfer of the blessing from his father. The emergence of this violence, I am suggesting, is a narrative expression of the urgency of the father-son relationship in this narrative of a nation's beginning—the father must achieve cultural continuity, must gain immortality through his son, but must come to terms with his own mortality, with his personal limitedness as a seeker of destiny.[63]

The following study of the patriarchal narrative takes as its starting point the symbolic understanding of kinship, and especially of father-son succession, proposed above. The study is organized as a series of analyses of the narrative, focusing respectively on kin relationships, on lexical patterns, and on broad narrative structure. The purpose of this organization is twofold. First, it is meant to demonstrate that an understanding of the nature of kinship in this text helps disclose narrative meaning; it serves as a tool in the interpretation of specific episodes and details as well as of the book as a whole. Second, the progressive levels of analysis constitute an attempt to test prior assumptions and interpretations.[64]

I begin, in Chapter Two, with an overview of the family narrative, focusing on specific episodes which I suggest are crucial stories of transfer from father to son and analyzing these episodes on the basis of my interpretation of the nature of conflict and resolution in literary texts. I move on, at the beginning of Chapter Three, to an analysis of a word pattern that appears in each of these transfer stories. This word pattern confirms the preceding overview in two basic ways: by singling out the same stories as the crucial elements in the family narrative and, more interestingly, by establishing the same structure of family relationships, for each generation, as had been suggested in the overview. The two levels of analysis support one another for, as we shall see, elements of the word pattern actually can be predicted on the basis of the kinship analysis and, conversely, details of kin relationships can be predicted by the linguistic pattern.

But the nature of kinship in Genesis cannot fully be understood out of the context of the whole narrative. And, as I have already noted, the study of kinship can help us more fully interpret the larger narrative. From an analysis of the details of kinship and of the word pattern that encapsulates the elements of succession, then, I proceed to an examination of the larger narrative. A number of problematic episodes, I shall suggest, become clearly and powerfully meaningful when we look at them from the perspective of kinship and, of course, we become able to explain some puzzling details of the family relationships through an understanding of the narrative context. The broad narrative analysis begins, in the second part of Chapter Three, with a study of narrative structure, for which I take my cue from the kinship and linguistic patterns, and goes on, in Chapter Four, to examine different elements of kinship and the destiny which the patriarchal family seeks. By the conclusion of Chapter Four, the three levels of kin relationships, linguistic patterns, and narrative structure fit together to form a clear picture of the quest for continuity of family and nation in the book of Genesis. Chapter Five places the patriarchal narrative in its broader context, the primeval history on the one side and the national history on the other, and suggests how the story of the transfer of the covenantal blessing and destiny within the family has significance for the biblical view of world history and of the history of the nation of Israel.

A few words are in order about my interpretive approach to the narrative at hand. First, I approach the biblical text with the assumption that it is a literary unit. Whether this unity derives from a mode of composition early in the history of the text or from later redactional work is not important for this study. What is important is that an assumption of literary unity yields analyses which explicate the text with great power and precision—a circular justification, perhaps, but one that allows the interpreter to go about the work of interpretation.

Second, I would like to emphasize that the approach to kinship in this study is literary, not psychoanalytic or anthropological, although it clearly is informed by these disciplines. I analyze kinship as a structure that symbolizes narrative concerns and conveys narrative meaning. How kinship functions in the experience of individual human beings and within human society is a separate question, though clearly a related one. Information about the specific elements of kinship—about which relationships are significant, about how these relationships are defined, about what they mean—comes, as much as possible, from the biblical text, not from universal assumptions about family structure or from data about specific cultures, even about the culture from which the biblical text emerged. We cannot readily assume, for example, that cross-cousin marriages, such as Jacob's to Rachel, are special, or that we can choose among numerous possible definitions of complicated kin relationships, such as Isaac's to Rebecca, or that we know the meaning of avunculate or maternal relationships, as represented by Laban or Sarah, which in fact vary from culture to culture and from text to text. In each of these cases, we shall try to determine the nature of the kin relationship as the biblical text, or indeed the individual episode within that text, defines it. At times this determination itself may illuminate the concerns of the text, for how a culture views kin relationships, especially paternity and maternity, speaks about most crucial issues of life and death, survival and decay.

Third, I recognize that many of the points that I make in the coming chapters are noted in classical rabbinic midrashim and in medieval biblical exegesis. For the most part, however, I have refrained from citing these works and have limited myself to citing the works of modern scholars. I have done this not out of low regard for the early interpreters of the biblical text; indeed, I think it beyond dispute that their sensitivity to the nuances of the text is unparalleled in modern times. But systematically to pick and choose midrashic or exegetical comments which seem to support my readings strikes me as overly audacious as well as premature. For, while I may at times be noticing the same textual details as the early exegetes, I think it is still an open question precisely how these exegetes understood the nature of the text and the way in which the text conveys its meaning. And I do not want to project my understanding of the biblical text onto the comments of these exegetes. Accordingly, I generally cite early interpretations only if they are particularly well-known or if they actively have shaped my reading. The major exception is Chapter Five, the typological argument of which is akin to one of the favored methods of midrash; there I freely cite and discuss in the notes early traditions which have bearing on my argument, especially those preserved in ancient retellings of the biblical narrative.

Finally, in this study I am attempting to offer neither a theory nor a poetics of biblical narrative, although without question the study has implications for both. But primarily this book is a work of interpretation. Taking as a starting point the narrative's concern for cultural continuity as epitomized by the father's transfer of the promise and blessing to his son, I hope to offer an interpretation of the patriarchal narrative which can contribute to the ongoing effort to understand the biblical text.

2

THE
GENESIS
OF
THE
FAMILY

The story of the patriarchal family begins with a command and a promise.[1] God commands Abraham to leave his father's house and settle a new land and simultaneously promises to make Abraham into a great nation. This promise is not simply a reward for obeying God's command; the promise and the command both are parts of the blessing which God offers to Abraham, and which Abraham is to become for others.[2] Neither makes sense without the other. Abraham must find the land, travel through it, define its limits, and take possession of it. But without the promise of succession his fulfillment of God's command is meaningless. A patriarch must have a son to carry on after his death, to inherit the land and the mission of building a nation—and to inherit the promise which will allow him, ultimately, to pass on the blessing to his own son, for all generations.

The fulfillment of the command depends upon the fulfillment of the promise, and the promise of descendants takes meaning from the mission inaugurated by the command. Once there is a mission the promise of a son makes sense, for the son is the bearer of his father's destiny. If Abraham is to be blessed, he must seek out both parts of the blessing—he must follow God's command to search for the land and he must seek the son through whom God promises to make him into a great nation.

In Chapter Three we will take a detailed look at Abraham's double quest and compare the structure of the Abraham narrative with the stories of the other patriarchs. For now, we will focus on the moment of transfer, on the episode in which each of the patriarchs designates his successor, noting only in passing the place of each episode within the larger narrative. Such a focus will allow us to trace a pattern throughout the entire book of Genesis, to identify the problem of succession and to follow its movement toward crisis or toward resolution. Looking back, afterward, at the context of each moment of transfer, we will be in a better position to understand the structure of the surrounding narratives and their meaning and to analyze the nature of each of the family relationships, maternal and fraternal, as well as paternal. Meanwhile we will only note the closeness of the various relationships in each generation, the corresponding intensity of the violence attendant on the transfer of the blessing from father to son, and the resulting need for a resolution that will allow for continuity of the patriarchal mission.

Abraham's successor

Of all the sons in Genesis, Isaac is the one most urgently sought. He is not born until almost the end of the Abraham narrative, yet Abraham had recognized his need for a son shortly after the beginning of his narrated career. After Abraham's most powerful moment, after the battle of the four kings against the five, in which Abraham proves not only his strength but his political independence, God must visit Abraham and tell him not to be afraid (15:1). At the peak of his strength, Abraham has the most to lose; he has watched his nephew, Lot, return to the land of Sodom, and he can envision no future for his family (15:2-3).[3] It is at this critical moment that he first complains of his childlessness, and God promises him a distant destiny through the heir that will be born (15:4, 13-16). But who this heir will be is a question which Abraham will have to answer, because he will eventually beget two sons, Ishmael and Isaac.

For Sarah, the problem of choosing between sons does not exist. She gives birth to only one son, and he, as she sees it, must be his father's heir. In fact, Sarah is the only matriarch who bears only one son, the only one who the text explicitly says is too old to conceive (18:11), and the only one whom God visits to announce the promise of a child (18:9-10). She jealously guards Isaac's rights, because, in her eyes, there is no possible contender.

Abraham ultimately is forced to acknowledge what Sarah recognizes. When the matriarch insists on sending Ishmael away, Abraham is distressed "because of his son" (21:11). But God speaks to Abraham, calling Ishmael not his son, but, echoing Sarah's words, "the son of the maidservant" (21:10, 13).[4] Ishmael, God grants, will become a nation, for he is Abraham's "seed." But Ishmael must be cast out for, God assures Abraham, "in Isaac shall your seed be called" (21:12). Once Ishmael is sent away, Abraham is left with only one son. Isaac will be his heir. And, with the recognition that Isaac is the fulfillment of the promise which Abraham had sought urgently his whole life, comes an eruption of that tension which characterizes the relationship between father and son.

The binding of Isaac is the result of Abraham's recognition of Isaac as his son and, in effect, is an enactment of that recognition.[5] Rashi, following the Midrash, points out the contradictory nature of God's words concerning Isaac. Isaac is to live on after Abraham, yet Abraham is commanded to kill Isaac.[6] The contradiction in God's words is an articulation of the ambivalent nature of paternity. The son poses both a promise and a threat to his father. Abraham has sought a son who would continue for him, but Isaac is to replace his father; he is the instrument of his father's immortality and thus a symbol of his approaching death. Abraham invests his son with all his hopes and visions of destiny, yet Abraham prepares to sacrifice the son who will carry out that mission in his father's place.

The paradoxical nature of the father-son relationship is expressed in the contradictory messages of God's promise and command. The moment of transfer from father to son is a moment of danger as the father must acknowledge his personal limitedness and his immortality through his son. This recognition involves a struggle to come to terms with oneself as merely the beginner of a destiny which depends on future generation for fulfillment; the struggle is expressed in the narrative through an outburst of violence.[7] But, in the book of Genesis, the violence does not take the form of hostility between father and son. Rather, the violence which accompanies the transfer of the blessing is channeled through the act of sacrifice.

This is an important point, because the manner in which the violence is expressed tells much about the understanding of paternity as well as the values that underlie the narrative. If the violence attendant on the transfer of the blessing from Abraham to Isaac is manifested in sacrifice, rather than in the open hostility characteristic of many other ancient narratives, then we must look at the nature of sacrifice, in addition to the more general phenomenon of violence between father and son, in order to understand the family narrative in the book of Genesis.

The act of sacrifice has often been seen, by both ancient and modern interpreters, as a ritual of substitution.[8] In order for the ritual to be effective, the substituting object must closely resemble the one who offers the sacrifice. Isaac, in this narrative, is the sacrificial object which will serve as Abraham's substitute in Abraham's ultimate act of self-dedication to God's commanding will. Isaac can serve as the sacrifice because he is, in essence, identical to Abraham; as we shall see, the entire course of his life is modelled upon the mission begun by his father. Isaac is the embodiment of the unique possibility of the survival of Abraham's mission; he offers the father the promise of the existence of his self beyond the limitations of his mortal self. By offering Isaac as a sacrifice, Abraham is offering himself on the altar. And, in so doing, Abraham enacts his complete dedication to his mission and, at the same time, destroys the possibility of the fulfillment of his mission.

In this story, then, there is a correspondence between the ambivalent nature of the father-son relationship, the contradictory nature of God's command, and the paradoxical nature of the act of sacrifice. All emerge from the identity between father and son, from the need for the father to live as through his son.

Abraham's near-sacrifice of Isaac, then, enacts his recognition that Isaac is the one through whom his mission will continue.[9] But, though the son's life must be threatened, it must, of course, also be saved if the son is to fulfill his cultural function. Isaac's life is saved through a second sacrificial substitute, as Abraham offers a ram on the altar in place of his son.[10] This substitution satisfies the need for a sacrificial victim for Abraham, fulfills by proxy God's command, and allows for a deflection of the violence which erupts at the moment of the transfer of the blessing.[11] But it is no solution to the underlying problem. If succession from father to son is to continue, then the danger inherent in the father-son relationship must be resolved, not merely deflected.

Isaac's closeness to his parents, then, results in the urgency of the tense paternal relationship. The son so clearly substitutes for his father that Abraham almost kills him, but this same identification ensures the continuity of the father's mission. Indeed, Isaac will do little in his lifetime that Abraham has not done before him; the events of the son's life closely parallel those of the father's. But this closeness between generations manifests itself, too, in an extreme form of the maternal bond. No mother in Genesis is as viciously protective of her son as Sarah is of Isaac. Isaac is the fulfillment of Sarah's life. To his mother, the son in no way represents a threat; his succession is not dependent upon her death. Sarah's death leaves Isaac saddened, and only in marrying can he be comforted for his loss: "Isaac took her [Rebecca] to the tent of Sarah, his mother . . . and he loved her, and Isaac was comforted for his mother" (24:67). Isaac, indeed, loves Rebecca, but his love is presented as a direct transfer of the bond which joined the son so tightly to his mother.

Isaac and his sons

If the first stage of the patriarchal family included an exceedingly close identification between father and son, the filial relationship in the next stage is somewhat weaker. Isaac's need for a successor appears less urgent than Abraham's. Isaac's accomplishments, in fact, are narrated only after the birth of his children; the continuity of his destiny is guaranteed from the start of his career. Moreover, neither of his sons is clearly the one who will replace his father. The boys are twins, born in a strange fashion which confuses the issue of first-born. While assured of an heir, then, Isaac is not portrayed as perceiving his sons as possible successors until the moment of the transfer of the blessing. Esau, as first-born, is likely to succeed him, but the issue of succession is less urgent, and the promise and threat are less clear. Toward the end of his life, Isaac wants to bless Esau simply because he loves him; he asks his elder son to bring him venison "so that my soul might bless you" (37:4).

The blessing here is more like a personal gift than a transmission of the family destiny. Yet the competition for the father's place does not simply fade away. If it is not a significant element in the paternal relationship, the competition, with its potential violence, is transferred to the brothers. While Esau is first-born and his father's favorite, Jacob has his own reasons for expecting the blessing of inheritance for himself. After all, Rebecca favors her younger son and intends to see him succeed Isaac (25:28; 27:10). But, unlike Sarah, Rebecca is the mother of both of her husband's children. While she is determined that her vision be realized, she cannot protect Jacob as exclusively as Sarah had protected Isaac, exiling the contending brother to the desert. Rebecca loves Jacob but is mother to two children; it is she who manages to avert the almost inevitable violence between the brothers.

Abraham's recognition that Isaac would succeed him was coupled with danger for his son which could only be deflected through the substitution of an animal sacrifice. When Isaac is about to recognize Esau formally as heir, through the transfer of the blessing, he takes a precaution against a similar eruption of paternal violence—he commands Esau to kill an animal and bring it to his father. Later in the story it becomes apparent that the slaughtered animal resembles Esau; its pelt reminds Isaac of the hairy arms of his older son (27:23). The animal, then, is a perfect surrogate victim for Esau.

Esau, in fact, has been performing this same act for his father all along; because of the constant slaughtering of animals for Isaac the father loves his heir-apparent (25:28). But at this moment the slaughtering of the animal takes on new significance. Isaac had walked up to Mount Moriah wondering at the absence of an animal for the sacrifice (22:7), and he was himself almost sacrificed by his father; only at the last moment did a surrogate victim appear. Avoiding such an act of violence against his own son, Isaac asks that Esau present an animal substitute, like the ram which Abraham finally sacrificed, before the son is to receive the blessing. Paternal violence will be deflected onto the animal, and only the father's love and his hopes for the future will remain to be passed on to the son.

While Isaac's request functions to avoid the eruption of paternal violence, a new violence is festering elsewhere. Rebecca knows that Jacob must receive the blessing, and she, who has felt the twins struggling within her (25:22), is afraid of what might happen between the two brothers.[12] The plan she proposes to Jacob is more than just a clever ruse to trick Isaac. The animal skins and the cloak do allow Jacob to pose as Esau, and the slaughtered animal allows him to receive his father's blessing without violence.[13] But Rebecca instructs Jacob to bring two animals (27:9), and the slaughtering serves two functions in this narrative. The animal which can deflect violence between father and son can deflect violence between brothers as well.[14] The two animals that Jacob brings allow him to take the place of his father and of his brother without the eruption of violence.

But Esau has no surrogate victim. The angry brother awaits only the death of his father, the moment when succession must occur and Jacob's usurpation becomes actualized, to allow his violence to emerge unchecked (27:41). Eventually, when Esau will set out against his brother with a large army, Jacob will be able to appease him with a gift of animals (32:13-20; 33:8-11). But meanwhile Esau's violence is smoldering within him. Rebecca understands the fraternal violence and begs Jacob to escape his brother's wrath (27:42-45).

His succession to Isaac assured, Jacob must now go to Rebecca's kin to find a wife. The woman he chooses is, indeed, related to his mother, and he finds her at the well, in precisely the spot where his mother was chosen to be Isaac's wife. But, while his quest for a wife is shaped by his relationship with his mother, we are not told that Jacob loves Rachel as a substitute for his mother, the way Isaac loved Rebecca. Jacob simply loves Rachel.

As the need for an heir becomes less urgent, the closeness between parent and child becomes less extreme. Abraham and Sarah could live on only through Isaac, and both the paternal and maternal relationships powerfully shaped the son's life. Almost killed by Abraham, Isaac imitates his father throughout his life; carefully protected by Sarah, Isaac knows no love but love for his mother. For Isaac and Rebecca, not the founders but the inheritors of a destiny already begun, the concern for continuity seems less pressing and the parental bond consequently less extreme. Moreover, both parents respond to the danger latent in the family relationships, taking precautions to avert violence before it can erupt. The son never becomes the object of his father's violence and, correspondingly, he is able to love a woman who is distinct from his mother. But with the safer loosening of the parental bond, the fraternal relationship gains in intensity and, consequently, in potential violence. The paternal and fraternal relationships are delicately balanced in Isaac's family—the same animal substitute, in fact, averts violence in both of them. But, again, the problem is only pushed aside, not solved. Violence still threatens the biblical family.

The sons of Jacob

If Isaac had to worry less than Abraham about the continuity of his mission, Jacob has no need for concern at all. Leah immediately bears him many children, the maidservants are fruitful as well, and Rachel's early barrenness seems to trouble him little (30:2). Jacob later favors one son, Joseph, but this favoritism has nothing to do with perceiving Joseph as a successor. Jacob never sought to beget this son and did not participate in his naming (30:23-24). He loves Joseph and gives him a fine cloak because he is "a son of his old age" (37:3), but there is no suggestion that Jacob means to choose him as successor. Paternal violence plays no role, because Jacob's relationship with

Joseph is unambiguous; the son in no way threatens to replace his father, because he has not been chosen as Jacob's heir.[15]

Joseph's brothers perceive this favoritism differently. The little boy is the eldest child of one of Jacob's two main wives—the second wife to be married, but the one who should have come first and, certainly, the preferred one. The sons of Leah and Rachel, then, stand in much the same confused relationship to one another as the twin sons of Isaac. Yet now one factor is missing. While Jacob and Esau were competitors in relation to their father, a single maternal bond joined them. But for Joseph and his brothers the maternal bonds are separate, and the boys' relationships to their mothers, for the first time, increase the fraternal competition.[16] The brother's mothers are absent from the narrative, and their father is nearly absent. While Isaac had played a partial role in determining his successor, Jacob remains almost completely passive, leaving the entire potential for violence in the hands of the brothers.

The ram on Mount Moriah prevented Abraham from slaughtering his son. Esau's meats were to protect the successor from his father's violence, and Rebecca made sure that Jacob would not appear before his father without a similar sacrificial object. While Esau's cloak and the animal skins disguised Jacob, allowing him to replace Esau in his father's mind, the slaughtered animal served another purpose as well, one for which only Rebecca could have perceived the need. Instructing Jacob to bring the Esau-like animal to be killed, Rebecca averted violence between the brothers. Neither Joseph nor his brothers, however, understand the consequences of their conflict or recognize how violence can be averted. Joseph's cloak, like Esau's, will allow the brothers to trick their father and avoid his curse (37:31-33). But the cloak, as symbol of unambiguous paternal love for Joseph, is symbol of the brothers' complete hatred (37:4). Rebecca gave Jacob Esau's cloak together with the slaughtered animal, but Joseph and his brothers share no mother who can insure that the fraternal violence will fall on a surrogate victim. Sacrificial substitution cannot function here, because the brothers do not see themselves as sharing a common destiny with Joseph.

Sacrifice, we noted in the story of the binding of Isaac, requires identification between the sacrificer and his victim. The sacrificer chooses to deflect the violence onto a surrogate victim, and so can preserve the real object of the violence. Even Jacob and Esau are closely enough identified for sacrificial substitution to function—Jacob can pass as Esau and later can offer gifts to his brother (33:10-11), Esau invites Jacob to travel with him (33:12), and the two brothers finally bury their father together (35:29). But Joseph's brothers seem to share nothing with Joseph. Their father favors Joseph and is distant from them; their mothers were competitors with Joseph's mother and no longer participate in their sons' affairs. Seeing Joseph approaching from afar (37:18), perhaps recognizing him by his cloak, the brothers think of their father's favor and their own hatred; before Joseph comes near, they remember their competition. There is no substitute. They are determined to kill him.

Only after Joseph disappears do the brothers come to terms with the consequences of their violent impulse. Ironically, they now perform the one act which they should have done earlier. Slaughtering a goat and dipping the cloak in its blood, the brothers manage to save themselves from their father's wrath, but they are too late to save Joseph from their own. Jacob is fooled by his sons, yet he perceives the truth. The bloody cloak is an empty symbol. It cannot achieve the sacrificial aim of averting violence; the violent act has already been committed. Jacob's response is correct—Joseph himself, in a sense, has been slaughtered (37:33); he is lost to his family. The brothers were determined to kill Joseph, and they can no longer do anything to save him. The boy, now in Egypt, is handed over to Pharaoh's Chief Slaughterer (37:36).

The dissolution of the family

The relieving of paternal tension increases fraternal competition. If Isaac's family stood in precarious balance, Jacob's family topples over. No conflict emerges between Jacob and his sons because the father never acts to choose a successor from among them.[17] Yet the violence still exists; it is simply transferred from the paternal to the fraternal relationship. Someone must succeed Jacob, and the brothers will fight it out. With the loosening of the paternal bond comes a diffusion of the maternal relationship. The relationships between mothers and sons, in this story, cannot save the brothers; they can only contribute to the emerging violence.

Joseph's brothers, in fact, misunderstand the situation. Jacob has not selected Joseph as his successor, and Joseph never replaces Jacob; his role is nothing like Jacob's, and the woman he marries is not related to Rachel.[18] Jacob's family, to this point, fails in every respect. The concept of destiny, of children continuing the parents' mission, has been totally lost, yet the violence of the family relationship has been allowed to burn uncontrolled. Clearly, the trend in Genesis must be reversed. Succession must regain its motivation toward destiny while removing the potential for violence once and for all.

Judah brings about the reversal. If all brotherhood means is competition and violence, Judah wants no part in it. The one who has tried to mitigate the violence directed against Joseph (37:26-27) can no longer remain with his brothers. He leaves his brothers and begins a new life for himself apart from his family, taking a Canaanite wife and begetting three sons (38:1-5). Yet, in leaving, Judah removes himself not only from fraternal violence but from familial destiny as well. For Judah the gain outweighs the loss—destiny can be a dangerous thing, and Judah chooses safety.

Judah takes Tamar as a wife for his eldest son, but Er dies without begetting a child (38:6-7). Understanding fraternal responsibility, having some notion that brothers share a common destiny, Judah asks his second son to marry Tamar and insure that his brother live on through the children that Tamar will bear (38:8). But Onan refuses to beget a son who will carry on for his brother instead of for himself and destroys his seed rather than giving it to Er (38:9). Angry at Onan's violence against his brother, God punishes the second son, too, with death (38:10). Now Judah encounters his earlier dilemma once again, and again he makes the same decision. If Er and Onan were inheritors of a single destiny, they were, inevitably, competitors. The fraternal relationship did not give Er a future; it merely brought about further destruction. The choice is clear. Allowing Tamar to marry the youngest brother is likely to result in violence; Er would remain childless, Shelah too might be killed, and Judah would be left with neither sons nor grandsons. The youngest child remains safe at home; Shelah will not be sent to redeem his brother (38:11).[19]

If Judah's tale were to end here, the entire biblical narrative would end here as well. Jacob sits alone, mourning for his son (37:34-35). The brothers have allowed one of themselves to be lost, and lack completely a sense of destiny. Joseph, away in Egypt, tries to forget his father's house (41:51). And Judah, the only one who seems capable of understanding that a family means the future of a mission, has excluded himself from his father's family and buried the notion of destiny within his own. The biblical family has reached its lowest point; there is no one left to ensure its future.

Tamar: the reconstruction of the family

We have traced the evolution of paternal violence to fraternal strife and linked it with the loosening of the paternal bond. Tamar seems to understand this link. If violence between brothers stems from the father, then fraternal responsibility must have its root in the father as well. Judah is correct: Shelah is not the one who must redeem his brother. Yet the future cannot be neglected, and this is what Tamar teaches Judah. The lost brother must be redeemed, if not through another brother, then through the father himself.

Tamar refuses to accept a substitute for Judah. She arranges that Judah sleep with her and, when Judah offers to send her a kid as payment, Tamar demands surety—she demands his signet, cord and staff, the symbols of Judah's identity (38: 14-18).[20] This scene presents the ultimate reversal of sacrificial substitution. Here, Judah symbolically substitutes himself for his own substitute; he gives his signet in place of the kid, and so he is forced to take responsibility for begetting Tamar's sons.[21] Substitution has meaning only when there is some identification between the person and his surrogate. But Judah sends the kid as something completely separate from himself, as a payment which will remove all obligation that he incurs through his action (38:20).[22] That is why he becomes frantic when his messenger cannot find Tamar (38:23); as long as Tamar has his pledge, Judah is still involved. But Tamar has no interest in the meaningless substitute; holding on to Judah's pledge, she finally uses it to clear herself of the accusation of harlotry. Tamar brings out the signet, cord and staff, and Judah acknowledges his responsibility; he has not given Shelah to Tamar, and so Tamar has forced the father to redeem his lost son (38:25-26).

Tamar has returned to the beginnings of the family. Destiny must be passed on from father to son, as Abraham passed it on to Isaac. Yet, by conceiving Er's successor through Judah, Tamar removes the threat of paternal violence. Judah's heir is established, but the potential object of his violence is missing—his son is dead. Er's line is assured of continuity, yet Er, of course, in no way threatens the sons. The twin sons, Perez and Zerah, so similar to Jacob and Esau, would seem to be in violent competition for succession, yet the story tells of no conflict between these brothers whose birth order is so ambiguous (38:28-30).[23]

While paternal violence in Isaac's family was transferred to the brothers, Tamar ensures that paternal violence never enters her family at all. Constructing the family carefully, Tamar makes sure that the paternal relationship is an instrument of destiny, for Judah is Er's predecessor and the twins are Er's successors. But the relationship is not an instrument of violence, for Er can be neither the recipient nor the inflicter of paternal violence. And, while tightening the paternal bond without its element of tension, Tamar tightens the maternal bond as well. If Jacob's sons had competing mothers, Judah's twins are born to a single mother; the boys can inherit a sense of destiny, yet they, at last, are free from the threat of violence.

Judah and the patriarchal family

Judah learns the lesson well and teaches it to the rest of his family. Following Tamar's example, he begins with the father, with Jacob. Joseph, in the guise of an Egyptian officer, has imprisoned Simeon and will release him only if Benjamin is brought to Egypt (42:19-20, 24). Further, the entire family is endangered by a famine, and only by delivering Benjamin will they receive any food (43:3-5). Yet when the brothers bring their message to Jacob, they hear him respond much as Judah had done when Onan died. The father has already lost two sons; he would rather keep his youngest safe at home, neglecting the family's destiny, than allow him to try to redeem his brother, thereby endangering his life (42:36).[24]

Reuven tries to reassure Jacob, offering to sacrifice his own sons (42:37), but only strengthens the very basis of Jacob's fear. If fraternal violence grows out of paternal violence, Reuven's offer only increases the danger. Judah, finally, understands. Offering himself for his brother (43:9), Judah demonstrates fraternal responsibility. As brothers, he explains to Jacob, they share a destiny; Judah will redeem Benjamin, but Jacob must be willing to send Benjamin to redeem Simeon and, indeed, the entire family. Jacob is reassured by this second offer and convinced by Judah's argument (43:11-14); he now learns what Tamar has taught Judah. It is the father's role to take responsibility for his family and to pass on a sense of destiny to his sons. Only by following their father's model can the brothers accept responsibility for one another, can they share a common destiny.

The brothers, of course, do precisely that. It is not enough for Judah and Jacob to understand their destiny; if the entire family is to be included in the mission, every member must perceive his role in it. When Joseph imprisons Benjamin, then, all of the brothers offer themselves, through Judah, to redeem him (44:16). Judah explains to Joseph what he has already taught his father and brothers—that father must take responsibility for his son, and brother for his brother—and Joseph, at last, sees his own life in terms of his family's destiny. Joseph can no longer torment his brothers and father. Breaking down in tears, he describes his part in God's mission; he has been sent by God to Egypt in order to save his family (45:1-8).

Joseph is both right and wrong. He is participating in God's plan, but not simply in providing food for his father and brothers; it is through him, too, that Jacob's family settles in the land of Egypt where they ultimately will become enslaved (45:9-13).

But Joseph participates in his family's destiny in another way as well, because it is only in coming to Egypt that Jacob and his children become a unified family for the first time. Joseph, Jacob, and all the brothers, through the lesson of Judah, become the first family to remain together in the book of Genesis.

Judah, then, reverses the process that has been unfolding throughout the patriarchal narrative. The narrative is concerned with the birth and continuity of a nation, and that nation is structured upon the framework of the families with which it began. The consciousness of a destiny, the urgent need for continuity, while creating a tight bond between parents and children, introduces an element of tension as well. The son is an extension of his mother and will be a replacement for his father—thus the paternal relationship is one of both hope and dread. To his father, the heir represents both life and death, and the recipient of his father's legacy can too easily become the object of violence. With the generations after Abraham, the issue of continuity gradually lost its urgency, and consequently the parental bond became looser. The father's consciousness of passing on a destiny to his children became weaker, and the potential for paternal violence lessened as well. But the maternal bond, holding fraternal strife in check, became more diffuse too. The fraternal relationship, then, replaced the paternal bond, and unleashed violence between brothers resulted in the family's total neglect of destiny.

But a nation is to be built, and the family has to be restructured. Tamar, an outsider, shapes the new family by strengthening the parental bond. Her children are conceived purely as replacements for her dead husband,[25] and the two brothers have the same mother. The brothers will inherit the destiny of their parents but will inherit jointly, without conflict or violence, because no paternal violence exists. Through Judah this family becomes the model for the entire house of Jacob—a family from which no one is excluded, a family with a shared mission. And Jacob recognizes, as he blesses all his sons at the end of his life (chs. 48, 49), that through the house of Judah a nation will be built—a nation of which every member has a part in a common destiny.

3

THE
QUEST
FOR
A
SUCCESSOR

The stories of the binding of Isaac, the blessing of Jacob, and the selling of Joseph seem the obvious points through which to trace the pattern of succession within the book of Genesis. Each story singles out the one son who is to succeed his father,[1] each signals a shift in narrative focus from the father to the son, and each tells of a potentially violent confrontation and an attempt to deflect the violence. I suggested, in Chapter Two, that these narratives form a pattern in which the fathers become progressively less involved in the issue of succession, while the competition between brothers correspondingly increases, until the identification which allows for sacrificial substitution has been lost, and all that is left is violence.

But besides the thematic connection between these three episodes, there is a stylistic link as well, a word pattern that appears, with variations, in each. The common linguistic details become apparent once the three episodes have been isolated on other, thematic grounds. But they serve, in turn, as a confirmation of the connection between these stories. And this is not, as it might at first appear, merely a circular justification of one kind of assumption by means of another. For the interrelationship of thematic and linguistic material actually will allow us to predict linguistic details, such as the absence of a key word or the presence of its opposite, on the basis of thematic details, such as the absence or reversal of a crucial motif.

The correspondence of linguistic and thematic material, then, will function as a test of the validity both of our choice of these three episodes for analysis and of our interpretation of their meaning. The linguistic details, like the thematic ones preliminarily discussed in Chapter Two, not only connect the stories to each other, but point to a progression from story to story and, finally, help us to understand both the stories themselves and their place within the longer narrative context.

Each of the three stories begins with a command and a response. The basic pattern is "go" (*lek*) and "here I am" (*hineni*). The command "go" is frequently paired with "take" (*qah*), and the response "here I am" is often accompanied by a statement introduced by "here" or "behold" (*hine*). "Take and go" (*qah velek*), in fact, is a common pair; both Pharaoh and Laban, for example, use the phrase when handing over Sarah and Rebecca, respectively (12:19; 24:51). And *hineni*, of course, is just a form of the word *hine*. While each of the stories includes both "go" (*lek*) and "here am I" (*hineni*), they vary in the occurrence of the accompanying words and, most significantly, in who commands and who responds.

The binding of Isaac

The most elaborate combination of these terms, yet the most straightforward, appears in the story of the binding of Isaac. God calls to Abraham, and Abraham responds "here I am" (*hineni*, 22:1). The command follows in the form of "take and go" (*qah velek*): "Take [*qah*] your son, your only child, whom you love, Isaac, and go [*velek*] to the land of Moriah, and bring him as an offering there . . ." (22:2). Abraham "takes" two lads and Isaac with him and sets out to "go" to the appointed place; after sighting the place on the third day of his journey, he "goes" on alone with his son (22:3-5). Abraham "takes" the wood and lays it on Isaac, he "takes" the fire and the knife and, as father and son "go" on together (22:6), the next sequence begins.

Isaac calls to his father, and Abraham responds "here I am" (*hineni*, 22:7). The conversation continues with "here" (*hine*) and focuses on the one thing that Abraham did *not* take with him: "Here [*hine*] is the fire and the wood, but where is the lamb for the offering?" (22:7). Abraham responds that God will provide the lamb, and the father and son "go" on together (22:8). Abraham builds the altar and prepares to sacrifice his son when, as he lifts his hand and "takes" the knife (22:9-10), the third sequence begins.

An angel calls to Abraham, and Abraham responds "here I am" (*hineni*, 22:11). The angel commends Abraham for his obedience, forbidding him to harm his son (22:12), and Abraham sees at last what he must do. The "take and go" (*qah velek*) of God's command and the "here" (*hine*) of Isaac's question come together as Abraham sees the ram: ". . . and behold [*hine*] a ram behind him entangled in the thicket, and Abraham went [*vayelek*] and took [*vayiqah*] the ram and brought it as an offering instead of his son" (22:13).[2] The resolution of the narrative coincides with the perfection of the linguistic pattern. Only in this third segment do all four terms appear: "here I am" (*hineni*), signalling the acceptance of the mission; "behold" (*hine*), introducing the circumstance that will allow the mission to be accomplished; "and he went" (*vayelek*), showing the person going to follow the command; "and he took" (*vayiqah*), offering the person an object which allows him to fulfill the command without danger. Abraham, finally, is able to fulfill God's command and also preserve his son through the offering of a sacrificial substitute.

God rewards Abraham's action by giving Abraham the promised blessing and guaranteeing its continuation through his seed (22:16-18). Isaac is not mentioned again in this story. Abraham simply returns to the lads he had left behind and "they go together" (22:19), as Abraham and Isaac had gone together before. The omission of Isaac's name is significant. It suggests that Isaac will receive the blessing automatically, simply because he is Abraham's son. Isaac receives the blessing through his experience on Mount Moriah because Abraham receives the blessing there, and Abraham receives the blessing and the guarantee that it will continue with his son through his double action of "taking" and "going" (*qah velek*), of preparing to sacrifice Isaac and killing the ram in his stead. In this story, it is the father who seeks the blessing—the father must accept his task with "here I am" (*hineni*), and it is he who must go, and he who must take.

The blessing of Jacob

The linguistic pattern is very different in Isaac's family, and so is the narrative pattern. Most significantly, it is the son who now must seek the blessing. While in the story of the transfer from Abraham to Isaac, God had commanded the father, in the story of the transfer from Isaac to Jacob, the father commands his son. This difference is striking and will warrant further investigation, but the father's command to the son can easily fit into the stylistic pattern established by the previous story. According to this pattern, we would expect the father to call to his chosen son and the son to respond "here I am" (*hineni*). The father ought to command his son to take something and to go on a mission, and the son ought to take and go, returning then to receive his father's blessing. This is, in fact, the basic narrative line of chapter 27, but many of the key words are glaringly absent where we would expect to find them.

As soon as the story begins, the style indicates that this is a parallel to the story of the binding of Isaac. After the formulaic introduction which is identical in both narratives, "And it came to pass" (*vayehi*), the story continues to sound just like its earlier counterpart: ". . . he called Esau, his bigger son,[3] and he said to him, 'My son,' and he said to him, 'Here I am [*hineni*].' And he said, 'Behold [*hine*] . . . ' " (27:1-2). Isaac proceeds to command his son to take his bow and arrow and to go hunt some food for his father, but suddenly, just when the text has established the familiar pattern, the language violates our expectations. Instead of "take and go" (*qah velek*), Isaac commands Esau "lift up and go out" (*sa' vetse'*) (27:3). Esau, the obedient son, "goes" (*vayelek*, 27:5).

Meanwhile, Rebecca has heard this conversation and speaks to her favorite son, Jacob. Suddenly, we find ourselves back within the pattern; Rebecca begins with "behold" (*hine*, 27:6). And the mother, speaking to the second son, supplies the missing words: "Go [*lek*] to the flock and take [*veqah*] for me from there two good kids . . ." (27:9). But from this conversation, too, something is missing; the son has not said "here I am" (*hineni*). The omission is emphasized by a redundant use of the verb "to say": "And Rebecca said to Jacob, her son, saying, 'Behold [*hine*] . . . ' " (27:6). The double use of the verb hints at what could have come in between, as in the exchange which we have just read between Isaac and Esau: ". . . he called Esau, his bigger son, and said to him, 'My son,' and he [Esau] said to him, 'Here I am [*hineni*].' And he [Isaac] said, 'Behold [*hine*] . . . .' "

Jacob does not say "here I am" (*hineni*) as his mother begins to speak, but he does respond after she finishes. Rebecca concludes her speech exactly as Isaac had finished his; the son must follow his parent's command in order to gain his father's blessing (27:9-10). While Esau obediently had set forth on his mission, Jacob hesitates: *"Hen"*—"But " (27:11). The word *hen* is closely related to *hine*; they are used almost identically, both with the meaning "behold." But while *hine* ("behold") is used by Isaac and Rebecca as the motivation for action, and Esau undertakes his task with *hineni* ("here I am"), Jacob uses *hen* ("but") as an excuse to forego action. And *hen* is the first word of Jacob's response to his mother's command, a response which we anticipated earlier. When Jacob finally speaks, we still listen for the expected *hineni*, but hear only a *hen*; instead of accepting his mission, Jacob objects.[4]

Why Isaac chooses Esau and why Jacob receives the blessing have always troubled interpreters of this story. But the distribution of these key words makes the issue much more complicated. We would expect, if the blessing is to be transferred from Isaac to Jacob, that Isaac would command with "go and take" and that Jacob would accept with "here I am." That this pattern does not occur in our story is not surprising because, we know, Isaac has no intention of giving the blessing to Jacob. But what does surprise us is that the pattern does not even follow the narrative plot; if Isaac intends to transfer his blessing to Esau, then Isaac must command Esau with "take and go" and Esau must accept with "here I am."

The absence of this pattern is surprising, especially because it is not Esau, the son who ultimately will be rejected, who deviates from the pattern; it is Isaac. In fact, neither Jacob, the son who ultimately will be chosen, nor Isaac, the parent who will transmit the blessing, uses the appropriate words. While Esau is willing to follow his father's command, Isaac does not know how to command him. And, while Rebecca knows how to command, Jacob is not willing to follow. When Jacob finally does fulfill the command, when he, like Esau, "goes"(*vayelek*) and, unlike Esau, "takes"(*vayiqah*, 27:14), he does so only because Rebecca has emphasized that he must take the animals to *her* (*veqah li*, 27:13). This is the closest we get to the expected pattern in a story which sets out to describe the transfer of the blessing from father to son. The mother commands, the son unwillingly follows, and the paternal blessing remains with a father who does not know how to transmit the blessing.

Another related word pattern here further stresses Jacob's inability to receive the blessing from his father and Isaac's inability to transmit the blessing to his son. While *sa' vetse'* ("lift up and go out") takes the place of *qah velek* ("take and go") in Isaac's command to Esau (27:3), *vehavi'a li* continues the command—"and bring it [the venison] to me " (27:4). The position of "bring" (*vehavi'a*) indicates that it is the crucial word, because the order of the commands throughout this story is first "go" and second "take." In fact, this is what Esau sets out to do—"and he went [*vayelek*] . . . to bring [*lehavi'*]" (27:5). Esau "goes" (*vayelek*) as an obedient son at his father's command; but "bring" (*vehavi'a*) is the wrong command.

When Rebecca commands Jacob with the appropriate words, "go [*lek*] . . . and take [*veqah*]," she does not omit the word "to bring" (*lehavi'*). She instructs Jacob with "take for me" (*qah li*), but she continues with "and you will bring it to your father" (*veheve'ta le'avika*, 27:10). Jacob objects to his mission for fear that "I will bring upon myself [*veheve'ti*] a curse and not a blessing" (27:12). It would seem that, while only "take" (*qah*) allows the transmission of the real blessing, "bring" (*have'*) can be the vehicle for some kind of blessing or curse. Rebecca reassures her son by taking the curse upon herself and repeats her command, this time leaving out the "bring" (*veheve'ta*). She says only "go, take for me" (*lek qah li*, 27:13). This mission the son accepts. Jacob "goes" (*vayelek*), "takes" (*vayiqah*), and, instead of bringing to his father, "brings to his mother" (*vayave' le'imo*, 27:14).

When Jacob later does visit his father, the word "he came" (*vayavo'*) is initially used (27:18). But when Isaac suspects Jacob, just as the son had feared, even this word is replaced. Isaac tells Jacob, "approach" (*gesha*) and "he approached" (*vayigash*, 27:21-22). The father commands again, "present before me" (*hagisha li*), and "he presented" (*vayagesh*, 27:25). After another double use of the verb, Isaac finally blesses Jacob (27:26-27). But, after Jacob leaves, Esau "comes" (*ba'*) back from the field and "brings" (*vayave'*) food to his father (27: 30-31). Esau had gone and returned exactly as Isaac had commanded him, but his blessing has already been given away. Yet Jacob, who received the blessing, has barely been able to come to his father, only through a hesitant *vayigash* and *vayagesh*, approach and presentation. If Jacob is truly to receive the blessing from his father, he must be able to come before him, to move from *vayigash/vayagesh* to *vayavo'/vayave'* and , finally, to receive the real command of *lek veqah*.

In Chapter 28, Isaac calls Jacob to him, sends him on a mission, and transfers to him the patriarchal blessing, "the blessing of Abraham" (28:4). Here, at last, Isaac uses the term "go and take" (*lek veqah*, 28:2). But, once again, it is Rebecca who has initiated the command (27:46), and it is to Rebecca's family that Isaac sends Jacob (28:2). In fact, the mother has already told her son to go and has promised to send for him when it becomes safe for him to return (27:43-45). Not until the end of chapter 35 does Jacob return home and, when he does, it is to his father that he returns: "Jacob came (*vayavo'*) to Isaac his father" (35:27). And not until chapter 46 does Jacob utter the word *hineni* ("here I am," 46:2).[5] The transfer of the patriarchal mission from Isaac to Jacob is not completed in the story of the blessing; it merely begins there. It begins as Isaac finally commands his son to "go and take" (*lek veqah*) and as Jacob sets out to seek the blessing which he has been promised.

The selling of Joseph

The pattern of "go" and "here I am" occurs one more time in the patriarchal narrative—predictably, in the story of the selling of Joseph. Here, as in the story of the blessing of Jacob, it is the father who commands and the son who must go, but little else seems to remain of the pattern which we have traced throughout the other stories of transfer. Jacob says "go" (*lek*) and Joseph accepts with "here I am" (*hineni*),[6] but we find neither the preface of "behold" (*hine*), nor the complementary command of "take" (*qah*, 37:13-14). If it was the father's "take" which insured the safety of the son, then the absence of the "take" in this story is to be expected. Joseph goes out empty-handed to his brothers. He has no sacrificial substitute which can incorporate both identification and conflict, which can allow him to come close while it deflects his brothers' violence. Such an offering makes sense only when identification already exists, as between Abraham and Isaac and between Isaac and his son. But between Joseph and his brothers there is only competition; Joseph cannot even come close to them before they decide to fall upon him (37:18).

This separateness is already expressed in Jacob's command, not only by the absence of "take," but by the new words filling the gaps in the pattern. Instead of "and take," a command to take something to the brothers, Jacob commands "and bring back to me" (*vahashiveni*, 37:14). While Jacob wants to send Joseph to his brothers, his command betrays the impossibility of a reunion. "See [*re'e*]," Jacob says, "whether there is *shalom* ['peace'] with your brothers and *shalom* with the flocks, and bring word back to me." The mission seems vaguely reminiscent of Esau's mission; Isaac sent Esau to hunt an animal for him because that was what the son was in the habit of doing, and that practice represented Esau's beloved status (25:28). Jacob sends Joseph to bring word back to him; that is what Joseph has been in the habit of doing, and that is what represents Joseph's beloved status. Joseph has always brought word of his brothers back to his father, "evil report" (37:2), and because of his favored position his brothers hate him—"and they could not talk to him in peace" (*dabero leshalom*, 37:4). Jacob's command, then, is impossible to fulfill—Joseph cannot see (*re'e*) the brothers' *shalom* and bring back word (*davar*), because the brothers cannot exchange words (*dabero*) in *shalom*. Instead of instructing Joseph to take a sacrificial object to his brothers, Jacob tells Joseph to bring to his father the thing which epitomizes the brothers' inability to get along.

The impossibility of this mission is apparent even before the command of "go . . . and bring back to me" (*lek . . . vahashiveni*). Jacob begins his speech with a description of the situation, just as Isaac and Rebecca had begun with the motivations for their commands, but, instead of *hine*, Jacob says *halo'* (37:13). Both words translate loosely into "behold," but the literal meanings are different—*hine* is affirmative, "here . . ."; *halo'* is negative interrogative, "is it not so. . . ?"[7] "Is it not so," Jacob says, "that your brothers are tending the flocks in Shechem? Go (*leka*) and I will send you to them." In fact, it is not so. Joseph cannot find his brothers in Shechem (37:14-17),[8] and, when he moves on toward their new location, they see him first. Instead of Joseph coming close to his brothers and seeing about their *shalom*, the brothers "saw Joseph from afar and, before he could come close to them, they plotted to kill him " (37:18). Jacob sends Joseph—*vayishlahehu* (37:14), not *vayelek*; that is, "Jacob sent" rather than "Joseph went"—on an impossible mission and Joseph never returns to his father.

While Jacob commands his son ("go" [*lek*]) and Joseph accepts his father's command ("here I am" [*hineni*]), Jacob has misassessed his family's situation. The impossibility of reconciliation, which Jacob fails to recognize, is suggested by the absence of the words "behold" (*hine*) and "take" (*qah*) and by their substitution with the inaccurate "is it not so?" (*halo'*) and the inappropriate "and bring back to me" (*vehashiveni*). The brothers soon take over the action and fill in the missing words. With an introduction, this time, of "behold" (*hine*) the brothers recognize Joseph and plot what to do—"let us go [*leku*] and kill him" (37:19-20). They are the ones who finally come to Jacob, and they do not come empty-handed—they take (*vayiqku*) Joseph's bloodied cloak with them, and they bring it (*vayavi'u*) to their father (37:31-32).

When Isaac had sent Jacob away from home (*vayishlah*), and Jacob went (*vayelek*, 28:5), it became Jacob's task to seek his destiny and return home. Joseph is sent away by his father (*vayishlahehu*, 37:14), and thrown into the pit by his brothers (*vayashliku*, 37:24); he does not leave his family willingly and he does not return to them.[9] While Joseph will, later, mold the experiences of his family, and while these events will lead to the family's ultimate reunion, it will remain the task of the brothers and father to return to Joseph.

And so, after Joseph finally reveals himself to his brothers, the plan for the family's reunion takes the form of the now familiar command. The brothers are told to "go" (*leku*) to Canaan and to "take" (*uqehu*)[10] their father back to Egypt with them (45:17-18); Joseph "sends" his brothers (*vayeshalah*), and they "go" (*vayeleku*, 45:24). When Jacob receives the message calling him to go to Egypt, he is being triply called: the brothers tell him what Joseph had told them which Pharaoh had told Joseph (45:17-21, 27). And yet, when Jacob agrees to go, he expresses personal motivation: "Joseph my son is alive; I will go and I will see him before I die" (*'elka ve'er'enu beterem 'amut*, 45:28).

Jacob's statement echoes the events of chapter 37. When Joseph is sent to see his brothers, the brothers see him first "before he came close" (*uveterem yiqrav*) and plan his death (*lehamito*, 37:18). To the news of Joseph's apparent death, Jacob responds, "I will go down ['*ered*] to my son a mourner into Sheol" (37:35). Now everything has reversed. Jacob will indeed "go down" (46:3) to his son, but not into Sheol; Jacob goes down to his son in Egypt, to see Joseph before he dies.[11]

Now, at last, Jacob will say the "here I am" which he never said to his father. Now, seeking his son, Jacob stops at his father's place, Be'er Sheba, and sacrifices to "the God of his father Isaac " (46:1). God calls to him just as he had called to Abraham on Mount Moriah—"Abraham, Abraham"—at the moment when Abraham was to claim his own son (22:1). God now calls "Jacob, Jacob," and Jacob responds "here I am" (*hineni*, 46:2). For the first time, Jacob fully accepts his role as son, and he knows that he must now become a father to his own son. Jacob goes down to Egypt not because of the brothers' command, or Joseph's, or Pharaoh's; he goes down because he has a mission to fulfill—the "God of his father" (46:3) has told him to go and seek his son.

Narrative doubling and the patriarchal quest

Having traced the pattern of "go and take" (*lek veqah*), "behold" (*hine*) and "here I am" (*hineni*) through the stories of transfer from father to son, I want to suggest that there is a connection between the words of command and the structure of the narrative. The command to "go" inaugurates a search; it does not introduce a simple mission which can be exhausted in a single episode. Each person who is commanded with "go" begins a long and difficult quest. That quest, the slow process of error and discovery and return, is expressed by the doubling of narrative events. The narrative moves forward and then retraces its steps, just as the protagonist embarks on his quest, loses his way, and finally returns having found what he was seeking.

In the Joseph story, the doubling emerges from Joseph's manipulation of events, when his brothers come to Egypt, to duplicate his family's experiences in Canaan.[12] Joseph favors the youngest brother and then attempts to keep him in Egypt as a slave, offering the other brothers the chance to return to their father in *shalom* (44:17). But this time, Joseph has slaughtered an animal in advance (43:16), and the brothers have prepared an offering to present to Joseph (43:25). And Joseph finally has been able to inquire after the *shalom* of his brothers and of his father (43:27). Joseph's plan serves ultimately to bring the brothers together and, eventually, to reunite all the brothers with their father, Jacob. Something has changed in Jacob's family—as we have seen, through Judah's experiences with Tamar—and the duplication of events within the Joseph narrative allows that change gradually to affect the entire family, the brothers, the father, and Joseph himself. The story of the selling of Joseph, then, with its variation of the pattern of "go" and "here I am," simply points a direction, the path which the son must take, which will take him away from his father's house, but which ultimately will restore him to Jacob's family.

In Isaac's family, too, the command to "go" begins a process in which the son leaves his family. Here, too, the son's experiences are duplicated; Jacob's experiences in Laban's house parallel his experiences in Canaan. And Jacob also changes through his travels in a way which allows him to be reconciled with his brother and to return to his father's house. The story of Jacob stealing the blessing, like the story of the selling of Joseph, begins a cycle in which the son leaves home, in which his experiences mirror his life at home, and through which he finally returns to his father and his destiny.

The story of the binding of Isaac, we noted, is also built on the pattern of "go" and "here I am." In this story the word "go" most obviously indicates a search—God commands Abraham to search for the place where he must sacrifice his son. Yet the search seems to begin and end within this one story; it does not involve a process of reenacting previous events and returning, changed, to the place of departure. And, while all three stories of "going" come toward the end of the fathers' lives and inaugurate the careers of the sons, the binding of Isaac seems to have little to do with the Isaac narrative. Isaac, throughout the story, is passive; here, it is Abraham, the father, who is commanded with "go."

Yet a closer examination of this story's context shows that it is not an isolated event, a quest unto itself. While the two later stories of "going" begin a search, this story culminates a search. And, while the two later stories tell of the son's quest, this story focuses on the father as seeker. Abraham's search, in fact, began at the beginning of his career, when God first commanded him—with "go"—to leave his father's house. And this "go" does begin a cyclical process in which the events of Abraham's life repeat. Abraham changes, and the change brings him to the "go" at the end of his life, to the culmination of his search with the acceptance of his son.

The occurrences of the word "go" (*lek*) in the stories of transfer from father to son suggest the same pattern that we followed, in Chapter Two, through the successive family narratives in Genesis. In Abraham's family, the father must seek his destiny and ultimately acknowledge his son. In Isaac's family, the son must go out, find his way toward reconciliation with his brother, and come back home to his father. In Jacob's family, the son is sent out, and the brothers and father must go, as well, to seek the lost brother and son and to reunite the family.

We have already noted this same progression within the stories of transfer themselves, with the shift from paternal to fraternal conflict and the need for a resolution which stems from both paternal and fraternal responsibility. The progressive inefficacy of sacrifice and the increasing need for resolution of the conflict rather than deflection of the violence, we now see, is expressed in the word "take" (*qah*), with its variations. The combination "go and take" (*lek veqah*) expresses the relationship between coming close and violent conflict, between identification and the possibility of sacrifice. Its parallels of "and he came/brought" (*vayavo'/vayave'*), "and he approached/presented" (*vayigash/vayagesh*), and finally "and he sent" (*vayishlah*) mark degrees of distancing and the degeneration of sacrifice from meaningful substitution into an empty symbolic act. Only for Abraham do "go" (*lek*) and "take" (*qah*) fit perfectly, together with "behold" (*hine*) and "here I am" (*hineni*), for in his family, at the very beginning of the nation, the father must accept the son as his identical replacement. That acceptance takes place at the end of Abraham's life, after he has built up a household and defined a mission which has to be passed on, as the culmination of the quest which itself began with "go."

The word pattern of "go and take," then, does not merely confirm the link between the transfer stories and the progression from each of these stories to the next. It forces us, as well, to look at the larger context of each of these transfer stories, to the sequence of episodes which constitute the narrative of each generation of the patriarchal family, because the very words "go and take" describe the quest which takes place during the lifetime of each of the patriarchs. The transfer story itself is the climax of each of the patriarchal narratives and the beginning of the next; if we are to understand fully how succession takes place in Genesis, we must look at the contexts of these stories. And, in analyzing the structure of these larger narratives, we will take our cue from the transfer stories and particularly from the variations of the basic word pattern in these stories.

We will seek to understand first how each patriarch functions as a father or as a son to his own father, and then how his ability to take his place within the patriarchal family is linked to the roles of other family members, especially of mothers and brothers. Our analysis of the larger narrative will proceed both sequentially and thematically; we will move from Abraham through Joseph, but highlighting different elements of the family and its quest at different points. Although at times we may seem to be far from our original inquiry into succession from father to son, all of the episodes at which we will look ultimately do participate in the definition of the biblical family. And, by the conclusion of the study of the patriarchal narratives, the parallel between the transfer stories, the word pattern of "go and take," and the narrative structure will have become clear.

Doubling in the Abraham narrative

We begin our narrative analysis with Abraham, the patriarch whose quest most clearly is shaped by the word "go" (*lek*). Abraham's career is enveloped by two divine commands to "go" (*lek leka*, 12:1; 22:2); between them all of his experiences repeat themselves.[13] Twice he leaves the land and identifies Sarah as his sister (chs. 12, 20); twice Lot sets out on a destiny distinct from Abraham's (chs. 13, 19); twice Abraham expresses concern with the fate of Sodom (chs. 14, 18); twice he enters into a covenant with God (chs. 15, 17); twice Hagar is forced to leave his home (chs. 16, 21); twice Abraham begets a son (chs. 16, 21); and twice Isaac's birth is announced (chs. 17, 18).

The doubling suggests a movement; the stories are very different the second time they appear, and they reflect a change in Abraham, a change suggested, too, by the change in Abraham's name which occurs at the center of the narrative.[14] At this point, too, a new motif is introduced in the narrative—the motif of laughter, which recurs a number of times in the second half of the Abraham cycle. Laughter, in this narrative, is evoked by the news of an occurrence which violates the expected order, repeatedly by the news of the birth of a child to elderly parents. And, so, laughter is related to the difficulty of true perception, to the lack of correspondence between what something appears to be and what it really is.[15]

Perception, I want to suggest, is the crucial issue for Abraham. Abraham's quest begins with finding the place and ends with finding a son, and the possibility of misperception, of finding the wrong thing or of losing sight of the quest, is the single greatest pitfall which Abraham will face. Abraham must define his own destiny, and what he sees must not be guided by his own lack of perception or by the misperceptions of others. The extent to which Abraham succeeds in retaining and clarifying his vision is what we will focus on as we compare the doubled stories in the Abraham narrative.

Biblical scholars, traditionally, have accounted for repeating stories by attributing them to different sources, and account for differences between the versions by discussing the different styles, traditions, and concerns of each source. The story of Abraham leaving the land and calling Sarah his sister has been seen as a prime example of the inclusion of parallel passages from different documents, because it appears not only twice in Abraham's life, but a third time in the life of Isaac.[16] Yet a comparison of the different Abraham stories with each other and with their contexts argues for closer attention to the details of each version, because Abraham's behavior in each fits with his behavior in the surrounding narratives, and because the particular action in each sets the stage for the action in the stories which immediately follow. Without attempting a complete analysis of the Abraham stories, we can at least trace the shape of the narrative and note the theme of perception through a brief comparison of some of the repeating episodes. We will begin with a look at the two "wife-sister" stories, in chapters 12 and 20.

Abraham and the "wife-sister" stories

The most obvious distinction between Abraham's early trip to Egypt and his later trip to Gerar is Abraham's lack of motivation throughout the second episode. Abraham had gone down to Egypt, the first narrative explains, because there was a famine in the land of Canaan (12:10). And he asks Sarah to pretend that she is his sister, because he is afraid that the Egyptians will kill him in order to take his wife (12:12). But the second narrative offers no reason for Abraham's trip, and Abraham gives no reason for claiming to the Gerarites that Sarah is his sister (20:1-2). Only after Abimelek self-righteously accuses him of trapping him into sinning, does Abraham give the expected response: he was afraid that he would be killed (20:11). But Abraham's response is strange, in what he says, in how he says it, and in the fact that he says anything at all. When Pharaoh had questioned his behavior, Abraham had not responded; he simply had left Egypt with his wife and possessions (12:20). This time, Abraham attempts to excuse himself, and he does so in a long-winded speech as self-righteously defensive as Abimelek's. He also gives more than one explanation, which suggests that no one explanation was good enough. Abraham's response, we are led to suspect, is an after-the-fact rationalization for an act which in fact lacked motivation.

Abraham's response consists of three parts. First, he explains to Abimelek what the reader already would have supposed—he was afraid that he would be killed because of his wife (20:11). But he goes on with the surprising claim that Sarah is, in fact, his sister (20:12). Even if, as some have suggested, Abraham's claim refers to a specific type of aristocratic marriage,[17] the information, in this context, is irrelevant. It is irrelevant, too, if Abraham's claim is literally true. Sarah is still Abraham's wife, and Abimelek is not free to take her.

Abraham's first excuse, then, is belied by Abraham's offer of a second excuse, and his second excuse is no excuse at all. As if in recognition that he as yet has offered no satisfactory explanation, Abraham moves on to a third statement: he has said that Sarah is his sister because that has been his practice all along (20:13). Abraham, like Abimelek, seems to be caught in a predicament from which he cannot emerge honorably. Like Abimelek, he has acted impulsively; he said that Sarah was his sister, we now see, simply because that is what he has always been doing, at least since his trip to Egypt. And Abraham, parenthetically, reveals something else about his travels; in his own mind, they have lacked direction. "When God caused me to wander from my father's house,' says Abraham, "I said to her: This is the kindness [hesed][18] which you shall do with me, in whatever place to which we come, say of me: He is my brother" (20:12). Looking back over his career, Abraham sees a life of aimless wandering. Moreover, Abraham blames God for having caused this wandering.[19] If Abraham can describe God's command with the term "caused to wander" (hit'u),[20] then Abraham, we see, has done more than lose his way. Abraham has forgotten that he is seeking something; he has forgotten the divine command, "go" (lek leka), with which his quest began.

Abraham has moved far from the sense of mission with which his career began, when God directed him to seek "the land which I will show you" (12:1). When Abraham first left that land to go to Egypt, it seemed to be almost by accident, as an extension of his southward travel through the land (12:9-10). And Abraham was motivated then by the danger of famine (12:10). Abraham allowed Sarah to be taken by the Egyptians because he clearly feared that his life would be endangered (12:11-13); in fact, the Egyptians take her without, as far as the narrative tells us, bothering to find out who she is (12:14-15). And Abraham, in giving up Sarah, at least had reason to believe that God's promise of becoming a great nation would be fulfilled though someone other than Sarah, for Sarah was barren (11:30), and God had not yet promised that Abraham's successor would be born to her.

But when Abraham leaves the land the second time, matters are quite different. Abraham goes to a foreign land suddenly and without motivation (20:1), and without motivation he allows his wife to be taken; in fact, Abraham declares Sarah to be his sister before anyone asks him, and Sarah is taken by Abimelek only after Abraham proclaims her to be available (20:2). And Abraham, by this point in the narrative, has been promised that Sarah is soon to give birth to his successor (17:16-21). Abraham, then, freely relinquishes both parts of the divine promise by leaving the land and giving up his wife. He has lost sight of his double mission, to seek the land and to seek the successor who, we now know, is about to be born to Sarah (18:10,14).

In fact, childbirth is a crucial element in the Gerar episode.[21] God punishes Abimelek's household with the cessation of childbirth, and the women bear children again only after Abraham prays for Abimelek (20:17-18). But this narrative endnote only underscores the concern with childbirth which is implicit in this story and explicit in its immediate context.

The narrative emphasizes that Abimelek did not sleep with Sarah (20:4,6). And, when Abimelek sends Abraham away with gifts and returns his wife, he makes a final statement to Sarah: "Behold, I have given a thousand in silver to your brother; behold, it [or he] is for you a covering of the eyes [kesut 'enayim] for all who are with you, and among all you are set right" (20:16).[22] Abimelek attempts to vindicate Sarah, to protect her reputation, just as the narrative has done in noting that Abimelek did not sleep with her. None of this, apparently, had been necessary during the episode in Egypt; we were not told that Pharaoh did not sleep with Sarah, and Pharaoh in no way attempted to vindicate her. These precautions are only necessary now because Sarah is about to give birth, and the paternity of Isaac must be unambiguous.[23] When Isaac is born, immediately after the sojourn in Gerar, the narrative will go out of its way to emphasize that Abraham is Isaac's father, detailing the joint parenthood of Sarah and Abraham through an unusually repetitive succession of verses (21:2-7). But this emphasis only makes more clear the basic problem of the Gerar episode—that Isaac would not have been born to Abraham had the outcome been left in Abraham's control.

Indeed, childbirth emerges as the crucial issue not only within the Gerar story and in the narrative which follows, but in the narrative which precedes as well. Immediately before the Gerar episode, children are born to Lot (19:36-38). The birth of the ancestors of Moab and Ammon raises the issue of childbirth, but more specifically necessitates the birth of a successor to Abraham. When Lot begets two sons who become new nations,

Lot's separation from Abraham and his destiny becomes complete. If, early in his career, perhaps still when he went down to Egypt, Abraham could hope that Lot would be his successor, now that can never happen. Lot has begotten children, he has become a separate nation, and now it is time for Abraham to beget a son who will be his successor, through whom Abraham will become a nation. And yet, before that can happen, Abraham goes to Gerar and gives up the future mother of that son.

Abraham and Lot

In order to understand how Abraham has come to this point, we must look at the larger context of the Gerar episode, noting always the parallels in the first half of the Abraham narrative. We will begin with the stories of the destruction of Sodom and the escape of Lot, the episodes which, as we noted, set the stage for the story of Abraham in Gerar.

Each of the stories is paralleled early in the Abraham narrative, in precisely reverse order: Abraham went to Egypt (12:10-20), Lot separated from him (ch. 13), and Abraham comes to the aid of Lot's endangered city (ch. 14). Now, Abraham comes to the aid of Sodom (18:16-33), Lot escapes and becomes the father of nations separate from Abraham (ch. 19), and Abraham goes down to Gerar (ch. 20). We have already noted one significant difference between Abraham's earlier and later behavior: in the later narrative, Abraham betrays a greater lack of concern for his wife, even while he has more reason for concern. Another difference between the two narratives is that, in the later one, Abraham betrays no concern at all for his nephew Lot.

Early in his career, even after Lot had separated from him, Abraham entered into battle with the four kings when he heard that "his brother was taken captive" (14:14). Now, Abraham also attempts to save Sodom from destruction, but this has nothing to do with concern for Lot. God shows concern for Lot; he sends angels to take him out of the doomed city, and he delivers Lot on account of Abraham (19:29). But Abraham, throughout his plea to God, never mentions Lot, nor does he take note of Lot's fate when he surveys Sodom's destruction

(19:28). Abraham has simply appealed to God's justice, asking him to spare the entire city if a group of righteous men be found within it. Such a group is not to be found, and God continues with his plan to destroy the wicked city.

Abraham's concern for Sodom, indeed, demonstrates his sense of justice, but his prayer also illustrates his lack of concern for Lot. Abraham never mentions the possibility that God would spare a righteous individual; according to the terms of his bargain, either the entire city will be spared or the entire city will be destroyed. Since God does not find the agreed-upon number of righteous men, according to the bargain struck with Abraham, Lot ought to perish together with the rest of the Sodomites. Lot, in fact, is spared because of Abraham (19:29), but not because Abraham has asked that he be spared.

Abraham has taken no interest in Lot, and Lot does not return to Abraham after he escapes from Sodom. When last we hear of him, he is alone in a cave with his two daughters, so isolated that his daughters think he is the last man on earth (19:30-31). They make him drunk, sleep with him, and conceive two children, the ancestors of two nations (19:32-38).

Lot, Abraham's nephew, had begun to separate from Abraham after the sojourn in Egypt, and his departure initiated Abraham's quest for a son (15:2-3). Now the separation between Abraham and Lot is complete, and the time has come for Abraham to have the son he has been promised through Sarah.[24] Yet it is at this point, as we have noted, that Abraham gives up his opportunity to have that promised son.

If we compare the first group of stories about Sarah, Lot, and Sodom with the second group, then, a significant pattern emerges. Abraham, throughout the second group of stories, displays no concern at all for his nephew and for his wife, for the two people whom he had brought with him on his mission to the promised land (12:5), the two people through whom he had a chance to achieve the promise of becoming a "great nation" (12:2).

Indeed, from Abraham's perspective, the quest for a son is over. Between the first and second groups of stories, Ishmael was born (16:15). Abraham no longer needs to seek a successor; he is satisfied with Ishmael as his son (17:18). But Abraham's perspective is wrong. It is true that Lot can no longer be his successor, as we shall discuss further in Chapter Four, but Abraham is wrong to give up on Sarah. Indeed, God has told him that Sarah's son, not Ishmael, would be the child of the promise (17:16). Yet Abraham laughingly rejects that possibility (17:17-18) and he goes on to abandon Sarah in Gerar, treating her as he treats his by now superfluous nephew Lot. In this second group of stories, Abraham has lost his vision.

Abraham and Abimelek

One disturbing sign of Abraham's fall is the similarity between his manner of speaking and Abimelek's. The first words that we hear Abimelek say echo Abraham's plea to God concerning Sodom. Abimelek, pleading for himself, says: "Will you kill the nation, the righteous one as well?" (20:4). Abraham, pleading for Sodom, said: "Will you also destroy the righteous with the wicked?" (18:23).[25] In the Sodom episode, as in Gerar, Abraham's argument is wrong; rather than attempting to save his kinsmen, as we have seen, Abraham offers arguments that would leave them to their fates. Now, we see, Abraham actually sounds like Abimelek. And this similarity of speech continues throughout the Gerar episode. Both men attempt to excuse their wrongdoing with repetitive claims which put the blame on everyone but themselves (20:5, 9, 11-13). Abraham and Abimelek are nearly indistinguishable. Like Abimelek, Abraham refuses to assume responsibility for his actions; he is no longer a shaper of his destiny.

But Abraham and Abimelek will meet again, and this time the two men stand in sharp contrast. Abimelek visits Abraham after Isaac is born and Ishmael is sent away; it is the last episode before the binding of Isaac. Abimelek behaves so characteristically that he becomes a figure of comedy. He arrives, on a supposedly friendly visit, together with his general and asks Abraham to take an oath not to lie to him or to his son or grandson (21:22-23). Abimelek's request plays ironically on the earlier events in Gerar, where Abraham did lie to Abimelek. Abimelek now speaks to Abraham of "kindness" (*hesed*), which can only recall the negative *hesed* which Sarah was forced to perform precisely because of the misdeeds of men such as Abimelek (20:13). "As the *hesed* which I have done with you, you shall do with me," continues Abimelek, "and with the land in which you have sojourned [*garta*]" (21:23). The verse echoes Abimelek's accusation in Gerar, the land of sojourning (20:1; cp. Gerar with *gur*, "to sojourn"), that "deeds which should not be done, you have done with me" (20:9). Now, Abimelek once again presents himself as innocent, as a man who performs only deeds of kindness; in contrast, he presents Abraham as an untrustworthy character in Abimelek's debt.

Abraham's brief response comes as a surprise; it contrasts sharply with his wordy response to Abimelek's accusation in the previous chapter. Now, he says only: "I will swear" (21:34). Then, suddenly, Abraham becomes the accuser, and Abimelek is put on the defensive much as he had been by God's accusation in his dream in Gerar (20:3-5). Abraham accuses Abimelek of stealing a well, and Abimelek responds with the same kind of repetitive excuse that he had uttered before—"I don't know . . . and also you didn't tell me . . . and also I hadn't heard until today" (21:26). Abimelek has not changed, but Abraham has. Abraham does not indulge in long speeches; he has business to do, and he does it with a minimum of words. We do not even hear Abraham's actual speech to Abimelek; the action simply is narrated to us with the word—"he rebuked" (*vehokiah*, 21:25). This word appeared also in the Gerar story, when Abimelek offered a "covering of the eyes" (*kesut 'enayim*) to vindicate Sarah (*venokahat*, 20:16). In Gerar, Abimelek and Abraham vied with each other to cover up their crookedness; now, Abimelek is still crooked and still tries to cover up, but Abraham sets Abimelek straight and behaves in a straightforward manner himself.

In Be'er Sheba Abraham establishes a covenant which, as Abimelek stipulates, will protect his children and grand-children (21:23). That he hinges the covenant on the issue of the well emphasizes this; in the preceding episode, his son Ishmael had been saved through the well in Be'er Sheba (21:14, 19). And soon, after Abraham establishes his lineage through Isaac by offering him as a sacrifice, he will return to Be'er Sheba (22:19), the place which guarantees the continued protection of children. In fact, Be'er Sheba will be established again, later, by Isaac, after he attempts to restore his father's wells against the opposition of Abimelek's people and as he, in turn, receives God's blessing of offspring (26:23-33). Be'er Sheba ultimately will symbolize Abraham's continuity through Isaac, but right now, notably, that is not clear. The episode of Abraham's covenant with Abimelek falls right between a story about Ishmael and a story about Isaac. Abraham establishes a covenant for his son—but who that son is has not yet been established.

That Abraham no longer resembles Abimelek in Be'er Sheba merely hints at what has changed in Abraham. In the Sodom and Gerar episodes, Abraham had not said a word about reclaiming Lot and Sarah; if anything, his prayer to God and his excuse to Abimelek argued against saving his nephew and wife. Suddenly, after Isaac is born to Sarah and after Ishmael is banished with Hagar, Abraham sets his mind on his future and on his children.

Actually, this orientation to the future represents less a change than a return to a previous state; Abraham certainly had begun his career with a concern for destiny. Only in the later part of his life does he, for a while, lose that concern. Abraham's most poignant statement of that loss is the beginning of his explanation to Abimelek: "And it came to pass, when God caused me to wander [hit'u] from my father's house . . ." (20:13). Looking at Abraham's behavior, at his lack of direction and lack of clarity, we might, together with Abimelek, ask the question: "What did you see [ma ra'ita], that you have done this?" (20:10). And we must ask as well what has changed that has allowed Abraham's vision to be restored.

Hagar

Abraham's blind wandering in Gerar is echoed a chapter later by Hagar's wandering (vateta', 21:14). Hagar has been banished from Abraham's house; she wanders through the desert of Be'er Sheba and, when Ishmael is about to die of thirst, she casts him under the shrubs. Hagar refuses to see ('al 'er'e) what will happen to her child (21:16). Her behavior contrasts with Abraham's behavior in the episode of the binding of Isaac. Hagar's eyes must be opened by God in order for her to see the well which will save her son (21:19). But Abraham will see by himself the ram entwined in the thicket which will save his son Isaac (22:13). What Abraham has been unable to see in Gerar is what Hagar never sees.[26] The expulsion of Hagar marks the end of the period of Abraham's blindness. After Hagar leaves, Abraham will be able to see how to save his son.

The story of Hagar's banishment has a parallel toward the beginning of the Abraham narrative (ch. 16). More precisely, the earlier episode comes after the stories of Abraham and Sarah in Egypt, the separation of Lot, Abraham's protection of Sodom, and God's first covenant with Abraham (chs. 12-15). Between the parallel Hagar episodes, each of these stories is paralleled as well, but the second group, beginning with Abraham's laughter at the promise of a son, and continuing through his lack of concern for his nephew and wife, show us a different Abraham. From the time Hagar enters his family (ch. 16) until the moment she is banished (ch. 21), Abraham loses sight of his destiny. In order to understand the problem that Hagar represents, we must look at the earlier Hagar episode and its context.

After God establishes his covenant with Abraham and, at Abraham's request, promises him a son, Sarah gives her maid Hagar to her husband in the hope of bearing a child through her.[27] From the moment Hagar conceives, the episode is full of words relating to sight. "And she saw [*vatere'*] that she had conceived, and her mistress became light in her eyes [*be-'eneha*]" (16:4). The fact is told twice, by the narrator and by Sarah (16:5), and what follows is a play on the word for eye (*'ayin*). Abraham tells Sarah to do what is good in her eyes (*be'enayik*), and Sarah makes Hagar suffer (*vate'aneha*, 16:6). Hagar escapes and is found by an angel "near a fountain [*'en*] of water in the desert, by the fountain [*ha'ayin*] on the road to Shur" (16:7).[28] The angel speaks three times before Hagar responds. Continuing the pun, he tells Hagar to return to her mistress and to suffer (*vehit'ani*), at her hands (16:9). Hagar says nothing, and the angel speaks again, promising to increase her seed until it will be too numerous to count (16:10). Again, there is no response. Finally, the angel foretells the birth of Ishmael, explaining the child's name and his nature (16:11-12). At last, Hagar responds. She names God, repeatedly using the word "to see" (16:13-14), and goes back to bear Ishmael to Abraham (16:15).

The conversation between Hagar and the angel takes meaning from its context; the episode follows a similar conversation between Abraham and God, during the episode of the covenant between the pieces. God begins with a promise of increase resembling the angel's second statement to Hagar— Abraham's seed will be, like the stars, too numerous to count (15:5). When Abraham asks for more sure knowledge, God responds with a strange prophecy about the future generations (15:13-16), a prophecy which we will have to examine before we can understand the link between God's promises to Abraham and to the angel's conversation with Hagar.

Abraham and the future of the nation

Within the narrative of the whole Pentateuch, God's prophecy to Abraham refers to the slavery in and exodus from Egypt. But the element of the prophecy which makes God's message so strange is the jumbled chronology. God tells Abraham that his descendants will be strangers (ger) in a land where they will be enslaved (va'avadum) and made to suffer (ve'inu), but that the enslavers will be judged, and the descendants will leave with much property (15:13-14). Then, as we are looking to the future, the prophecy suddenly shifts to the present generation: "And you will come to your fathers in peace [beshalom], shall be buried in a good old age" (15:15). And then it shifts just as suddenly back to the future: "And the fourth generation will return here, because the iniquity of the Amorites is not complete (shalem) until this" (15:16).

The shifting chronology, which moves smoothly from future to present and from present to distant future, implies an identification between the destiny of Abraham and the destiny of his descendants. It suggests that the future history of the nation is already in progress, and that Abraham's experiences are a part of that history.[29] Moreover, the prophecy ends at a beginning, at the point when the people return to the promised land, at the moment when the fulfillment of their destiny is to begin.

A parallel to this prophecy, which may illuminate the strange sequence, can be found at the beginning of the book of Exodus. Moses, like Abraham, has been promised by God that his people would possess the land of Canaan. And, like Abraham, Moses questions God and receives a response: ". . . this is the sign that I have sent you—when you take the nation out of Egypt, you [plural] will worship God on this mountain" (Exod 3:11). The sign seems hardly reassuring; instead of showing Moses something that betokens the future, God gives him a sign which will come to be only after the event which it betokens.[30]

The sign is the fulfillment of the event. It only makes sense if Moses can understand his mission as a process already in motion, controlled by the God who was with his forefathers and who will continue to be with Moses and with the nation (3:12-15). Moses is the link between that past and that future; he, first, must understand his mission and then must teach it to the people (3:6-10,16-17). Moses' encounter on the mountain with the God of his fathers is a part of the nation's destiny; they, too, God tells Moses, will encounter the God of their fathers on the mountain after they leave Egypt. The best guarantee of the nation's destiny, then, is precisely the sign that God offers to Moses, because that sign suggests that the nation's future has already begun through Moses.

To Abraham's question, "By what will I know that I will inherit it [the land]?" (Gen 15:8), God responds by speaking in the future. But the future of the nation, he is saying, is a fulfillment of Abraham's present. Abraham's own experience, like Moses' encounter with God in the mountain, is the model for the later experience of the nation. The shifting chronology suggests that the elements of God's prophecy refer both to the future of the nation and to Abraham's own life. When we reach the third verse of the prophecy, then, and find that it tells of Abraham's own future, we sense that the previous verses ought to have been talking about what preceded this in time—that is, of course, about Abraham's own past. And, in a way, the first two verses, the prophecy for the future of the nation, do describe Abraham's past. Abraham has just sojourned in Egypt, God has judged the Egyptians and stricken them, and Abraham has left with much property (12:10-13:2). And, if the first three verses speak of Abraham's past and future, then the fourth verse, concerning the "fourth generation," ought to be talking about the fourth generation from Abraham—that is, about the sons of Jacob. The sons of Jacob do, of course, return to the land after a period of exile; they even take possession of a portion of the land when the "Amorite" inhabitants sin (ch. 34; cp. 48:22).

I will discuss more fully the typological nature of Abraham's and Jacob's experiences in Chapter Five, but for now it is important to note that Abraham lives out, in his own lifetime, the future history of the nation. That history consists of events which have begun in Abraham's lifetime and which will continue through his children, grandchildren, and great-grandchildren. The prophecy is connected to the promise of a son, and the son who will inherit Abraham's blessing must be capable of accepting this destiny and of passing it on, in turn, to his children.

Hagar's blindness

Immediately after this episode, a son is finally to be born to Abraham. And this son, if he is to be Abraham's successor, must be capable of having the covenant fulfilled through him. It is precisely the terms of the covenant which the angel offers to Hagar for the son whom she is about to bear to Abraham. Hagar is an Egyptian, a stranger in the land of Canaan, as her name suggests (cp. *gur*, "to sojourn"). She is the slave of Sarah, and the angel tells her to return to her mistress—and to be afflicted (*vehit'ani*) at her hand (16:9).[31] In sum, the angel is telling Hagar to accept the suffering—the sojourning, enslavement, and affliction (*gur*, *'avoda*, and *'oni*)—that is a part of the covenant of Abraham and his descendants (15:13). But Hagar does not respond.[32] The angel speaks again, adding the promise which God had just made to Abraham (15:5), the promise of innumerable descendants (16:10). But again Hagar does not respond.

Hagar has rejected both the suffering of the present and the promise of the future. Instead, the angel goes on to offer her alleviation of her suffering and the promise of the present. Speaking a third time, he uses language that, in contrast to what preceded, is markedly uncovenantal: "Behold you are pregnant, and you will bear a son, and you shall call his name Ishmael, because God has heard [shama'] your suffering ['onyek]" (16:11).

The word for suffering has played throughout the passage on the word "eye" ('ayin) and so has echoed the motif of sight; its juxtaposition here with the word "heard" (shama'), rather than "saw," is ironic. Hagar adds to the irony by calling God 'El Ro'i, "the God who sees me," because, she says, "I have seen [ra'iti] him who sees me [ro'i]." (16:13). In a final twist, the well, until now also called 'ayin (16:7), takes on this name, Be'er Lahai Ro'i, "the well of the living one who sees me" (16:14).

Ra'oh, "to see," seems to be the normal verb for the object 'oni, "suffering"; both Leah and Jacob will say that God "saw" their suffering (29:32; 31:42), and God will tell Moses that he has seen the 'oni of his enslaved nation (Exod 3:7; 4:31). The use of the verb shama' ("heard") with 'oni ("suffering") is unusual, as is emphasized by Hagar's own assessment that God has "seen" her; she employs the verb that we would have expected the angel to use. But the angel has not used the term "to see the affliction," because this is a term reserved for God's response to his covenantal people. And Hagar has just rejected the opportunity to participate in God's covenant and to share, with her son, in the destiny of God's people. God ultimately offers her a promise for the present, instead of the promise for the distant future, which she has rejected; and God "hears" her affliction and alleviates it,[33] rather than responding covenantally to her affliction, for she has rejected that as well.

Hagar believes that God has "seen" her and that she, in turn, has "seen" God (16:13). But God has not seen her and she, we must conclude, has not seen God. Hagar is blind to divine destiny; she cannot accept affliction in the present, because she does not possess a vision for the future (16:9-10). She is, indeed, directionless; just as she will wander later in the desert (21:14), she has no sense of direction now. When the angel first "finds" her (16:7), he asks where she is coming from and where she is going, but Hagar responds only to the first question (16:8). She wants to escape servitude and affliction, but she has no idea where she wants to go.

Hagar is blind to destiny, as she will be blind, later, to her dying son and to the well which is capable of reviving him (21:16,19). Ishmael is the son of a woman whose suffering is heard, and his cries, later, will be heard (21:17). But he is not the son of a woman who sees clearly. The only thing that Hagar does "see" in this episode is that she is now pregnant (16:4); she perceives only the present, as she responds only to the angel's promise for the present—"behold, you are pregnant . . ." (16:11). But even this Hagar misunderstands; when she sees that she is pregnant, "her mistress became light in her eyes [be'eneha]"(16:5). Hagar misperceives her role and she does not return, as the angel commands, to her mistress.

Sarah had wanted to bear a child through Hagar, but Hagar bears her child only to Abraham, and it is Abraham who names the child Ishmael (16:15-16). Ishmael is not born within the terms of the covenant, and he will not be the son to succeed Abraham. God establishes another covenant with Abraham, foretelling the birth of Isaac through Sarah, but Abraham cannot understand why he must have another son (17:1-17). He prays for the son he already has begotten: "If only Ishmael might live before you" (17:18). God responds, once more, that he has "heard" him (uleyishma'e'l shema'tika, 17:20), and that Ishmael will be blessed with increase; but the covenant, he says, will be established through Sarah's son, Isaac.

Abraham's loss of vision

Immediately after the episode of Hagar and Ishmael, the second part of the Abraham narrative begins, paralleling the first part. There is a covenant between God and Abraham with the announcement of the birth of a child, Abraham's intercession on behalf of Sodom, Lot's final separation from Abraham, the journey to a foreign land where Sarah is taken and, finally, the banishment of Hagar and Ishmael.

This second sequence begins with Abraham's laughing disbelief at God's words concerning his destiny through his son (17:17) and continues, as we have noted, with Abraham's lack of concern for Lot and for Sarah. Thus, when Abimelek asks Abraham, "What did you see . . . [ma ra'ita]?" (20:10), we find that Abraham has seen no more than Hagar has seen. He has lost sight of the covenant—"God caused me to wander [hit'u]" (20:13). The sequence of episodes leads to the birth of Isaac, whose name reflects Abraham's laughter (21:1-3), and with the laughter of Ishmael (21:9). Ishmael's laughter parallels his mother's mockery of Sarah[34] and expresses what has been wrong with Abraham's family since Hagar joined it—Isaac, the son who is to carry on Abraham's mission, has been seen as a superfluous addition to the family.

From the moment Hagar joined the family and conceived Abraham's son, relationships have been reversed, the order of things has been violated, and the fulfillment of God's promise has been met by laughter. And now, Sarah's demand to banish Hagar and Ishmael is "very bad in Abraham's eyes [be'ene 'Avraham]" (21:11). Abraham is unable to see properly, but God tells Abraham to listen (shema') to Sarah so that he may see clearly—the banishment, God says, should not "seem bad in his eyes [be'eneha]" (21:12). Abraham, once again and for the last time, cannot see what he must do, but he does listen to Sarah, who is able to see. He rises early in the morning and sends Hagar away with Ishmael, to "wander" (vateta')—unseeing as ever—in the desert (21:14).

Ishmael's laughter and Hagar's blindness do not originate in this episode; they are simply more extreme manifestations of Hagar's earlier lack of perception. Similarly with Abraham. His laughter at the news of a son and his lack of concern for his nephew and wife do not originate during the second part of his life, when Hagar is incorporated into his family. They develop from a problem already inherent in Abraham's family, a problem which Hagar personifies, but does not introduce.

When God commanded Abraham with the first "go" (lek), he called the destination "the land which I will show you ['asher 'ar'eka]" (12:1). The verb is a form of ra'oh, "to see"; God will cause Abraham to see the land. As his grandson Jacob will later do, Abraham first stops in the city of Shechem, at 'Elon More, where God appears to him (vayera'), and Abraham builds an altar to "the God who appeared [hanir'e] to him" (12:6-7). Abraham continues to travel southward through the land (12: 10), and his arrival in Egypt, motivated by a famine, is just one step further on his southward journey, but one step too far. Seen in this way, Abraham's journey to Egypt seems not so much sinful as unperceptive. Abraham, at this point, is not able to define the boundaries of the land. In fact, he was not able to find the chosen place without God causing him to see it. Without God showing him the way, Abraham cannot choose where he must go and where he must not go. And, thus, he oversteps the bounds and goes to Egypt.

Egypt is a land where people follow what they see, but what they see leads them to misperceive what they should do. It is this characteristic of the Egyptians that Abraham fears; they see the beauty of his wife and they take her (12:12, 14). This same characteristic, soon after, is what causes Lot to be lost to Abraham.

After the family returns from Egypt, Lot and Abraham find that they have too much property to allow them to live near each other (13:6). Abraham offers Lot the choice of moving northward or southward and agrees to go the other way (13:9), but Lot chooses neither of these directions. Instead, he chooses to move eastward, toward the land of Sodom (13:11-12). He chooses this region because it looks fertile—"Lot lifted up his eyes and saw [vayar']"—but the text tells us that the land resembles Egypt (13:10). Sodom, like Egypt, is a place of blindness; in fact, later the Sodomites become literally blind (19:11). Lot's choice of Sodom contrasts with Abraham's tie to the land of Canaan, but it also says something about Abraham's recent willingness to leave the land for Egypt, a land which is compared to Sodom, where, we are told, the people are very evil (13:13).[35]

Now, after Lot's departure, God tells Abraham to look, as Lot has just done: "Lift up your eyes and see [ure'e], from the place where you are . . ." (13:14). God promises Abraham the entire land which he can see (ro'e) for himself and for his descendants and commands him to walk throughout the land (13:14-7). Abraham must define the limits of the land, but he must not overstep them as he did once before. The land is defined by what Abraham sees, and Abraham's mission is to go (hithalek) where his sight leads him. And his vision will be correct when he looks about him from the place which he has already been caused to see.

While it is the Egyptians and Lot who allow their eyes to mislead them, Abraham is a partner to their misperception. He undertakes the trip to Egypt, he misdefines Sarah as his sister, and he suggests that Lot separate from him, defining his nephew as his brother (13:8). "Brother" ('ah) is a common term for any relative, but in this episode it plays against the repeated "sister" ('ahot) in the previous episode. Both, of course, contrast with the true relationships defined earlier in the narrative: "and Abram took Sarai, his wife, and Lot, the son of his brother . . ." (12:5).

Property does not separate a man from his wife or a man from his nephew or foster-son; but it does separate siblings. When the shepherds of Lot and Abraham quarrel, Abraham tells Lot that they should not quarrel "because we are men who are brothers" (13:8). We might expect him to leave it at that or to reiterate that they should live together in peace, but Abraham goes on to suggest that they separate.

Siblings, then, are competitors; they cannot share a single heritage in peace. By misdefining Lot as "brother" and Sarah as "sister," Abraham loses each of these relatives and the chance of finding his destiny through them. Lot, in fact, never returns, because the separation is mutual; Abraham suggests that they separate, but it is Lot who chooses Sodom as his dwelling place. Sarah, ultimately, will share in Abraham's destiny because, although twice Abraham misdefines her and relinquishes her, she herself never chooses to separate from his destiny. Yet, initially, by misperceiving the two relatives whom

81

he brought with him to the land of promise, Abraham precludes the possibility of transmitting his heritage to Lot or to a son who might be born to Sarah.

Through this exclusion of Lot and Sarah, Hagar the Egyptian is evoked;[36] she becomes essential now because Abraham seems not to have any other way of begetting a son. Like Abraham, Hagar misperceives relationships, and she is incapable of possessing a vision of destiny. She is Abraham's lack of perception made tangible, and this quality pervades the later episodes in Abraham's life. Hagar's banishment, for which only Sarah perceives the need, but which Abraham is forced to effect, marks the restoration of Abraham's vision. Sarah defines the relationships properly. Hagar is "the maidservant," Ishmael is "the son of the maidservant,"[37] and Isaac is Sarah's son (21:10). God confirms these definitions and promises that Abraham's destiny will continue through Isaac (21:12). Hagar, banished, wanders in the desert, unseeing, but Abraham no longer wanders. Meeting Abimelek, he answers him straightforwardly and makes a covenant for his descendants.

Seeing the place from afar

At this point, Abraham's sight is tested. Earlier, his misperception of his family had coincided with his misperception of the land and, so, when God commands him once again with "go" (lek leka), he sends Abraham again on the original quest —to find the land and to find a son, to seek the blessing and to ensure its continuation.

Abraham fulfills the double command of "go and take" (lek veqah) by seeing clearly.[38] God no longer offers to show Abraham the land (as in 12:1); he intends simply to "tell" ('omar) Abraham where to go (22:2). And, while earlier God had fulfilled his intention of causing Abraham to see the place (12:7), now God never tells Abraham which is the chosen mountain. God need neither show nor tell Abraham which is the chosen place, because Abraham can see it himself. In fact, Abraham "saw the place from afar" (22:4), in a sense preempting God's showing the way.

At the beginning of his career, God appeared to Abraham after Abraham unknowingly had reached the place (12:6-7); Abraham simply had walked through the land—and, as we have seen, eventually walked out of the land—and God stopped him as he passed through the chosen place. Now Abraham travels directedly—"he went to the place of which God had told him" (22:3)—and finds the place before he nears it (22:4) and before God might have to inform him that he has reached his destination. Each of Abraham's journeys leads to a place with a similar name—'Elon More (12:6) and 'Erets Hamoria (22:2). Both names seem to stem from the root yrh, "to instruct," and play as well on the words ra'oh, "to see," and 'amor, "to say."[39] In both episodes, God instructs Abraham, but now God no longer has to show him; God tells Abraham what to do, but Abraham sees for himself how it must be done.

Abraham's sight in this episode contrasts with Hagar's lack of sight in the preceding episode.[40] In both, Abraham "rose early in the morning" (21:14; 22:3), but it is not he who departs with Ishmael as he does, later, with Isaac. Hagar leaves with Ishmael. She now is his significant parent; that is why she finally will take a wife for him from her nation (21:21), as Abraham later will do for Isaac. Hagar wanders, directionless, in the desert and casts her son under the shrubs when their water runs out. Refusing to see ('al 'er'e) her dying child, she sits far away (harheq) and "lifted up her voice and cried" (vatisa' 'et qolah vatevk) (21:16). Abraham does the opposite. He sees the place (vayar'), even though he is far away (merahoq) when he "lifted up his eyes" (vayisa' 'Avraham 'et 'enav, 22:4).

While Hagar cries in desperation, unable to see what she can do to save her child, God, ironically, "heard [vayishma'] the voice of the lad" (21:17).[41] An angel "called to Hagar from heaven" (21:17) and tells her what to do and, finally, God "opened her eyes" so that she could "see" (vayifqah 'elohim 'et 'eneha vatere') the well which would save her son (21:19). Abraham has been able to lift up his eyes to see the place, but he does not yet see how he must save his son. To Isaac's question—"Where is the lamb for the sacrifice?"—Abraham can only answer that God "will see [yir'e] for himself" (22:7-8). And yet, after the angel "called to him from heaven" (22:11) and tells him not to kill his son, Abraham is able to see for himself how he can save Isaac. "Abraham lifted up his eyes and saw" (*vayisa' 'Avraham 'et 'enav vayar'*) the ram, which would substitute for and save his son (22:13).[42] Just as he saw the place though still far away, he sees the ram though it is hidden from his view—"behold [*hine*], a ram behind him, caught in the thicket by his horns" (22:13).

Hagar is unable to see the well which can save her son; in despair, she moves far away from her son, refusing to see him die. Ishmael is saved only when an angel calls to Hagar and God forces her to see the well to which she had been blind. Abraham, in contrast, is able to see throughout this episode; though told that his son must die, he remains with him—"and the two went together" (22:6, 8). Isaac is saved not only by the angel calling to Abraham and interrupting the sacrifice, but by Abraham seeing for himself how to resolve the paradox of God's command—by seeing something which ought to be impossible to see.

When Hagar first left Abraham's house, she called the place *Be'er Lahai Ro'i*, mistakenly thinking that she saw God and that God saw her (16:13). But Hagar cannot see. She lacks direction and vision, she does not see her son and cannot see how to save him. And God does not see her. In fact, by this later episode, he does not even hear her voice; he hears instead the voice of the child who is far from her (21:16-17). Abraham names the place to which he has gone YHWH *Yir'e* —"God will see" (22:14), echoing his assurance to Isaac that God would provide—or "see"—the animal to be sacrificed (22:8).[43] Yet it is Abraham who sees, and what he sees, the animal to be sacrificed, is precisely what he had told Isaac that God would "see." Not only does Abraham see, then, but he sees what God sees; his vision and God's are one.

The relationship between God's vision and Abraham's was expressed at the very beginning of Abraham's career by the words "which I will show you/cause you to see" (*'asher 'ar'eka*, 12:1) and in Abraham's ability to "lift up his eyes and see" (*sa' na' 'eneka ure'e*) once he is standing in the right "place" (*hamaqom*, 13:14). Now Abraham names the "place" (*ha-maqom*) "God will see," and "to this day," the narrative adds, "it is said, in the mountain of God he (or it) will be seen [*yera'e*]" (22:14).[44] The narrative conflates God's seeing with man's seeing; Abraham is able to see for himself once he is able to find the place (*hamaqom*) from which one can see.

Abraham offers Isaac as a sacrifice after he loses Lot and banishes Ishmael, when he has only one possible heir remaining and when he sees clearly that Isaac will succeed him. The episode is an affirmation of paternity, fraught with danger for the son who is about to receive his father's blessing. Indeed, Isaac and Abraham are so closely identified that the son never actually need be given the blessing by his father; he is blessed automatically, as an extension of his father's being blessed. The blessing of Abraham is confirmed now, after the resolution of the near-sacrifice of Isaac (22:16-18); and, by implication, this blessing shall be inherited by Isaac.[45]

Abraham's perception of Isaac is bound to his vision of his mission; Isaac is the son who will carry on the mission after Abraham's death. The sacrifice of Isaac depends upon Abraham seeing "the place" (22:4), because the need for a son results from the promise of the land (12:1-2), from the promise of a special destiny. When Abraham finally is able to see "the place," he sees his son as successor and he nearly kills him. But, if Isaac is to continue on for Abraham, the father must see one more thing—the substitute which will allow him to save his son. Abraham both kills his son and does not kill him, and that very paradox is what makes him the father of his son.[46] Abraham has enacted the double blessing of land and descendants; as father, he is blessed, and his son will inherit the blessing.

4

MOTHERS,
BROTHERS,
AND
THE
LAND

When Abraham offers Isaac as a sacrifice, he ensures that his son will continue his mission after him. But, if the nation which will arise from Abraham is to be modeled on the patriarchal family, the relationship between father and son must lose the element of conflict which almost leads to the son's death. And, of course, the paternal relationship is not the only one that must be accounted for. In Chapter Three we noted the recurring events in Abraham's life which formed a sequence centering on the announcement of Isaac's birth and bordered by Abraham's double quest for the land and for a son. The recurring stories on which we focused concerned a sojourn in a foreign land, Lot and Sodom, and Hagar and Ishmael. These narratives suggest factors other than paternity which determine the nature of the family: the choice between self-definition and assimilation into an alternate society, the relationship between brothers, and the role of wife and mother with respect to father and son. We have already seen how these elements are interwoven in the Abraham narrative, particularly through the motifs of laughter and seeing. They are, indeed, crucial elements throughout the book of Genesis, and an analysis of these elements is indispensable to an understanding of how the narrative establishes succession from father to son.

The Jacob and Joseph narratives have been studied in great detail by biblical scholars in recent years, and much attention has been paid to the meaning of the doubling of events in each of these narratives.[1] But, while many scholars have noted the doubling of events within the Abraham narrative, little has been made of the meaning of this structural phenomenon. Yet the doubling structure, suggested by the word pattern central to the transfer stories, seems to me to be a crucial element of the narrative meaning, and it is for that reason that I chose the structure of the Abraham narrative for detailed analysis.

The doubling structure of all the patriarchal narratives is a function of the patriarchal quest; it parallels the journey into a foreign land and the threat of assimilating into an alternate society, and it allows for the possibility of return to the land and to identification with familial destiny. If the theme of a sojourn in a foreign land is interwoven with the elements of fraternity and maternity, as I have suggested, then we can expect an especially close connection between the structure of the narrative and its meaning as a quest for familial and national destiny. By establishing the structural pattern, as we have done for one of the narratives, and analyzing the plot elements, as we are about to do for the others, we can begin to approach the patriarchal narrative as a whole and establish a framework for analyzing each of its details.

Isaac and Rebecca

Almost immediately after the binding of Isaac, following a brief genealogy leading to Rebecca's birth (22:20-24), the narrative tells of Sarah's death and burial (ch. 23). Abraham's establishment of a gravesite seems to result from the episode on Mount Moriah in two ways. Abraham, for the first time, shows concern for Sarah, who has finally become the mother of the chosen son. And Abraham, again for the first time, claims a portion of the land as his own; he purchases a field in Hebron as an eternal possession (*'ahuza*, 23:20). Abraham doubly affirms the end of his quest, the search for a son and for the land, by purchasing this field for Isaac's mother.

Both the binding of Isaac and the burial of Sarah, then, lead to the next episode, the search for a wife for Isaac (ch. 24). If Isaac is the chosen son, he must have a wife with whom he can build a family.[2] The choosing of Isaac necessitates his marriage; hence the announcement of Rebecca's birth immediately following the binding of Isaac. And the birth of Rebecca obviates the need for Sarah; immediately after the genealogy we hear of Sarah's death. In terms of the family, Sarah has fulfilled her mission once Abraham has chosen her son to be his successor. If Isaac is chosen and is to have the appropriate wife, Sarah has no more purpose. Rebecca, in fact, will take over for Sarah (24:67), and she will make sure, in her turn, that her husband chooses the son who will take over for him.

But Abraham, although his quest has come to an end, still must perform certain acts to insure the continuity of his family. If he affirms the importance of his wife and the land by purchasing the burial plot, he reaffirms it by sending his servant to find a wife for Isaac. Isaac must have a wife from his father's homeland, but he must not undertake the journey which such a search usually entails, as it will for Jacob and as the servant thinks it might for Isaac (24:5). Abraham will not allow Isaac to leave the land which has been chosen for him.

Isaac never does leave the land, and he never has to find his way back to it. Isaac never undertakes a quest at all, never is he commanded with "go" (lek), and never does he seek or receive his father's blessing. His experiences, unlike Abraham's, Jacob's and Joseph's, do not repeat. We see no development in Isaac, no wandering away from or movement toward his destiny, and no change of name which would signal that a change of character had taken place. As his brief stay in Gerar (ch. 26) shows, Isaac will always model himself on Abraham, the father with whom he had to be so closely identified, and he will always be the metsaheq, the one who laughs (26:8). He will never see clearly, and will never have to, for it is not his task to find the land, to find a son, or to find a wife. The land has been chosen by his father, the wife is chosen for him by his father's servant, and the son is chosen for him by his wife.

Rebecca, in fact, chooses the land and chooses to be Isaac's wife, as well.[3] It is she who agrees to go to Isaac in Canaan (*'elek*; 24:58), against the wishes of her brother and mother. And it is she who falls off her camel when she recognizes that she has reached her destination and come to her husband (24:64). Isaac is coming (*ba'*), from Be'er Lahai Ro'i, "the well of seeing"—a name which had played ironically on Hagar's and Ishmael's blindness. "And he lifted up his eyes and saw, behold [*hine*], camels coming" (24:62-63). But Abraham's servant has taken Rebecca and gone on his way (*vayiqah . . . vayelak*; 24:61). "And Rebecca lifted up her eyes and she saw Isaac and she fell from the camel" (24:64). Isaac sees only the camels, but Rebecca sees Isaac.[4]

Isaac's role is not to seek a destiny, but to continue a destiny; he is not to make choices, but rather to maintain what has already been established, as he will do with the wells which his father had dug (26:18). The crucial task for Isaac is not to stray from the path which his parents have paved for him. He accepts Rebecca for a wife as a substitute for his mother (24:67); he brings her to Sarah's tent and, like Abraham, will say that she is his sister (26:7).

Exiled brothers

The relationship between finding a wife and leaving the land will warrant further discussion in the context of the stories about Jacob and Rachel. For now, it simply is important to note that Isaac may not leave the land, even to find a wife. In contrast, Isaac's brothers must leave the land. The last act that Abraham performs, after burying his wife and finding a wife for Isaac, is to send away the sons of his concubines. Abraham gives all his possessions to Isaac, reserving only gifts for his other sons, and he sends these sons (*vayeshalekem*) away from Isaac "eastward, to the east country" (25:6).

The word "east" (*qedem*) recalls an earlier episode in Abraham's life in which possessions were distributed between brothers and one brother went east. When the possessions of Abra-

ham and Lot increase too greatly for the kinsmen "to dwell together" in the same land (13:6), Abraham addresses Lot as *'ah*,
"brother," and suggests that Lot move either northward or
southward, and that he will move in the opposite direction
(13:8-9). "Lot lifted up his eyes and saw" the fertile Jordan
plain, "like the garden of YHWH"; he chooses this region and
travels eastward (*miqedem*)—"and the brothers separated from
each other" (13:10-11). We have already discussed the significance of Lot's choice of Sodom, a city "like the land of Egypt"
(13:10), and Lot's misperception. Most noteworthy is that Lot
and Abraham do not share the land of Canaan; Lot leaves it
and his "brother" Abraham is given the entire land, for himself
and his descendants (13:15).

Furthermore, although Lot will be forced out of Sodom in
the parallel episode of chapter 19, he will not return to the land
of Canaan. Instructed by the angel to escape from the entire
plain and to reach the mountain (19:17), Lot pleads to be
allowed to run only to Zoar (*Tso'ar*; 19:20-22). That Lot will
remain in this insignificant (*mits'ar*; 19:20)[5] town is foreshadowed already as he looks out and sees the garden-like plain of
Sodom, "on the way to Zoar" (13:10). Lot's choice of Sodom,
like Hagar's mocking of Sarah, is an early indicator of the direction which the character later will take.[6] The later, parallel
episodes confirm that Abraham's potential heirs both have
disqualified themselves—Lot through his move to Zoar, Hagar's
son Ishmael through his laughter. Unlike Abraham, they keep
going in the direction which they took at first; they do not
return to a sense of mission.

Both Lot and the sons of Abraham's concubines go eastward (*qedma*) and never return. And the eastern land which Lot
chooses is described as "like the garden of YHWH." The combination of "east" and "garden" unmistakably conjures up the
Garden of Eden. God plants the "garden in Eden in the east
[*qedem*]" (2:8). Adam is exiled from the garden and God places
the cherubim and the flaming sword "eastward [*miqedem*] of
the garden of Eden" (3:24). Even more significantly, Cain
dwells "in the land of Nod, eastward [*qidmat*] of Eden" (4:16),

which is to say, of course, that he settles nowhere at all, since *nad*, "wander," is the essence of his punishment (4:12).[7]

A man who cannot live in peace with his brother has no choice but to leave the land, and to leave the land means not to have a place, to wander. The narrative tells how Cain's descendants build cities and develop technology and the arts (4:17-22). Their names signify fruitfulness (*Yaval, Yuval*) and pleasantness (*Na'ama*), but they are, after all, the descendants of a fratricide. The name of Lemek's youngest son, *Tuval-Cain*, reminds us of the destructive ancestor of this creative family, while combining echoes of the names of the brothers who could not live together, Cain and Abel (4:20-22). Lemek, finally, boasts of a crime with more violent repercussions than Cain's (4:23-24), and at this point the narrative confirms that the family living in the land of Nod cannot be a link in the generations of man. Adam and Eve have another son, Seth, to replace the murdered Abel (4:25). Seth will bring forth descendants with names which parallel the descendants of Cain, but only with Seth is the sequence of generations significant; his line replaces the line of Cain. After Lemek nothing more is heard of the descendants of the brother who was exiled from the land. But Seth begets *'Enosh*, "humankind" (4:26) and the narrative continues—"This is the book of the generations [*toledot*] of Man, *'Adam* . . ." (5:1).[8]

After Abraham sends the sons of the concubines eastward (25:6),[9] we also read of "generations." In fact, two consecutive segments are introduced by the words "and these are the generations [*toledot*]" and the two contrast sharply with each other. The "generations" of Ishmael consist of a straightforward genealogy (25:13-18), while the text offers no genealogy of Isaac's descendants; the words "and these are the generations of Isaac the son of Abraham" (25:19) introduce a narrative instead. The text pauses only to mention Isaac's lineage—"Abraham begat Isaac"—before it swerves from the genealogy and resumes the narrative. Ishmael's "generations" also begin with his own lineage, and this, like what follows, contrasts significantly with Isaac's lineage—"And these are the generations [*toledot*] of Ishmael the son of Abraham, whom Hagar the Egyptian, the maid of Sarah, bore to Abraham" (25:12). The text qualifies Ishmael's link to Abraham with his maternal lineage, while it confirms Isaac's link to Abraham through a repetition of his paternal lineage. And Ishmael's fate, as described in his genealogy, conforms to God's promises to both Abraham and Hagar.

"Hearing" Abraham's concern for his elder son, God had promised that twelve tribes would arise from Ishmael (17:20) and, "hearing" Hagar's suffering, the angel had foretold that Ishmael would "encamp upon the face of all his brothers" (16: 11-12). These promises, we have already noted, were for the near future and contrasted with God's promise of a distant destiny for Abraham's descendants (15:13-16). God juxtaposed Ishmael's fate with the "eternal covenant" through Isaac (17: 19), and the angel pronounced the immediate fate of Ishmael only after Hagar silently rejected the promise for the future (16:9-10). And so, with the beginning of Ishmael's "generations," comes the immediate fulfillment of his fate. Ishmael begets twelve sons, and they encamp upon their brothers.[10] But here the twelve tribal heads (*nesi'im*) represent separate nations (*le'umotam*; 25:16), and the verb "he will encamp" (*yishkon*) is replaced by the verb "he fell" (*nafal*; 25:18).

These details suggest that the promise for Ishmael of immediate increase contains a destructive element. Ishmael's twelve sons do not lead distinct tribes within a single nation; they bring forth separate nations.[11] And these nations do not inhabit a specific land; they encamp all along an area bordered by Havila and Shur (25:18). It was on the road to Shur that the angel had found Hagar and foretold Ishmael's future (16:7), and Shur is described now as "on the face of Egypt," Hagar's birthplace. The lifestyle of these twelve nations is summed up in the last statement we hear about Ishmael—"on the face of all his brothers he fell." The word *nafal* can carry both senses of the word "fall": "to fall upon" and "to fall down."[12] Accordingly, the fate of Ishmael seems to be both of conflict between brothers and of destruction. Ishmael's future fulfills the promises to Abraham and to Hagar, but his destiny is exhausted in a single generation. Ishmael, like Cain, Lot, and the concubines' sons, is the brother who is sent away. The name of his youngest son,

Qedma ("eastward"), reinforces this link (25:15).[13] Ishmael was exiled in order to avoid precisely the kind of conflict between him and his brother that we glimpse within his family. Brothers, at this point in the narrative, still are unable to live together.

Ishmael's twelve sons who cannot coexist in a single nation recall the twelve sons who will form the nation of Israel. It is the burden of Genesis to make sure that these twelve sons can form a single nation, not only that they can take over without conflict from their father, but that they can share a common destiny without conflict among themselves. These twelve sons, therefore, are not yet ready to be born. They will form the distant fourth generation about which Abraham had been promised (15:16). But the members of the third generation, the sons of Ishmael and of Isaac, are still not able to coexist as brothers. Ishmael gives rise to twelve nations (*le'umim*) who fall upon each other and disappear from the narrative, and Isaac gives rise to two nations (*le'umim*; 25:23) as well.[14] If anything is to be preserved in a generation in which brothers destroy each other, one brother will have to be sent away, as Ishmael, the concubines' sons, and Lot were cast out to preserve the family destiny through the remaining "brother." And so, when it will become clear that Jacob and Esau cannot remain together in peace, one of them will be sent out, and he will go "to the land of the sons of the East (*qedem*)" (29:1), the place where brothers are sent when they are excluded from their family's destiny. The exiled brother is Jacob.

Jacob, of course, ultimately will return to the land, unlike the other exiled brothers. But his return will coincide with Esau's departure from the land, described in words very similar to those describing Lot's departure: "For their property was too great for them to dwell together, and the land of their sojourning was not able to carry them because of their livestock" (36:7; cp. 13:6). The departure of Esau coincides with a long genealogy introduced, once again, by the words "And these are the generations [*toledot*]" (ch. 36). And the "generations" of Esau are juxtaposed with those of Jacob in much the same fashion as those of Ishmael and Isaac.

The words "These are the generations [*toledot*] of Jacob" (37:2) lead not to a genealogy but to a narrative.[15] The narrative, as we by now expect, will tell of conflict between brothers, but this time the problem cannot be solved by sending one brother away and allowing the other to inherit the paternal legacy. Now there are twelve brothers; each will give rise to a family of his own and, if the families are to become twelve tribes within a single nation rather than twelve separate nations, the problem of fraternal conflict must finally be solved. Jacob will be the first who is able to forge a unified family in Genesis just as, when forced to leave his family, he is the first who is able to find his way back. He brings his family together, though, only at the point where they are all about to be lost, when all of the brothers have left the land and gone down to Egypt. Never within the book of Genesis will the land be able to "carry brothers dwelling together," but Jacob does bring his sons together, and the final return of this fourth generation to the land remains, at the end of the book, a promise yet to be fulfilled.[16]

Isaac as Abraham's son

While Jacob will leave the land and return and will beget twelve sons who will remain together, Isaac bides the family's time, remaining in the land and begetting two sons, only one of whom will succeed him. The delay in the formation of the family is reflected by the interrupted "generations" of Isaac. Isaac received the blessing as a result of his father's quest; he did not actively seek it. He will not be able actively to pass it on, and he will not be the father of brothers who share a common paternal heritage. If one of his sons is to receive the paternal blessing, he will have to seek it for himself, and if the father passively refrains from choosing between his sons, then the brothers will compete for the blessing which they cannot share.

Significantly, the competition between the brothers for the paternal blessing and the transfer from father to son occur at precisely the point within the Isaac narrative as the transfer from father to son within the Abraham narrative. After Abraham sojourns in Gerar and returns to the land, and after Ishmael is cast out on account of his laughter, Abimelek visits Abraham and they establish a covenant at Be'er Sheba for their descendants. This covenant, which implies that Abraham's descendants, like him, will continue to dwell in the land, leads directly to the episode of the binding of Isaac, the outburst of paternal violence and the moment of transfer from father to son.

Isaac also sojourns in a foreign land, but only once, in contrast to the doubling of the episode in the Abraham narrative. Isaac, as we have noted, does not undergo a change, and this episode clearly demonstrates both his constant nature and his tenacity in copying his father's model. And, as if to call attention to the fact that Isaac imitates his father but never undertakes a quest, the narrative relates God's admonition to Isaac not to leave the land for Egypt after it has already told of Isaac's move to Gerar (26:1-2). God tells Isaac to "dwell [gur] in this land" (26:3), and Isaac remains in Gerar (26:6). The Gerar episode seems designed to show both that Isaac, as God commands, never leaves the land to undertake a quest and that Isaac copies his father's departure and return to the land.[17]

The account of Abraham's sojourn in Gerar was bound up with the issue of childbirth and led into the birth of Isaac and the banishment of Ishmael. But Isaac's sojourn in Gerar has nothing to do with childbirth. Both of Isaac's sons already have been born and, moreover, Rebecca is never taken by the Philistines; Abimelek, in fact, sees Isaac in intimate play [tsehoq] with his wife (26:8). The episode is followed neither by the birth of one son nor by the casting out of another. Having children and choosing a successor are not issues in Isaac's life; the issue is for Isaac to be a son to his father.

The Gerar episode, therefore, is followed by a brief account of Isaac restoring the wells which his father had dug and calling them by the names which his father had given them (26:18). Then, Isaac travels to Be'er Sheba, the place where Abraham had established a covenant protecting his descendants. As we noted in Chapter Three, the account of Abraham's covenant appeared between an episode about Ishmael and an episode about Isaac. At the time it was not clear to which son the covenant referred. But now, with Isaac's move from Be'er Lahai Ro'i (25:11), associated with Hagar and Ishmael, to Be'er

Sheba (26:23), Isaac confirms that he is the son to whom the covenant referred. And God articulates the confirmation by blessing Isaac and promising him many descendants "for the sake of Abraham" (26:24).[18]

At Be'er Sheba, Abimelek visits Isaac and the two establish a covenant (26:26-31) much as Abimelek had done with Abraham after his return from Gerar. It is at this point, when Isaac has returned to the land, has identified with his own paternal destiny, and has been assured that the destiny of his father will be continued through his own descendants, that the moment of transfer and the conflict over succession occur. The conflict emerges between the brothers because Isaac has not chosen a successor. Abraham's sojourn in Gerar and his later meeting with Abimelek were episodes concerned with the quest for a son. But Isaac's parallel encounters with Abimelek confirm Isaac as his father's son; they ignore completely Isaac's relationship to his own sons. Isaac's return to the land, immediately following, signifies an identification with paternal destiny and, if that destiny is to continue, it must be transferred once again from father to son. Jacob's theft of the blessing, then, comes at exactly the point in the Isaac narrative at which the binding of Isaac had come in the Abraham narrative.

Isaac and Esau, Rebecca and Jacob

To be more precise, two verses interrupt between Isaac's covenant at Be'er Sheba and the account of the blessing (26:34-35). These verses tell of Esau's marriage and of his parents' dissatisfaction with his choice of wives, but they hint at much more. Esau marries Canaanite women, a choice which we know from Abraham's instructions to his servant is inappropriate for a member of this family (24:3). Esau, however, marries at the age of forty, the same age at which his father married Rebecca (25:20).[19] And the names of his wives further reflect Esau's bond to Isaac. One is the daughter of *Be'eri*, a name meaning "well" and reminiscent of Isaac's choices of dwelling places and his occupation with wells. The other is called "*Basemat* the daughter of '*Elon*," names meaning "spice" and "tree," respectively. These two names recall that both Isaac and Esau are "men of the field"; Isaac was walking in the field when he met his wife (24:63), and Esau is described as a "man of the field" (25:27).[20] In fact, when the blind Isaac remains unconvinced that the disguised Jacob is really Esau, he reassures himself by smelling his son's garments and recognizing (*re'e*) the "aroma of a field" (27:27).[21]

Esau's marriage, then, hints at a problem which will be developed in the following episode; Esau resembles his father and strives to be like him, but he goes about it in the wrong way. And his marriage also indicates that Isaac has not assumed the role of a father; unlike Abraham, he has not made sure that his son take a non-Canaanite wife. These two verses, then, subtly encapsulate the problem which the ensuing narrative develops and tries to solve, Isaac's inability to be a father to his son, but they perform a simpler and more obvious function as well. At the moment that Isaac returns to the land and must transfer the paternal heritage to his son, but at the moment before he actually blesses his son, the narrative tells us that Esau has disqualified himself from becoming Isaac's successor.[22]

That Jacob, not Esau, will receive his father's blessing, in fact, we suspect already. Jacob has bought his brother's birthright (25:33), and the blessing must accompany the birthright. Esau does not understand the connection between the two; he complains that Jacob has cheated him on two distinct occasions: "he took [*laqah*] my birthright and, behold [*hine*], now he has taken [*laqah*] my blessing" (27:36). Esau has willingly relinquished his birthright, but he does not want to give up the blessing, and the distinction which he draws between the two betrays his misunderstanding of both.

The words for "birthright" and "blessing" are nearly identical in Hebrew (*bekora* and *beraka*) and the narrative plays extensively on the connection between them.[23] The *bekora* is the right to succeed the father, and the *beraka* is the blessing received from the father. The blessing promises the land and descendants, and includes the paternal mission which is to be passed on, together with the land, to the descendants. Esau has no interest in the birthright (*bekora*) because, he says, "Behold [*hine*], I am going [*holek*] to die" (25:32). Esau lacks a sense of destiny, and so the birthright is not significant to him,[24] and the blessing is not appropriate for him.

But that Esau has no concern for the birthright (*bekora*) does not mean that he does not want the blessing (*beraka*), because there is more than one kind of blessing in this episode. The blessing which Esau desires and which Jacob steals is not the blessing of the paternal heritage. That, "the blessing of Abraham," will be transferred later in this episode (28:4). The first blessing, the one which Isaac intends to give to Esau, is a purely material one, which speaks only of the present (27:27-29). And, like Esau, Isaac seems to be aware of no other kind of blessing (27:37).

Esau's willingness to imitate his father combined with Isaac's inability to offer his son direction, indicated by Esau's marriage to Canaanite women, corresponds precisely to the complex which we identified in Chapter Three through the word pattern of "take/go" (*qah/lek*) and "behold/here I am" (*hine/hineni*): Esau is willing to follow his father's command, but Isaac is incapable of commanding him. Isaac wants to bless Esau, the son who resembles him and who takes care of him (25:28), but he understands neither the nature of the blessing nor how to give it to his son; he does not command Esau with "take and go."

Rebecca, we noted, does know how to command her son, but she is not the one who can transfer the blessing to her son. And Jacob has no relationship to his father; he bears no resemblance to him nor does he take care of him or try to imitate him. In fact, even upon Rebecca's command, he is unwilling to bring his father the slaughtered animals. He finally agrees to bring the animals for his mother (27:13-14), but he never accepts the parental command with "here I am." Rebecca alone understands the command and she alone understands the nature of the blessing which Isaac must transfer to his son; while Isaac refers to a personal blessing (27:4), Rebecca talks of a blessing "before God" (27:7).

Rebecca's understanding in this episode corresponds to her earlier ability to come to the land and to see her husband and contrasts with Isaac's inability to leave the land and return to it and to seek a wife or even to see her. Isaac, also, is blind to his sons and to the blessing (27:1); Rebecca has sought counsel regarding her sons and knows who must receive the blessing (25:22-23).[25] It is Rebecca who sends Jacob to her brother Laban for protection from Esau, and it is she who tells her son that he will return at her bidding: "I will send and take you from there" (*veshalahti uleqahtika misham*; 27:45).

Rebecca tells Isaac something different, and this conversation is what compels Isaac, at last, to command Jacob "go and take" (28:2). Rebecca complains of her disgust with the Canaanite women and speaks of her fear that Jacob might marry such women himself (27:46). By not mentioning Esau explicitly as the one who misstepped in taking these women, Rebecca avoids the suggestion that such women are not fitting for her older son, saying only that her chosen son, Jacob, must not marry Canaanites "such as these."

Rebecca's statement leads directly to Isaac's transfer of the paternal blessing to Jacob. The episode of the binding of Isaac, designating Isaac as Abraham's successor, had made it necessary to seek a wife for Isaac. If Rebecca emphasizes to Isaac that Jacob must have a proper wife, this can mean only one thing— that Jacob is to be Isaac's successor.

Thus Isaac's command to Jacob to seek a wife and his transfer of the blessing to Jacob are interwoven. The "go and take" with which the father commands his son consists of instructions to seek a wife yet remains an integral part of the blessing—"and he blessed him and commanded him . . ." (28: 1).[26] And this blessing is different from the one which Isaac had planned to give to Esau but had given hesitantly to Jacob. This blessing promises descendants who will form a nation, and it promises "the blessing of Abraham" to Jacob and his descendants, guaranteeing inheritance of the land "which God gave to Abraham" (28:3-4).

Isaac had been blind to his own wife and to the need for a wife for his son, and he had not recognized either his sons or the nature of the blessing. Now, Isaac's wife has made him see the need for a wife for his son, and only now does Isaac recognize which son must be blessed and understand of what that blessing consists. The "blessing of Abraham" is a blessing for the future; it must be given to a son who is mindful of the future, and that son must have a wife through whom he can build that future. Rebecca insures that Jacob receive that blessing before he leaves the land.

Esau's choice of wives is what had shown Esau to be unqualified to receive the blessing. Now Esau sees that Isaac has blessed Jacob again and has sent him to take a wife from Padan Aram (28:6), and he understands that Canaanite women are unacceptable to his father (28:8).[27] In response, Esau takes an additional wife, this time from the children of Ishmael (28:9).

Esau's two marriages border the episode of the blessing, marking the beginning and end of this story. Like the parallel episodes in the Abraham narrative, the doubling here allows a comparison; one episode can be measured against the other to determine whether the protagonist has changed his ways or whether he has continued to move in the same direction.

Esau's second marriage does not indicate a change. Most noticeably, Esau does not send away the Canaanite women; he merely takes another wife, keeping the two he had taken at first.[28] But Esau's first marriage hinted at a more subtle problem, the son's attempt to follow a father unable to command him, and the second marriage confirms that problem. Once again, Esau tries to please his father by imitating him. He chooses a wife from his father's kin, both binding himself more closely to Isaac and following Isaac's example, for Isaac had married a woman from his father's kin.

Esau's choice, of course, is wrong once again; much of the Abraham narrative had been directed at separating Isaac's family from Ishmael's. By marrying Ishmael's daughter, Esau reforges a link which was forcibly broken and identifies himself with the line which is not chosen.[29] Esau makes the wrong choice, once again, because his father has not commanded him. Although he strives to do what his father wishes, he does not know what he must do. But while, earlier, Isaac was not able to command at all, by the end of the episode he is able to be a father, yet he does not choose now to command Esau or to bless him. Esau will not share in the patriarchal destiny.

Jacob leaves the land

Isaac does, by the end of this episode, command and bless Jacob. But the problem in this story, we have noted, is two-sided; Isaac's inability to be a father to his son is paralleled by Jacob's inability to be a son to his father. Now, at last, Isaac is able to command his son with "go and take," but Jacob still has not defined himself as a son to his father. He leaves on the instructions of both his father and his mother (28:7); his father has actually "sent" him away (*vayishlak*; 28:5-6), while his mother has instructed him to return to her (27:45). If Jacob is to succeed his father, he will have to return to the land and, more specifically, to his father's home. His acceptance of his father's command of "go" is only the beginning of the search which will end back in the land. Jacob must leave the land, as Isaac never was to do, because he must learn how to return to the land of his destiny and become a son to his father.

Jacob must leave, too—and go eastward (*qedma*)—because his competitor, Esau, is the brother who stays. And Esau stays because he is the brother who resembles the father. Jacob is allied with his mother and, as we shall soon see, resembles his mother's family. But the mother's family, throughout the patriarchal narrative, constitutes outsiders. Ishmael's alliance with his mother, his *tsehoq* ("laughter"), caused him to be sent away; he married an Egyptian woman, chosen by his mother, and his descendants encamped near Egypt, his mother's birthplace. If Jacob follows his mother, he will not continue the paternal line; he must go to Padan Aram, his mother's birthplace, and his descendants can be expected to remain there.

Of course, marriage to an Aramean is not strictly exogamous. In fact, for the previous generation such marriage was considered endogamous. Abraham, instructing his servant to find a wife for Isaac, calls Padan Aram "my land" and "my birthplace" (24:4); Isaac marries an Aramean woman who is his paternal kin. When Jacob is sent to find a wife, however, Padan Aram is described as the home of his maternal kin (28:2). It is

Esau who chooses a wife from his paternal kin. The two marriages are exactly parallel; Esau marries his father's brother's daughter, and Jacob marries his mother's brother's daughter.[30]

To make matters more complicated, Esau allies himself to the paternal line, as his father did, which should allow him to remain in the land and succeed his father. Yet the alliance is with a family which has already been disqualified, and the alliance is suggested by neither of his parents. Jacob allies himself to the maternal line, unlike his father, which takes him out of the land and should exclude him from the paternal lineage. Yet his alliance is with a family which is really his paternal kin as well, and the alliance is suggested by both his mother and his father. Similarly, Isaac's wife was related to him through both his father and his mother, since Sarah and Abraham came from the same paternal home. But if Abraham calls Padan Aram his son's paternal home and Isaac calls it his son's maternal home, the terms become significant and contrasting definitions.[31] The people of Padan Aram, that is, are gradually becoming excluded from Abraham's family[32] and, by the end of the Jacob narrative, the break will be complete. Meanwhile, the link to Padan Aram is still necessary, and the Arameans are still members of the extended family—thus Jacob, as we shall see, never becomes totally separated from his father's kin.

Jacob must go to Aram, according to his father, to seek a wife, but his mother has already instructed him to go for a different reason. Jacob cannot stay in the same place as his brother, because Esau plans to kill him as soon as his father dies (27:41-42), to receive the paternal blessing by default when the issue of succession becomes relevant.[33] But, if Jacob cannot live together with his own brother ('ah), he can visit his mother's brother ('ah) and be protected by him (27:42-44).

Rebecca's instructions, with their reiteration of the word 'ah, contrast Rebecca's brother, Laban, with Jacob's brother, Esau, but the ensuing narrative sets Laban, Jacob's father-in-law, in contrast to Isaac, Jacob's father.[34] Jacob is endangered in his father's home, and he seeks safety in the home of his maternal uncle. His father has the ability to bless him, but also has the power to curse him (27:12); Laban is powerful but is not able "to speak to Jacob either good or bad" (31:29). Isaac's father and maternal uncle were the same person. Abraham and Isaac were doubly related, and Isaac had no way to avoid conflict with his father. For Jacob, though, the paternal figure is split into father and maternal uncle. Isaac can harm him; Laban cannot. But Isaac can harm his son for precisely the same reason that he can transfer the blessing to him; Laban cannot harm Jacob because, ultimately, they do not share the same destiny.[35]

In Laban's house

Soon after Jacob sets out, he arrives at "the place" (hamaqom), and God appears to him in a dream, identifying himself as "the God of your father Abraham and the God of Isaac" (28:11-13). God promises to "return" Jacob to the land which will be given to him and his descendants (28:15), and Jacob begins to speak of "returning in peace to his father's house" (veshavti beshalom 'el bet 'avi; 28:21).[36] Jacob leaves the land as the son of his mother, but will return as the son of his father. His experiences with Laban, his maternal uncle, and his ultimate break from his mother's birthplace will bring about the transition.

That Jacob's experiences in Laban's house parallel his experiences in his father's house has frequently been noted by biblical scholars. Fishbane and Fokkelman both have analyzed the structure of the entire Jacob narrative in detail and have noted the resolution achieved by the doubling of the episodes. We can forego an analysis of each episode, then, and concentrate on the place of this narrative, with its particular family structure, within the sequence of family narratives in Genesis.

The most striking clue that Laban's house mirrors Isaac's is the parallel between Leah and Rachel and Esau and Jacob.[37] As before, Jacob seeks to put the younger sibling before the older. Here, however, it is Laban who does the cheating; he switches Leah for Rachel and self-righteously explains: "It is not done thus in our place to put the younger before the elder" (29:26).[38] "In our place" (bimqomenu) recalls that exactly this has just been done in a different place, in Canaan. While in both incidents Jacob attempted to violate the order, here it is

Laban who acts deceitfully. Jacob has met a person similar to himself. Deceitfulness becomes Laban's most outstanding characteristic (29:25); Esau has already recognized it as Jacob's (27:36), and Jacob was tutored in deceit by his mother, the sister of Laban.[39] Throughout his stay in Padan Aram, Jacob will be forced to respond to Laban's deceitfulness in kind.

Unlike Abraham, who wanted a son but did not care whether Sarah was the mother, and unlike Isaac, who prayed for his wife to bear a child (25:21) but never was concerned about his own childlessness, Jacob does not seek a son either for himself or for his wives. His wives, in contrast, are desperate to bear children. Leah, indeed, sees her childbearing as a way to gain her husband's favor (29:32-34), though we are not told of any response on the part of Jacob to the birth of her sons. And Jacob's marriage to Rachel is never linked to a desire to beget children; he chooses Rachel and waits for her simply because he loves her (29:18-20). Leah's and Rachel's all-absorbing desire to bear children, then, emphasizes Jacob's apathy and passivity. He takes no part in naming his children, and he allows his wives to bargain with each other for mandrake roots and conjugal rights (30:14-16). Childbirth, in this story, is the arena in which the sisters compete, and Rachel, jealous of her sister, demands that Jacob give her children (30:1). When Jacob rebuffs her, Rachel gives Jacob her maid, as Sarah had given Hagar to Abraham, using similar words—"I too will be built ['ibaneh], through her" (30:3).[40] But the emphatic "I too" pinpoints Rachel's motive, not simply to bear a child to her husband, who already has children, but to compete with her sister.[41]

Jacob, too, had competed with his brother, both for the birthright (bekora) and for the blessing (beraka), but without a clear sense of what the blessing means. Being sent to find a wife was a function of that blessing, for the family's destiny depends on the continuity of the family, but Jacob does not seem to understand the significance of Isaac's command. The scene in which he finds Rachel echoes the scene in which Abraham's servant finds Rebecca, but Rebecca was chosen so that Abraham's line could continue through Isaac and his descendants, while Jacob chooses Rachel without thinking of begetting children through her. Jacob's response to his wife's demand—"Am I in the place of God?" (30:2)—expresses his lack of concern about children. It begins to reveal, as well, a breach between him and Rachel. Of the two sisters, Rachel is more Laban's daughter than is Leah, as we shall see, just as Jacob is more Rebecca's son than is Esau. After Jacob will finally break from Laban and Padan Aram, when he is about to return to his father and to the land of Canaan, he will be forced to leave Rachel behind.

Meanwhile, however, God hears Rachel's complaint and Joseph is born (30:22-23). And, when Jacob has a son from the wife he was sent to find, Jacob decides to return home (30:25). Once again, return to the land is linked to establishing a family. Although Jacob did not seek to beget a child through Rachel, the birth of their son seems to convince Jacob that he must establish his own family in his own land. In much the same way, Isaac had understood that Jacob was his chosen son, that Jacob must build a family and receive the blessing, once Rebecca explains that Jacob must have a suitable wife. If Jacob's family, now, is to be distinct from Laban's, if Jacob is to receive his father's blessing for himself and his children, then Jacob will have to return to the land which the blessing promises and to his father's house.[42]

When Jacob asks Laban to "send" him home (shalheni), Laban offers to pay Jacob wages for his work (30:25-28).[43] The episode which follows, in which Laban and Jacob cheat each other, is reminiscent of Abraham's experience in Gerar, where Abraham and Abimelek rivalled each other in deceitfulness. Uncle and nephew steal from each other and switch flocks in an incident which reveals both how much at home Jacob is in his uncle's house and how crucial it is for him to leave.

Laban himself, while he does not want Jacob to leave, has not accepted him as a member of his family. He gives flocks to his own sons rather than to Jacob (30:35), while his sons resent Jacob's accumulation of their father's wealth (31:1). Jacob now is in a position parallel to his position in Isaac's house; he has taken what the sons of his father-in-law, or surrogate father, feel is rightfully theirs. But the fraternal competition at which the narrative hints is secondary here. Jacob hears Laban's sons complaining, but they complain that Jacob has taken, not their property, but the property of their father. And it is Laban, not his sons, from whom Jacob flees (31:1-2). The story of Isaac's blessing shifted the focus from paternal to fraternal conflict. This narrative refocuses on the paternal relationship. Through Jacob's experiences with Laban, he resolves to return to his father and, once he understands the meaning of this return, he will be able to encounter his brother.

After Joseph's birth, Jacob seemed to want to leave immediately; he did not ask Laban for wages (30:25-26). Once he is offered property and gains wealth, however, he is not quick to leave. Jacob resembles Laban's family, and the likelihood that he will become a member of Laban's family increases with the danger posed to him by Laban and his sons. Jacob must leave Padan Aram, then, not so much because Laban and his sons have become a threat, but because Jacob is threatened by the possibility of assimilation into Laban's family.[44] Jacob does not leave spontaneously, and Laban does not "send" him;[45] God has to appear to him and command him to return (*shuv*) to his father's house (31:3). Jacob convinces his wives to leave their father (31:14) and departs toward "his father Isaac in the land of Canaan" (31:18).

Jacob, Laban, and Rachel

When Laban hears that Jacob has departed, he chases after him, and the meeting between uncle and nephew parallels Abraham's and Isaac's second meetings with Abimelek, after each had left Gerar. Between Jacob's speech to his wives and Laban's discovery of his escape, five verses set the background for the ensuing narrative, and this brief passage is parallel in function to the passages which bridge Abraham's and Isaac's sojourns in Gerar and their later meetings and covenants with Abimelek. Abraham, after leaving Gerar, begot Isaac and banished Ishmael, thus paving the way for the succession of the chosen son. Isaac, at the same narrative juncture, restored Abraham's wells and received God's assurance of blessing on

Abraham's account, thus confirming that he was Abraham's chosen son.

Jacob, too, defines his kinship, and so his nature, at this point in the narrative. On leaving Padan Aram, Jacob differentiates his entire family from the family of Laban, and thus rejects kinship with his surrogate father. He takes his sons and his wives, all of whom Laban will soon claim as his own (31:43), and departs with his family from Laban's home toward Isaac's. But, just before the family leaves, Rachel performs an act which identifies her both with Jacob, as he has been, and with Laban, linking her husband to her father once again. Rachel steals (*vatignov*) her father's idols and, the passage continues, Jacob steals (*vayignov*) Laban's heart (31:19-20).[46] If these idols are household gods, possession of which indicates the right to inherit an estate, then Rachel is asserting that her family will continue in the line of her father Laban.[47] Certainly, however, the theft is typical for a member of Laban's family, and its juxtaposition with Jacob's theft recalls that Jacob too has always behaved like a member of Laban's family. Yet the nature of his theft, this time, reveals that Jacob has begun to break from Laban.

Jacob has stolen Laban's heart by "not telling him that he was escaping" (31:20). The verse not only remains silent about Jacob's Laban-like appropriation of the flocks, an act to which we might have expected the word "stole" (*vayignov*) to refer,[48] but which would link Jacob to Laban once more; it actually indicates that Jacob has severed his tie to Laban. The figurative use of the verb to steal (*gnv*), juxtaposed with the actual theft in the previous verse, suggests that Jacob is caught between belonging to Laban's family—for he is still a thief—and separating from it—for this particular kind of theft distances him from Laban. Rachel's theft, though, reinforces the bond. Rachel's theft, in fact, serves as a pretext for Laban's pursuit of Jacob and attempt to appropriate his family, and it finally will cause Jacob unknowingly to reject Rachel as a member of his household.

Jacob's encounter with Laban is parallel to Abraham's and Isaac's encounters with Abimelek, each occurring after the patriarch's self-definition with respect to his family. In addition, Jacob's encounter echoes his earlier encounter with his true father, when Jacob deceived his father and stole the blessing. Now, Laban is the father who has been deceived and, like Isaac, he searches (*vayemashesh*) to uncover the deceit (31:34; 27:21-22).[49] But Jacob has not stolen, this time, and he does not respond to Laban as to a father. He has no reason to fear Laban because, unlike Jacob's father, Laban has no power over Jacob. Laban explains, in a redundant speech characteristic of Abimelek's style, that he has power to harm Jacob but that God prevents him from so doing. In contrast to Isaac, who can bless or curse his son, Laban cannot speak to Jacob either good or evil (31:29). Laban is a stranger, and Jacob addresses him as such. Using the same verb which described Abraham's dealings with Abimelek, *vayokihu* ("judge," "reprove"), Jacob calls Laban to task for his actions and vindicates himself (31:37; 21:25).

If earlier Jacob and Laban were related through action as well as through kinship, now Jacob disassociates himself from Laban. He has stolen nothing from his host, while Laban has cheated him repeatedly (31:39-41). And, while Laban insists that Jacob and he are members of a single family, Jacob differentiates between the two families. When Laban finally initiates the covenant which parallels the covenant with Abimelek at Be'er Sheba and which takes effect for future generations (31:43-44), he calls on "the God of Abraham and the God of Nahor . . . the God of their father" (31:53). But Jacob does not look back to the common ancestor or even to the brothers from whom he and Laban are descended. Jacob swears, instead, by the God of "his father Isaac." Jacob's lineage is separate from Laban's, and the two men go separate ways, each to his own place (*maqom*; 32:1-3).

The oaths between Jacob and Laban emphasize the link between each one's father and his god, a motif which has appeared frequently within this episode. Laban introduces the notion when he tells Jacob of his dream: "the God of your father spoke to me saying, beware of speaking with Jacob good or bad" (31:29). Laban goes on, seemingly to make a separate point, but his next sentence really follows directly from what he has just said. "And now that you are going because you long for your father's house—why did you steal my gods?" (31:30). Laban's question is not a simple rhetorical condemnation of Jacob's suspected theft; it is, in the context of what precedes it, a real question. If Jacob's father has his own God, and if Jacob is returning to his father, then why does Jacob want Laban's gods?

The sequence reinforces the parallel between Laban and Isaac, heads of distinct families with separate gods, and it raises another issue. Jacob, it is true, has no use for Laban's gods, but Rachel does want them. For Rachel to take Laban's gods is for her to affirm that Laban is her father, and Jacob, unwittingly, condemns Rachel as a result—"He with whom you find your gods shall not live; before our brothers recognize what is with me, and take it for yourself" (31:32). Jacob then emphasizes the growing distinction between the two families as he challenges Laban to display the findings of his search for the idols "before my brothers and your brothers" (31:37).[50] Jacob's family is separate from Laban's, and Rachel has shown herself to be a member of her father's house. When Jacob goes on to accept responsibility for any of Laban's livestock that has been stolen under his charge, he does so with one qualification: "I would compensate for it, from my hand you would demand it, that stolen from me by day and that stolen from me by night" (31: 39). This emphatic statement, an echo of which will reappear many episodes later, excludes Jacob's responsibility for Rachel's deed, as Jacob does not take responsibility for a theft of something not in his charge, such as Laban's gods.

Rachel is doomed as a member of Jacob's family when Jacob separates from Laban and Rachel is unable to do so. Jacob differentiates himself completely from Laban's family, finally, by speaking of the God of his fathers, Abraham and Isaac (31:42). Laban hastily counters that wives, children and livestock all belong to him (31:43). He no longer attempts to incorporate Jacob into his family, because Jacob has made it clear that he has separated from Laban's family. Accepting the distinction, Laban half-heartedly makes one attempt to claim everything for himself, and finally decides to initiate a covenant, an agreement between two separate peoples (31:44).

Jacob has separated himself from Laban and his family, both in character and in kinship. He had gone to Padan Aram, initially, to find a wife through whom he could inherit the paternal blessing but also in order to escape the danger of his paternal home and seek haven in the home of his maternal kinsman. The maternal home is safe—Laban can harm Jacob neither physically nor spiritually —but nevertheless threatens to destroy Jacob as part of the patriarchal family. If Jacob were to stay with Laban, he would be forever lost to his special destiny.

Reconciliation, separation, and return

Jacob's journey from his father's home in Canaan to his uncle's home in Padan Aram exemplifies the two opposite but equivalent dangers discussed in Chapter One: the son can remain close to his father and be destroyed or he can preserve his life in exile but become lost to his heritage. Either choice is disastrous, because neither allows for the continuity of the father's destiny through his son. The son is safe in exile precisely because his place of exile lacks cultural significance; it has no blessing to offer and it has no curse to give. The son is threatened at home precisely because his land represents his cultural heritage; it is a place of promise and a place of danger. Exile, in Genesis, is the place of the maternal kin; the land of Canaan is the place of the paternal kin. The father is the bearer of the blessing; the mother is not. If Jacob is to inherit his father's blessing, then he will have to return to his father in the land of Canaan. And, in returning, he will have to resolve the conflict inherent in the family relationships. His stay in Padan Aram and, especially, his break with Laban and with his own Laban-like character, will have prepared him for his return home and his reconciliation with his family.

First, Jacob must settle the conflict with his brother, the conflict which directly led to his exile in the house of Laban. As soon as Jacob leaves Laban, he sends a gift to appease Esau who, Jacob finds out, is coming toward him with a troop of men. But the cattle which Jacob sends are more than just a gift.

Jacob begins by calling the animals a present (*minha*; 32:19), but goes on to speak of atonement (*'akapera*; 32:21).[51] The gift of atonement implies a sacrificial offering, and the sacrificial nature of this episode is confirmed by Jacob's encounter with the "man" called Elohim. Jacob uses the word "face" (*panim*) repeatedly to describe both his meeting with Elohim and with Esau, particularly as the object of the verb "to atone" (32:20-21, 30), and finally compares the two encounters explicitly: "take my gift from my hand, for I have seen your face as if seeing the face of Elohim" (33:10). By presenting these animals to his brother, Jacob is offering a sacrifice, much like the sacrificial animals which Rebecca had instructed him to bring to his father in order to receive the blessing which was to have been his brother's.

In the episode of the encounter with the "man," too, Jacob solicits a blessing (32:26). The "man" changes his name and offers him a blessing which God confirms later as the blessing of Abraham, the double blessing of land and descendants (32:28-29; 35:9-12). This element of Jacob's encounter with Elohim makes Jacob's gift to Esau significant in one more way. Jacob returns to Esau the stolen blessing (*beraka*).[52] After he speaks both of present (*minha*) and of atonement (*kapara*), Jacob is able to convince Esau to accept his offering only by calling it a blessing (*beraka*): "take, please, my blessing which is brought to you" (33:11). Jacob can return this blessing because it is not the significant blessing. Isaac had given him a different blessing before he left home; that blessing has been confirmed by the "man" and will be further confirmed by God.[53] And that second blessing, the blessing of Abraham, Jacob did not obtain through deceit.

When Jacob presents his material wealth to Esau, he rids himself both of the blessing which he had obtained by deceiving his father and of the wealth which he had obtained by deceiving Laban (30:43; 32:5, 14-15). Jacob relinquishes the legacy that he had received by being Rebecca's son and, accepting the second blessing of his father, he rejects conclusively his tie to Laban and to Padan Aram. Esau accepts what Jacob rejects. He receives the material wealth and the blessing for the present and finally, like Lot and Ishmael, he leaves the land which cannot contain the property of both brothers (36:6-7; cp. 13:6).[54]

Jacob enters the land and comes "complete" (*shalem*) to the city of Shechem (33:18), fulfilling a part of God's covenant with Abraham (16:17). A few episodes intervene before the narrative speaks of Jacob's return to his father (35:27), each of which describes the distinctness of Jacob's family and their separation from outsiders.

Like Abraham, Jacob purchases a field, affirming his possession of the land and the exclusiveness of that possession (33:19). Jacob's dealings with the sons of Hamor, Shechem's father, lead to the episode of the rape of Dinah and to Hamor's offer of an alliance with Jacob's family. Hamor, we find in his speech to the people of Shechem, is eager to become "one nation" with Jacob's family and to take possession of their property (34:22-23).[55] Jacob's sons accept Hamor's offer only on condition that the men of Shechem become circumcised. The stipulation, of course, expresses the uniqueness of Jacob's family (34:14-15), who alone are partners to God's covenant; the brothers have no intention of joining with the people of Shechem, and they avenge their sister while the Shechemites are weak from their circumcision (34:25-27). Jacob's family then travels on, pausing to build an altar to God and to discard their "strange gods" (35:2-4). And, finally, the family is completed as Jacob's twelfth son is born to the dying Rachel, and Jacob for the first time participates in naming his son (35:17-19).

Distant father, absent mother

When Jacob at last returns to his father, he has separated himself from his maternal uncle, from his brother and from the Canaanites, he has taken possession of a part of the land, and he has begotten twelve sons. He has also established a pattern of behavior with respect to his children. Jacob, both after the rape of Dinah and after Reuven sleeps with Bilhah, remains passive (34:5; 35:22); he allows his sons to take control. Abraham, in contrast, had taken an active role regarding his children, banishing Ishmael and sending away the concubines' sons, and Isaac ultimately chose between his sons as well.

Jacob is passive, but his passivity, at first, allows the fourth generation to form a single family. His sons reclaim their sister after she is taken by Shechem. And Reuven is included in the family despite his act of usurpation. The verse which tells of Jacob's lack of response to Reuven's act concludes with an apparent *non sequitur*: ". . . and the sons of Jacob were twelve" (35:22).[56] Reuven would seem to have disqualified himself as a member of Jacob's family, but Jacob refuses to exclude any of his children. He establishes his family in the land, but allows his sons to act as they please as long as they remain together. When Joseph will dream of power over his family, Jacob will rebuke him mildly but, once again, will wait to see what happens (37:10-11). Meanwhile, he will send his favorite son to join his brothers and see to their "peace" (*shalom*) in Shechem, the place where they have already recognized and acted upon their responsibility toward a sibling.[57]

Joseph and his brothers have a passive father, and they have no mother. Rachel dies as they enter the land, and Leah is never mentioned again. Rachel's death follows the sequence of episodes which confirms the separateness of Jacob's family as they enter the land of Canaan, and it severs the last tie to Padan Aram.[58] Rachel was a typical member of Laban's family. Her thievery underscores her family character, and the possession of Laban's idols reifies her permanent link to her father. Jacob relinquished both his deceitfulness and his tie to Laban when he left Padan Aram for his own father's home, and he rejected the person who took Laban's idols (31:32). Rachel can no longer be a part of Jacob's family once Jacob separates from Laban.

Looking back over the Jacob narrative, we can now see the connection between the issues of brothers, wife and mother, and the land. We noted these issues in Abraham's final experiences with Lot, Hagar, and Abimelek as well as in Abraham's preparations for Isaac to take over. Now we have examined these same issues in the Jacob narrative, in Jacob's conflict with Esau, his experiences with Rebecca and with Rachel, and his return to the land.

The relationship between these elements becomes clear in the context of the most crucial relationship—between the paternal heritage and the land. The blessing and command which God first gave to Abraham focused on the land, and the blessing which each father passes on to his son promises the land as well. Living in the land, then, implies identification with familial destiny, and leaving the land means giving up a share in that destiny. The blessing of the land can be passed on only to a son who is able to understand its meaning. A son who looks to the land only for prosperity must leave. As a physical entity, the land cannot be shared; the prosperity which the land offers motivates competition between brothers. Prosperity can be found elsewhere by a brother who chooses to seek it. The brother who chooses to remain in the land seeks, instead, the blessing of Abraham, his paternal heritage.

Mothers are instrumental in the transfer of the paternal heritage from father to son but, in the patriarchal narratives, the father's lineage is the culturally significant one. The transfer from father to son is dangerous because of its significance; the mother can protect her son, but she cannot transfer to him his destiny. The mother, then, offers her son an alternate lineage, one which is safe precisely because it is not culturally significant. The mother can neither bless nor curse her son, although she can ensure, through her perception of the family's destiny, that her son receive his father's blessing.[59]

The son who follows his father remains in the land; the brother who follows his mother leaves the land. The function of the maternal relationship is complicated, though, by the degree to which the mother is related to the father. Hagar, for example, is completely foreign to Abraham's kin, while Sarah is closely related. Ishmael, following his mother, leaves the land, while Isaac, whose relationship to his mother reinforces his relationship to his father, never leaves the land at all. Rebecca is more distantly related to Isaac than Sarah is to Abraham, but she is not a foreigner like Hagar. She is able, like Sarah, to insure the paternal blessing for her favored son, and Jacob, although he leaves the land for his maternal home, is able to return to his father.

For Jacob's sons, though, the maternal relationship offers neither guarantee of blessing nor safety. Rachel is more distantly related to Jacob than either Sarah was to Abraham or Rebecca was to Isaac. The alternate lineage which she would be able to offer her son would remove him too far from Jacob's family. And Padan Aram, once Jacob leaves, is defined as completely separate from Canaan. Never again will a member of the patriarchal family go to Padan Aram to seek a wife; like the Egyptian Hagar, such a wife would be a foreigner. Maternal lineage for Jacob's sons, then, is an alternative which would not allow the son to remain a member of Jacob's family. Rachel is an outsider, and she dies outside the patriarchal home.

Jacob's sons have neither a mother who can provide an alternate lineage, separate from but related to their father's, nor a mother who can insure that they receive their father's blessing. They lack a mother who can define their relationship to their father or their relationship to each other. Joseph and his brothers do not identify with each other. Similarly, Hagar's son did not identify with Sarah's son. But Esau and Jacob did recognize their relationship to the extent that they could exchange rights and blessings and, most importantly, they identified enough to allow sacrificial substitution to function. Jacob's sons do not share a mother who can define them as brothers, and they lack the identification which allows for sacrifice. When Rachel was alive, her relationship with Leah was much like Jacob's with Esau. The sisters competed with one another, yet they were able to bargain for each other's conjugal rights and to substitute in marriage for one another. The birth of their sons, however, was a manifestation of the sisters' competition and, once Rachel dies, the element of identification is lost and only competition remains.

In Abraham's family, with its close identification between father and son, paternal violence was deflected through sacrifice. In Isaac's family, both paternal and fraternal violence were averted through both sacrifice and doubling; Jacob presented sacrifices to his father and to his brother, and he left, temporarily, to a surrogate maternal family. But Jacob's family, with its distant father and absent mother, has no way to remain together without the eruption of violence. The brothers lack the identification which would allow sacrifice to deflect fraternal violence, and they have no alternate lineage which could protect the threatened son and allow him later to return to his father and brothers.

When the inevitable fraternal conflict arises, then, only two possibilities remain: the son will be lost to his family either through death or through exile. Joseph must either be killed, in the absence of sacrificial substitution, or he must be separated completely from his family, in the absence of an alternate lineage. Joseph suffers both fates; exile is equated with death as Joseph is sold to the Chief Slaughterer (*Sar Hatabahim*) and is lost to his family's destiny.

Jacob's passivity as a father ultimately does not allow his family to remain together; it results, instead, in the eruption of fraternal conflict and the exclusion of the favorite son from the paternal heritage. Joseph's fate, then, reflects both his father's relationship to his sons and his mother's relationship to the family. In fact, his separation from his family is really different from Jacob's move to his maternal kin only in degree. Jacob had moved to an alternate, maternal home which had not yet been defined as completely separate from his paternal home. But, leaving Padan Aram, Jacob broke all ties between his family and Laban's, and Rachel's lingering tie to Padan Aram and to her father prevented her inclusion in Jacob's family. The banishment of Rachel's son, then, is equivalent to Joseph's move to an alternate home which is completely separate from his own, as Padan Aram, his maternal home, is now.

The nature of this banishment, and its relevance to the definition of kin relationships in the extended narrative, is hinted at by Judah's suggestion to his brothers that they sell Joseph at the moment that he sees Ishmaelite merchants passing by.[60] Ishmael was a son who was banished; he was excluded from his paternal home and joined his mother's totally separate kin, marrying an Egyptian and settling near Egypt. Judah uses the model of Ishmael to banish the brother who is excluded from the paternal home. Joseph is taken to Egypt, to a place totally separate from his paternal home, a place equivalent, in a sense, to Rachel's Padan Aram as defined by Jacob; the Ishmaelites take the excluded brother to the foreign place from which a brother never returns. Like the exiled Jacob, Joseph will take a wife and his name will be changed (41:45). But, like Ishmael, Joseph marries an Egyptian woman, and Joseph's new name, which defines his transformation, is Egyptian as well. His children are not born as members of the patriarchal family; they represent, instead, Joseph's total separation from his family. Joseph names his firstborn Menasheh "because God has caused me to forget all my travail and all of my father's house" (41:51).

The loss of Joseph signals the end of the patriarchal family. Unlike Abraham and Isaac, each of whom needed only one son to succeed him, Jacob has twelve sons; he is the father of a nation. And if any one of these sons is lost, the remaining sons amount to nothing. Eleven sons are simply eleven sons; they are not a nation. Unless Joseph can be reincorporated into Jacob's family, the nation of Israel will never emerge.

Judah and Tamar

As we noted in Chapter Two, the turning point of the family narrative occurs at precisely this crucial moment, in the story of Judah and Tamar. Tamar, we saw, is able to restore paternal responsibility, eliminating conflict between father and son and between brothers. And Judah, once among his family again, will be able to draw both his father and his brothers back toward family responsibility. Looking once again at the Tamar story, we can now take note of other elements, particularly the problem of perception, which we discussed in Chapter Three, and the separation of brothers, departure from the land, and choice of wife and mother. The episode of Judah and Tamar addresses all of these elements, as well as the father-son conflict and sacrificial substitution, and transforms the biblical family with respect to each.

The story begins when Judah leaves his brothers, moves to a different region, and takes a wife (38:1). Judah sees (*vayar'*) "the daughter of a Canaanite man," although the woman is not called a Canaanite herself (38:2). We suspect that Judah's choice confirms his separation from his family, as had Esau's marriage to Canaanite women, and we expect that his own sons will be unable to identify with each other as heirs to a common heritage. Judah begets three sons. He names the first and finds him a wife, performing the duties of a father, but his other two sons are named by their mother (38:3-6). Judah, in fact, is absent when his last son, Shelah, is born. The father is in *Keziv*, which name suggests Judah's future deceitfulness toward Tamar regarding his youngest son; his passive refusal in the future to fulfill his responsibility as a father is foreshadowed now as he takes no part in the birth of Shelah.[61] The distance between father and son, implied by the father's lack of involvement in the child's birth and naming, increases with the birth of each of Judah's sons to their Canaanite mother, and this progression is paralleled by the increasing inability of each son to accept family responsibility, in the form of begetting a son to carry on for a deceased brother.

In contrast with Judah's Canaanite wife, Tamar, who will restore the proper family relationships, is not described as a Canaanite, nor is she linked to any other nation.[62] When Er dies without a son, and Onan is killed for refusing to give his brother an heir, Judah tells Tamar to return to her "father's house" until Shelah is old enough to marry (38:7-11). Tamar does return to "her father's house" (38:11), but once again her family and nationality remain unnamed. Tamar, as far as this story is concerned, has no significant family. She is not a foreigner; she is meant to be a part of Judah's family, and she is determined to be reincorporated into it and to make sure that the family continues.

Tamar, in her manipulation of events, resembles Rebecca, who had chosen to be a part of the patriarchal family and had striven for the continuation of the familial destiny, and a number of details confirm the similarity. The first of these appear during her seduction of Judah. Tamar covers her face with a veil and sits at the entrance to Enayim (*petah 'Enayim*) because "she saw [*ra'ata*] that Shelah had grown up and she had not been given to him as a wife." Judah sees her (*vayir'eha*) and thinks that she is a prostitute, "for she had covered her face" (38:14-15). Rebecca, too, covered her face with a veil and

Isaac, we have noted, was unable to see her. Rebecca, however, was able to see Isaac (*vatere'*) and to recognize him from afar as her husband (24:63-65).

The locations of the two encounters are similar as well, and each plays on the theme of perception. Isaac is on his way from Be'er Lahai Ro'i, the well of seeing or, at least in Hagar's case, of unseeing, and Rebecca has been chosen for him at a well, described as an *'ayin*, also meaning "eye" (24:62, 16). The place at which Tamar awaits Judah is called 'Enayim, "eyes," and the name plays, especially in conjunction with the word *petah*, "entrance" or "opening," on Tamar's perception and Judah's inability to see.

Tamar, ultimately, restores Judah's ability to recognize his responsibilities by sending the surety (*'eravon*) which Judah had given her in promise of the goats: "Recognize [*haker na'*] to whom belong this seal, cord, and staff" (38:25). The words *haker na'* recall the demand of Joseph's brothers of their father: "Recognize [*haker na'*], is this your son's cloak or not?" (37:32). And recognition will be the key to the story of the brothers in Egypt: "Joseph recognized [*vayaker*] his brothers but they did not recognize him [*hikiruhu*]" (42:8).[63] Once Judah recognizes his surety and acknowledges that he was wrong not to give Tamar a husband (28:26), Tamar gives birth, and the episode completes the parallel to Rebecca.[64] Tamar gives birth to twins and, as with Jacob and Esau, the issue of the firstborn is confused. In this story, though, the characters deliberately designate first and second born. The child who begins to come out first pulls back, and the other child comes out before him. Unlike the birth of Rebecca's twins, here neither brother holds the other back; Zerah is born second because he does not move forward, and Perez is born first because the other stays back while he jumps ahead (38:27-30).

Tamar is a mother who does not represent an alternate lineage; the text assigns her no nationality, and she refuses to stay in her father's house. Instead, she returns to Judah's family and defines the relationship between father and son and between brothers. Perez and Zerah are both sons and grandsons of Judah. Judah, as grandfather, is a father once removed, yet he is also, as both grandfather and father, a father twice related. Judah is a patriarch.

If the closeness between father and son leads to violence, then the distance between grandfather and grandson insures the child's safety. But this distance is not the geographical distance that protected Jacob but forced him into an alternate alliance with his maternal kin, or that has removed Joseph from any identification with his family. The safety of the relationship between grandfather and grandson does not imply the absence of a blessing, as in Padan Aram,[65] or of family destiny, as in Egypt. A patriarch is precisely the one who can pass on a blessing to his descendants, yet he does not come into conflict with them if one or more generations intervene. Jacob was blessed with the "blessing of Abraham," his grandfather, and, as we shall discuss later, Joseph's sons will be blessed by their grandfather as well. Judah is a model patriarch, a grandfather who sets the standard for the relationship to grandsons, because his grandsons, Perez and Zerah, are really his sons.[66]

Reclaiming Rachel's son

Tamar traces the lack of fraternal responsibility back to the father. Judah relinquished paternal responsibility by not giving Shelah to his deceased brother's wife, and Tamar forces Judah, by having him perform the duty of a brother, to assume the responsibility of a father. As we noted in Chapter Two, Judah will go on to lead his father to assume paternal responsibility, when Simeon is imprisoned, and to lead his brothers to assume fraternal responsibility, when Benjamin is threatened. And the family's reformation, at Judah's hands, will force Joseph to reveal himself to his brothers and will cause the reunion of the entire family. The actions of Jacob and his sons during the famine play against their earlier behavior toward Joseph, especially through the constant mention of the "one who is no more," Joseph, in the context of the "little brother," Benjamin, who must be protected at all costs, and the "one brother," Simeon, who is imprisoned in Egypt (42:13, 15, 19-21, 33-34, 36).

The experiences of Joseph and his brothers in Egypt reenact in reverse their experiences in Canaan, allowing Joseph to be reincorporated into his family. But Tamar established Judah's family by redefining kin relationships. And the disintegration of Jacob's family had coincided with the absence of a mother who could define her son's relationship to his father and brothers. The reacceptance of Joseph into Jacob's family, then, coincides with an implied acceptance of Joseph's mother, Rachel. Both Joseph and Rachel are reclaimed through the family's treatment of Benjamin, Rachel's younger son.

When Judah approaches his father to allow Benjamin to go with his brothers to Egypt, he makes a pledge which echoes from a previous episode: "I will stand as surety for him ['e'erve-nu]; from my hand you shall demand him" (43:9). The statement repeats almost exactly Jacob's statement to Laban concerning property that was stolen from him (31:39). But Jacob, we noted, did not take responsibility for Laban's idols, stolen by Rachel. He had already vindicated himself with the demand to "recognize" (haker na'), challenging Laban to find his idols and condemning to death the person who stole them: "He with whom you find your gods shall not live . . ." (31:32). In the process of separating from Laban and establishing his own family, Jacob had unwittingly excluded Rachel.

Judah, though, has learned from Tamar the meaning of surety ('eravon; 38:17-18, 20), and he offers himself as surety for his brother   ('e'ervenu).[67] Bringing Tamar back into the family, he had conflated paternal and fraternal responsibility. Now, by offering to stand as surety ('eravon) for his brother, Judah gives Jacob the opportunity to reclaim his lost son as well as, in some measure, his wife. Judah introduces his proposal with the words, "The man has testified against us . . ." (ha'ed he'id; 43:3). These words, too, remind us of Jacob's last encounter with Laban and the covenant which they established when the two families separated: "It shall be a witness ['ed] between me and you" (31:44, 48, 52). Judah's offer to his father, expressed in Jacob's own words and recalling his past experiences, convinces Jacob to send Benjamin to Egypt.

Judah's words—"The man has testified against us, saying, you shall not see my face unless your brother is with you" (43:3)—recall another incident from Jacob's past. Almost immediately after Jacob's covenant with Laban, Jacob prepared to meet Esau. Sending a gift (*minha*) to his brother, Jacob hoped to appease him and to be able to "see his face" (33:10). Now, sending Benjamin with Judah, Jacob allows his sons to "see the face" of Joseph (43:3). He prepares his sons for their encounter with their brother by sending a gift (*minha*; 43:11) and the gift consists of much the same items carried by the Ishmaelite merchants to whom Judah convinced his brothers to sell Joseph (37:25).[68] This gift, copying the one which allowed Jacob to make peace with his brother, reverses, as well, the proposed sale which separated Joseph from his brothers. Offering the goods which symbolize Joseph's sale and returning the money which seemingly they have stolen from Joseph (43:11-12), the brothers imitate Jacob's restoration of the blessing to Esau.

When Joseph sees his brothers coming with Benjamin, he commands his servant to slaughter animals for a meal (*utevoah tevah*; 43:16). The words recall Joseph's fate after he was drawn out of the pit; he was handed over to Potiphar the Chief Slaughterer—*Sar Hatabahim* (37:36). Potiphar's title confirms Jacob's response to the brothers' question of recognition (*haker na'*) regarding the bloody cloak—"Joseph has been ripped apart" (37:32-33). But Joseph's command to slaughter animals comes in the context of the brothers' gift (*minha*) and, more significantly, is a response to the arrival of Benjamin. The slaughtering which once signified the murder of a brother now becomes a sacrificial act, the kind of response to conflict which presupposes identification.

Jacob and Esau, sharing a single mother, were able to engage in sacrificial substitution; Joseph and his brothers were not. But, when Jacob is about to send Benjamin, he instructs the brothers to bring a gift (*minha*) and, when Joseph sees the only brother with whom he shares a mother, he is able to respond with the slaughter (*tevah*) of an animal. The link between the gift and the slaughter is reinforced by the verb used in the context of both—"prepare" (*haken*); both Joseph and his brothers are preparing for the moment of encounter (43:16, 25). Jacob, at last, has behaved like a father. By sending Benjamin to redeem his brother and by instructing the brothers to bring a gift, he allows the brothers to approach Joseph and to tame the potentially deadly encounter through an act of sacrifice.[69]

Meanwhile, the brothers' conversation with Joseph's servant extends the parallel between this episode and both Jacob's encounter with Esau and the selling of Joseph. When the brothers offer to return the money which they seem to have taken wrongfully, Joseph's servant refuses to accept it. He explains that he has received his money, and that the money which the brothers have was not taken from him (43:23). Jacob, too, had tried to return to Esau the property which he owed him, but Esau had rejected the offer, explaining that he had enough and that Jacob should keep what is his (33:9). Furthermore, Joseph's servant responds with the word *shalom*, recalling Jacob's condition after his separation from Esau—*shalem*, "whole" (33:18). The word recalls also the mission on which Jacob sent Joseph, but which separated Joseph from his brothers, and which Joseph never completed—"See [*re'e*] the peace [*shalom*] of your brothers and the peace of the flocks" (37:14). Now, when Joseph arrives and the brothers present their gift, bowing to him as in the young boy's dreams (37:7, 9), Joseph finally does ask after their *shalom* and the *shalom* of their father (43:26-27).[70]

The relationship of Joseph to his brothers has shifted. It began, in the story of the selling of Joseph and his descent to Egypt, as parallel to the relationship between Ishmael and Isaac, who had different mothers, and has moved on, as the brothers prepare to meet and appease Joseph, to be parallel to the relationship between Esau and Jacob, who had a single mother. But, while Esau and Jacob identified as brothers, they still were not able to live together; after the exchange of the gifts, the brothers separated. If Joseph and his brothers are to be able to live together, they must move beyond *tevah* ("slaughter") and *minha* ("gift"). The movement, indeed, continues when Joseph meets Benjamin, his brother from the same mother, and forces his family to reaccept both himself and his mother through Benjamin.

123

When the brothers separate once again from Joseph, Joseph forces them to return. We have noted already the verbal echoes of Jacob's separation from Laban, and his consequent loss of Rachel, in this narrative. Now, the plots become parallel. Joseph commands his servant to "chase" after his brothers and to "overtake" them (44:4), as Laban had "chased" after and "overtaken" Jacob (31:23,25). The servant accuses the brothers of taking Joseph's cup, as Laban had accused Jacob of stealing his gods, and the brothers, using the verb "steal" (gnv), deny the charge (44:8). Like Jacob, they condemn the wrongdoer to death—"the one of your servants with whom it is found shall die" (44:9).[71] But unlike Jacob, they do not exclude themselves completely—"and we too shall be slaves to my master" (44:9). Joseph's servant accepts the offer of slavery but changes the terms to resemble more closely Jacob's refusal to be held responsible: the one who has the cup shall be a slave and the rest shall go free (44:10).

Judah cannot accept this offer. When the brothers are accused by Joseph himself,[72] Judah adopts the reduced penalty of slavery for the thief, but, speaking throughout in the plural, he refuses to allow Benjamin alone to be punished: "God has found the sin of your servants; we are [hinenu] slaves to my master, both we and he in whose hand the cup was found" (44:16). Joseph rejects Judah's offer, reiterating his servant's terms and sending away all of the brothers except for Benjamin: "and you (plural), go up in peace [shalom] to your father" (44:17).[73] Joseph's offer clearly plays on both the brothers' treatment of Joseph and Jacob's treatment of Rachel. The youngest brother, he says, will remain in Egypt as a slave; he alone of the brothers, like Joseph before him, will not be able to return in peace to his father. And Rachel's son, the one who, like Rachel, is accused of stealing, will alone be culpable for his action; the rest of Jacob's sons will return safely to the land, as Jacob had returned "whole" (shalem).

Judah now attempts to fulfil the pledge which he has made to Jacob. He steps before Joseph and explains what has happened, but without trying to vindicate either Benjamin or the other brothers. Judah omits the issue of theft and of guilt.

Instead, he discusses his family and the relationship between his father and the two sons of Rachel. Speaking of his father's sorrow were he to lose Benjamin, Judah repeats his promise to Jacob: "For your servant became surety ['arav] for the youth to my father" (44:32). Becoming surety goes beyond sharing responsibility; Judah had already offered to share his brother's slavery (44:16). Now, Judah offers something different: "And now, let your servant stay in place of the youth as a slave to my master, and the youth shall go up with his brothers" (44:33).

Judah's willingness to accept exile and slavery in place of Benjamin comes as a response to Jacob's loss of both Rachel and Joseph: "We have an old father and a little child of his old age, and his brother died, and he alone remains to his mother, and his father loves him" (44:20). If Benjamin does not return, his father will die of grief (44:29, 34), having lost Rachel's entire family. Judah's offer to become surety not only saves his father by restoring Benjamin; it makes possible the return to his father of Rachel's other son as well, for Joseph can no longer conceal his identity. He reveals himself to his brothers and, at the same time, manifests his sense of identification with Benjamin, implicit throughout the narrative. Judah's description of Jacob's grief should Benjamin, the son of Rachel and the "child of his old age," be lost (44:20, 29, 31) echoes the description of Jacob's grief when Joseph, Rachel's other child and "the son of his old age," was lost (37:3, 35). Hearing of the "evil" that may befall his father when he finds that the lad is missing (44:34; cp. 37:30), Joseph cannot help but question Jacob's survival of Joseph's own disappearance: "I am Joseph; is my father still alive?" (45:3).[74]

The failure of Jacob to include Rachel in his family had culminated in his inability to stand as surety for her, but it had begun when Jacob rebuffed Rachel's request for children with the response "Am I in place of God?" (30:2). When Judah repeats the words which had signified Jacob's ultimate rejection of Rachel, he transforms the import of those words, expressing now an acceptance of responsibility for Rachel's children and a reincorporation into the family of the previously excluded members. Joseph later confirms that reversal by repeating the words which his father used in response to Rachel's request for children.

After Jacob dies, his sons are afraid of Joseph; they fear that he, like Esau, plans to avenge himself after his father's death (50:15).[75] Presenting themselves first as brothers, then as "the servants of the God of your father," the brothers appeal to Joseph through the wishes of their father, as Judah had done many years before, and finally offer themselves as slaves in the same words that Judah had used: "We are [*hinenu*] slaves" (50:16-18). Joseph reassures them with an ominous question: "Am I in place of God?" (50:19). Like Jacob, Joseph presents himself as a passive agent through whom God works. But Jacob's statement constituted a refusal to help a member of his family, while Joseph's statement is a guarantee that no member of his family will be harmed. All of the sons of all of Jacob's wives are included in the nation which Joseph believes he was sent to save (50:20).

Joseph does save his brothers by giving them food during the famine, and he saves the family by bringing them together into a single nation. But he also brings the family down to Egypt.

In a sense, through the exclusion of Joseph, the entire family is excluded, temporarily at least, from the paternal heritage. Abraham had two children of different mothers, one of whom was banished with his mother, the other of whom remained in the land. Isaac had two sons of a single mother, one of whom was banished to his mother's home but returned to encounter his brother and, trading places with him, to settle in the land of his father. Jacob also has two sons of a single mother, one of whom is banished from his paternal home never to return, and the other of whom is forced to join his brother in exile. This is the family portrait that Judah paints, in the name of Jacob, in his appeal to Joseph: ". . . my wife bore me two [sons]. And one went away from me, and I said: 'Surely he is torn in pieces; and I have not seen him until now. And if you take this one too from before me, and an accident befall him, you shall bring down my white hair in sorrow to Sheol.' " (44:27-29).

In a sense, this narrative is accurate. Jacob was sent by his father to find a wife. He saw Rachel at the well in Padan Aram, married her, and begot two sons. The older son was born without his father's active involvement, and his mother named him. The younger son was born as his mother died, and the father gave the infant a name in addition to the name given by the mother. The older son is banished from the land, and the younger son stays home with his father, replacing his brother as the "child of old age" (37:3; 44:20). This younger son, Jacob says, is all that is left him (44:20). When Joseph calls Benjamin down to Egypt, then, Jacob has, from this perspective, no son remaining in the land. And if Joseph, as he threatens, will force Benjamin to remain in Egypt, Jacob will have no son to carry on after him; his entire family is in exile.

But it is in exile that Jacob's family finally can be united. We have noticed the parallels between Joseph and, progressively, both Ishmael and Esau, and we have recognized the need for a more permanent reunion between Joseph and his brothers than that between Esau and Jacob. That reunion is what Joseph initiates by forcing Benjamin down to Egypt. Joseph greets Benjamin—"He fell on the neck of Benjamin and he cried and Benjamin cried on his neck" (45:14)—much as Esau had greeted Jacob—"he embraced him and he fell on his neck and kissed him, and they cried" (33:4). But Jacob and Esau, although able to meet in peace, did not remain together. Esau departed "on the same day" to Se'ir (33:16), and only Jacob returned to his father. Jacob's sons must go beyond this temporary reunion. Joseph's identification with Benjamin allows him to bring about a permanent reunion with his brother, but only by drawing him into his own exile and by defining him, as a thief, as a son of the same mother.

Jacob and the sons of Joseph

Jacob's youngest son, then, is able to live together with his brother, but he must join him outside the land, and Jacob is forced to leave the land and go into exile together with his sons. The entire family finally can live together in peace outside of the land, where there is no issue of a paternal heritage to engender conflict between father and son or between brothers. But even in exile from the patriarchal homeland, Jacob, before his death, transmits the patriarchal blessing. In fact, he distributes two sets of blessings, to Joseph's two sons as well as to his own twelve sons.

Jacob's blessing of Joseph's sons recalls earlier episodes in which a father had two sons and had to choose the one who would receive the blessing. Abraham, at the end of his life, came to see that Isaac, not Ishmael, was the chosen son. Isaac, planning to give only one blessing, blindly gave it to the son whom he had not planned to bless at all. He then learned that he could bless both sons, but that only Jacob would receive "the blessing of Abraham." Now Jacob is blind (48:10), but he sees clearly how the blessing may be transferred.[76] He acts not as a father but as a grandfather, and he is able to choose the appropriate child while giving the blessing to both children. Ephraim and Menasheh are to Jacob what Perez and Zerah are to Judah. In both pairs, the second son gains ascendancy over his brother, but in neither pair is there a hint of conflict. And, just as Perez and Zerah's grandfather is their father as well, Ephraim and Menasheh are adopted as sons by their grandfather.

Jacob adopts the sons born to Joseph before Jacob's arrival in Egypt, during Joseph's separation from his father; the rest of Joseph's children will be included automatically in Jacob's family, now that Joseph himself has rejoined the family (48:5-6). Menasheh and Ephraim had been born outside of the patriarchal family; Joseph had tried to forget his father's house, and the names of his sons reflect that separation (41:51-52). Jacob now remembers that God had promised to make him fruitful (48:3) but that Rachel had died immediately thereafter (48:7; cf. 35:6-19), and he asks Joseph to "take" his sons (*qahem*) to him so that he can bless them (48:9). Jacob's temporary loss of Joseph is juxtaposed with his loss of Rachel; Jacob wants to reclaim both Rachel and Joseph by completing his family—and so realizing God's promise of increase—with Joseph's sons.

Jacob places the younger son, Ephraim, before his older brother, Menasheh (48:14-20). Menasheh represents Joseph's desire to forget his father's house (41:51); Ephraim represents Joseph's fruitfulness in the land of his affliction (41:52). Clearly Menasheh's naming was more negative than Ephraim's. While Joseph celebrated his fruitfulness in Egypt upon the birth of his second son, and while Joseph's fruitfulness was linked by the narrative to the plentifulness of the land of Egypt itself (41:49-50), still Joseph had come to recognize that Egypt is the land of his affliction ('erets 'onyi; 41:52). Jacob's words to Joseph here play on the name of Ephraim, the child whom Jacob recognizes will be greater than his brother. Jacob explains that, as he entered the land after his sojourn in Padan Aram, God had promised that he would make him fruitful (hineni maphreka; 48:4)—but that Rachel had died on the road to 'Ephrat (48:7). Jacob fulfills the promise of fruitfulness (maphreka), as yet unfulfilled because Rachel died at Ephrat, by adopting Ephraim, the child of Rachel's lost son, Joseph. Like Joseph, Jacob also had begotten his children in exile, in a land of affliction ('onyi; 31:42); and Reuven, one of the two sons to whom Jacob now compares his adopted sons, derives his name from his mother's affliction ('onyi; 29:32). Both Jacob and Joseph had children in exile, before they were reunited with their fathers. Jacob recognizes the fulfillment of his promise of increase in the sons born to Joseph under the same circumstances under which Jacob's sons were born to him.

Jacob, like Judah, has lost a son, but he is able, again like Judah, to reclaim him through his grandsons. And Joseph is able to return to his father by "taking" his sons to him, and he receives his father's blessing through Jacob's blessing of Joseph's sons: "And he blessed Joseph and said . . . may the angel who has redeemed me from all evil bless the lads . . ." (48:15-16).[77] Joseph, the father of the boys, cannot see which one is chosen; he "sees" (vayar') that Jacob has switched his hands and "it was bad in his eyes" (48:17). But the blind Jacob, who "cannot see" and who never expected "to see [Joseph's] face," has been "allowed to see" Joseph's children (48:10-11), and he, the grandfather, is able to distinguish between the two children, as Perez was distinguished from Zerah, and to accept them both.

129

Jacob the patriarch

Jacob, then, is more than a father; he is the patriarch, Israel. As a patriarch, he is able to talk not only of the present but of the future, and his words echo the words of God's covenant with Abraham for the future: "Behold [*hine*], I am dying, and God will be with you and will return you to the land of your fathers. And I have given you one portion [*shekem*] over your brothers, which I took from the hand of the Amorites with my sword and with my bow" (48:21-22; cp. 15:15-16)). Acting as a patriarch, looking toward the future, Jacob gathers all his sons together to tell them "what will happen to you in the end of days" (49:1). Jacob speaks to each son individually, characterizing each and telling what his future will be. Only at the conclusion of his long speech does the text explain that Jacob has blessed his sons. "All these," it sums up, "are the tribes of Israel, twelve, and this is what their father spoke to them, and he blessed them; each according to his blessing he blessed them" (49:28).

Jacob, as the patriarch, Israel, accomplishes what no father in Genesis has been able to do. He includes all of his sons within a single nation, but he precludes conflict between brothers and between father and son. Each brother has been designated his own place within the family, and the heritage which the father passes on to his sons is one which reaches from the distant past to the distant future. If brothers, until now, could only get along when they were distant from the land and the paternal heritage, Jacob ensures, through a different kind of distancing, that his sons will return to the land and continue to live together in their paternal home. Instead of competing for the father's blessing, the brothers will share the patriarchal heritage.

Jacob expresses his commitment to the land, and ensures that his descendants will return to the patriarchal home, by asking his sons to bury him in the land of Canaan. In fact, the blessings of Joseph's sons and of the twelve brothers are framed by Jacob's commands to bury him in the grave of his fathers (47:30; 49:29-32). The first command, to Joseph, is especially striking because it takes the form of an imposed oath which resembles the oath that Abraham imposed on his servant. The servant's oath-taking occurred immediately after Abraham bought the gravesite to which Jacob now refers, and Abraham commanded his servant with exactly the same words which Jacob speaks to Joseph: "Place, please, your hand under my thigh [*yereki*]" (24:2; 47:29). Abraham commanded his servant not to allow Isaac to leave the land, while Jacob commands Joseph not to leave his remains in Egypt but to bury him in his forefathers' burial-place, and the fulfillment of both fathers' wishes is linked to the word *hesed*, "kindness" (24:6, 12; 47:29-30). The oath taken by placing the hand under the thigh, then, is connected with establishing a paternal home and creates a bond between father and son in relation to that home.

The thigh is mentioned one other time in Genesis, in the episode of Jacob's encounter with the "man." Jacob is about to enter the land and establish his own family as a separate nation. He moves his wives and children across the stream of Yaboq, but he remains alone on the other side. It is at that moment that he meets the "man" and enters into a night-long struggle with him, which plays on the name of the stream (*vaye'aveq*; 32:23-25). At the break of dawn, when the "man" sees that he cannot subdue Jacob, he strikes the hollow of Jacob's thigh (32:26). Jacob still refuses to release the "man" until he receives a blessing, and the "man" grants his request by changing Jacob's name to Israel, "for you have contended with Elohim and with men, and you have prevailed" (32:29). The "man's" blessing is simply an affirmation of what Jacob himself has just demonstrated, and it anticipates God's revelation to Jacob at Beth El, when God will change Jacob's name to Israel and will give him the blessing of land and descendants (35:9-12).

Jacob's encounter prompts him to rename the stream Peni-'el, reflecting his ability to "see Elohim face to face [*panim 'el panim*]," and as the sun rises Jacob crosses the stream, "limping on his thigh" (32:31-32). Only after his ambiguously successful encounter can the transformed Jacob cross the stream; he goes on, limping, to meet Esau and finally enters the land "whole" (*shalem*; 33:18). He immediately buys a field in the land (33:19),[78] and his purchase leads directly to the incident of Dinah's rape, with its emphasis on circumcision (ch. 34). This incident, in turn, immediately precedes God's command to Jacob to go to Beth El (35:11), where his change of name and his blessing are confirmed (35:9-12).

We noted already that in the Abraham narrative the purchase of the field is connected with the thigh-oath and the importance of remaining in the land, just as at the end of the Jacob narrative burial in the field is connected with the thigh-oath and the importance of return to the land. The Yabok episode and its context contain the same elements; Jacob purchases a field when he returns to the land after "the man" touches his thigh. But in the Yabok episode the touching of the thigh is linked to a blessing and a change of name, and the touching wounds Jacob.

The blessing, change of name, and wounding of a patriarch occur in an episode within the Abraham narrative as well. When God appears to Abraham and foretells the birth of Isaac, God changes Abraham's name and gives him a blessing (17:5-8) closely resembling the blessing which Jacob receives when his name is changed by God. Abraham, God promises, will be the progenitor of nations. The name change reflects the transition from *Avram*, "a great father," to *Avraham*, etymologized as "the father of many nations" (17:5). Jacob's name change, too, signals the transformation of the father of a family to the patriarch of a nation, Israel (35:11). And both namings and blessings are accompanied by God's promise of the land to the patriarchs' descendants (17:8; 35:12). While Jacob's transformation from a father to a patriarch occurred at the moment he received a thigh-wound, Abram's transformation to Abraham depends on the performance of circumcision. In each case, the father's own virility is impaired as he becomes the progenitor of a nation.[79]

Circumcision and the thigh-wound, then, symbolize the ambivalent nature of paternity.[80] The father's acceptance of the son who will succeed him carries a recognition of the father's personal mortality, but of his continued existence through his son. Thus, paradoxically, Jacob comes to the land "whole" (*shalem*; 33:18) though he limps from the wound to his thigh (32:32). The father is personally limited, but the patriarch's mission lives on through his descendants. Similarly, Abraham and Jacob impose an oath on the thigh (*yerek*) at the end of their lives, when each patriarch wants to ensure that his son and his son's sons will be able to succeed him.[81] Abraham makes sure that his son will remain in the land and will marry a woman who will allow the family to continue in the land. And Jacob makes sure that his descendants will return to the land.

Jacob asks Joseph to take an oath on his thigh and then, recalling the blessing of increase which he had received when his thigh was hurt—and which, therefore, he could never personally realize—Jacob claims his son's sons as his own. Joseph removes his sons "from between his knees [*birkav*]" (48:12) and brings the boys to Jacob to receive their grandfather's blessing (*beraka*).[82] At the end of his life, Jacob becomes the father of his grandsons, and he gives them the blessing of his own father and grandfather (48:16). Jacob confirms his transformation to Israel and, as a patriarch whose descendants continue his mission without conflict, he goes on to bless his own sons.

5

THE
FAMILY
IN
CONTEXT

We have traced the transfer of the blessing from father to son throughout the patriarchal narratives in the book of Genesis and have suggested that the achievement of a stable family structure, one which allows for the sharing of a common destiny without conflict, is essential if the family is to be a firm foundation on which the nation may be built. In this chapter, I would like to expand the focus of this study somewhat, to place the patriarchal narratives in their context and to see how they connect to what comes after, the story of the nation, and to what comes before, the primeval history of the world. I shall suggest a typological reading of the covenant and blessing of Abraham, one which sees the promise to the fathers as prefiguring the later experiences of the nation and as fulfilling the earlier design of creation.[1]

In Chapter Three, when contrasting Hagar and Abraham, we looked briefly at the covenant between the pieces and suggested that the terms of the covenant may be read as referring not only to the future nation but also to the experiences of Jacob and his children, the fourth generation, and indeed to Abraham himself. This point was important in that context because it shows that Abraham, even though he is silent during and after God's announcement of the terms of the covenant, nevertheless through his actions accepts his destiny, with its present suffering and its delayed fulfillment.

Moreover, anyone who is to participate in that destiny must similarly accept the terms of the covenant: sojourning, enslavement, and affliction (ger, 'avoda, and 'oni) for the present, inheritance of the land and God's blessing in the distant future. Such acceptance requires clarity of perception, for only one who has vision, who "surely knows" (15:13), will be able to endure the suffering and strive toward the future promise. This, in fact, is the fundamental test of the characters in the book of Genesis. Characters can change and grow, shedding bad qualities such as deceitfulness, but they must begin with a sense of future; if they are imbedded in the present—like Lot, Hagar, Ishmael, and Esau—no matter what other positive traits they may possess, they can never become part of the covenantal nation.

The basic idea of Abraham's acceptance of the covenant, then, was important for the development of the theme of vision in the Abraham narrative. At this point, however, I would like to expand upon the links between the covenant and the experiences of Abraham and Jacob, in order to show how the patriarchal experiences prefigure later events in the history of the nation.

Family and nation

God introduces the promise of land which precedes the covenant with a sentence strangely reminiscent of the preamble to his later covenant with the nation at Sinai (Exod 20:2): "I am God who took you out of Ur Kasdim" (15:7).[2] The text takes a past event in Abraham's life and doubly reinterprets it. First, it recounts the event in language and in a context which make Abraham's personal experience of leaving a strange land and entering into a covenant with God parallel to the nation's experience of leaving Egypt and entering into the covenant of Sinai. Second, and I think even more striking, it reinterprets Abraham's past, even of those elements which were not initially presented as responses to God's call, as having been a part of God's plan for Abraham. When Abraham originally left Ur Kasdim (11:31), the text gives no hint that Abraham was following God's command or that this move was part of God's plan at all. But, in retrospect, our passage interprets this earlier event as a part of the working out of God's covenant through Abraham.

This preamble offers a clue as to how we are to read the terms of the covenant (15:13-16). Abraham's past experiences parallel those of the nation, and this is true whether Abraham was aware of it at the time of those events or not.

This last point is especially important, because it accounts for why Abraham's prior experiences in Egypt, although corresponding to the terms of the covenant, are not recounted using all of the key words of the covenant, while Hagar's story and, we shall see, Jacob's story do include these words. Abraham's story is not narrated in the language of the covenant, because the covenant has not yet come into existence. But this does not mean that Abraham's experiences are not a part of the covenant. One's personal experience, in the book of Genesis, is covenantal to the extent that one recognizes it to be such, even if that recognition comes after the fact. This is a point to which we shall return when we move on to the Jacob narrative.

While most of the words describing the future suffering of the nation do not appear in the story of Abraham in Egypt, the ideas of sojourning, enslavement, and affliction are alluded to. Abraham goes to sojourn (*lagur*) in a land which is not his, in which he is a stranger (12:10); his wife is misappropriated (12:15), one of the primary meanings of the word '*oni*, "affliction"; and he remains in Egypt until Pharaoh releases him (*vayishalhu 'oto*; 12:20).[3] God's judgment (*dan/din*) of the nation and the attainment of wealth (*rekush*) also occur in this story, as Abraham is given gifts by Pharaoh, and as God strikes Pharaoh and his household with great plagues (12:16-17).

In fact, the actual words *dan* and *rekush* appear, together with the word *shalem*, "whole," in the episode immediately preceding the covenant between the pieces, the story of the battle of the four kings against the five. They appear once Abraham enters the narrative, and they appear in precisely the order in which they later are spoken in the covenant. Abraham's kinsman has been taken captive,[4] and Abraham fights to free him, chasing the enemy first to *Dan*, then to *Hova* (14:14-

136

15)—in a sense, the enemy has been judged and found guilty.[5] Abraham frees Lot and the Sodomites, allowing them to return with their wealth (rekush; 14:16),[6] and finally Abraham meets Melchizedek, the king of Shalem (14:18).[7]

Abraham, then, both has undergone suffering and oppression in Egypt and has come back to the land of Canaan and done battle to free it from those who possess it illegitimately; he has experienced the future of his descendants in miniature.[8] It is these events (hadevarim ha'eleh) that lead to God's promise that he will protect Abraham in the future as he did in the past (mgn; 15:1 and 14:20)[9] and to God's covenant with Abraham for his descendants. The nation's destiny will take its particular form because that is the shape of the destiny which their forefather Abraham carved out for them. And Abraham's past experiences become covenantal as Abraham comes to understand that his past is the beginning of the long road toward nationhood.

Jacob, too, undergoes exile, oppression, and redemption; he is the other patriarch in the book of Genesis who seeks his own way and thus shapes the future of his descendants. He also, as we mentioned in Chapter Three, can be seen as forming, together with his children, the fourth generation which returns to the land (15:16); as such his family's experiences are the fulfillment of the covenant made to their forefather Abraham. Jacob, then, is both ancestor and descendant, prefiguring the nation's future and fulfilling his family's past—as we have seen, he is both father to his sons and son to his fathers.

In the story of Jacob, not only do the themes of the covenant appear, but the key words of the covenant appear as well; and not only do the words appear, but they appear in configurations significant for the covenantal context and, indeed, identical to the configurations of these terms found in the later story of the nation, at the beginning of the book of Exodus.

Perhaps the first clue that we should read the story of Jacob in Laban's house as a fulfillment of the covenant is the puzzling verse which introduces the conception and birth of Joseph: "And God remembered Rachel, and God heard her, and he opened her womb" (30:22). The verse is intrinsically difficult as well as troubling in its context. First, what is God remembering and hearing? We have been told neither of a promise to Rachel which God might now be remembering, nor of a plea to God which he might now be heeding. Second, how does the account of Rachel's conception and birth of Joseph relate to what immediately precedes it, the birth of Dinah, and what immediately follows, Jacob's decision to leave Laban's house? The last question we have already begun to answer in our earlier discussion of the Jacob narrative—Jacob thinks of leaving now because, when his chosen wife bears him a son, he recalls the mission on which his father had sent him and realizes that he must return to his land and establish his own family (30:25-30).

If Joseph's birth forces Jacob to think of returning home, and thus leads to the founding of the house of Israel, then God's notice of Rachel takes on significance beyond the divine favor to an individual in need. Joseph's birth is a mechanism for the fulfillment of the promise of national destiny. The words "remembered" (vayizkor) and "heard" (vayishma‘), then, refer not only to God's response to Rachel but to God's response to his covenant with this family about to become nation. Indeed these same words appear in the book of Exodus specifically in reference to God's responses to his covenant: "And God heard their moaning and God remembered his covenant with Abraham, with Isaac, and with Jacob" (Exod 2:24); "And also I have heard the moaning of the children of Israel, that Egypt is enslaving them, and I have remembered my covenant" (Exod 6:5).[10] Both in Genesis and in Exodus, God "hears" the distress of people who are in trouble, even though they have not called out to God, and responds to this distress by "remembering" a covenant which he had made much earlier; in a sense, God is reinterpreting the suffering of Jacob's family and of the children of Israel in terms of the covenant.[11]

God's covenantal response to Israel's suffering comes at specific moments in the book of Exodus: the words "remembered" and "heard" appear each time after the root ‘vd (signifying servitude or enslavement) has occurred seven times.[12] The number seven is a number of covenant;[13] once the enslavement of the Israelites has reached covenantal proportions,

God's covenantal response is evoked. In the Jacob narrative, too, the words "remembered" and "heard" appear after the root *'vd* has occurred seven times.[14] Here, as in Exodus, God takes notice of the suffering, sees it as a fulfillment of the covenant, and is moved to act to keep his part of the covenant.

That is why the birth of Dinah is narrated immediately before our puzzling verse, and that is why Jacob asks Laban to send him off immediately after Joseph's birth. God's response to enslavement (*'avoda*) and the beginning of the redemption are heralded in the covenant by the word "judge" (*dan*): "And also the nation which they will serve (*ya'avodu*) I shall judge (*dan*), and afterward they will leave with great wealth" (15:14). Now *Dinah* is born (30:21; cp. *dyn*, "to judge"),[15] God remembers the covenant (30:22), and Jacob appeals to Laban to let him go (30:25).

"Send me" (*shalheni*) sounds like Moses' plea to Pharaoh; it is the request to a master to free his slave.[16] And, indeed, Jacob is treated as a slave in the house of Laban: Laban attempts to withhold his payment, he chases after Jacob to prevent him from leaving, he tries to claim Jacob's wives and children as well as his property as his own.[17] Jacob, then, has been enslaved, the moment of judgment has come, and Jacob asks to be released; but, if the terms of the covenant are to be fulfilled and Jacob is to prefigure the nation's experiences in Egypt, Jacob will not be able to leave until he has accumulated "great wealth" (*rekush gadol*; 15:14). And that is exactly what Jacob goes on to do. He stays in Laban's house long enough to become wealthy and, when he leaves to rejoin his father in the land of Canaan, it is with thrice-mentioned wealth (*rekush*; 31:18).[18]

So far we have accounted for the sevenfold repetition of "enslavement" (*'avoda*), the name Dinah, and the words "remembered" (*vayizkor*) and "heard" (*vayishma'*), "send me" (*shalheni*) and "wealth" (*rekush*), as well as for the order of these terms and the relationship between them. But the interpretation of this narrative as a fulfillment of the covenant is not yet complete, for certain difficulties remain. First, we must expect to find in this narrative not just the term "enslavement," but the two other terms mentioned in the covenant to describe the suffering of Abraham's descendants, "sojourning" (*gur*) and "affliction" (*'oni*). Second, while it is true that the term "enslavement" (*'avoda*) occurs seven times before God's remembrance of Rachel, the seventh occurrence actually precedes this event by many verses, occurring in 29:30, before the birth of Jacob's first child, Reuven.

The location of this seventh occurrence of "enslavement" forces us to see the birth of all of Jacob's children as the beginning of God's response to the family's suffering, and to see Jacob's wives as included in the covenantal suffering and hence, together with their children, in the covenantal family/ nation.[19] Immediately after the seventh occurrence (*vaya'avod*; 29:30), God "sees" (*vayar'*) that Leah is "despised" and opens her womb (29:31). The names of Leah's first two children reflect God's perception of her suffering: Reuven is etymologized using the word "to see" (*ra'a*) and Simeon using the word "despised" (29:32-33). In fact, when her first child is born, Leah asserts that God has "seen" her "affliction" (*ra'a YHWH 'et 'onyi*), mentioning the covenantal term "affliction" and using the verb which expresses God's covenantal response to that affliction, "see."[20] And the birth of Rachel's first surrogate child, *Dan*, introduces the idea of judgment in response to suffering (30:6).[21]

The birth of Dinah and God's remembering of Rachel, then, do not mark the beginning of God's response to the family's suffering. They mark, rather, the moment at which God's response reaches covenantal fullness and the turning point of the narrative from concern with the needs of individuals to concern with the future of the family.[22]

They mark, as well, the beginning of a new series of occurrences of the word "enslavement," paralleling the second group of seven in Exodus (ch. 5). And here, too, the word is mentioned seven times, beginning right after Jacob asks Laban to release him (30:26) and ending when Jacob finally breaks away from Laban (31:41).[23] As we have seen, both series in Exodus lead up to God's hearing and remembering, and the first series in the Jacob narrative leads to God's remembering and hearing and, even more immediately, to God's seeing of affliction. So, too, this second series of the term "enslavement" reaches the covenantal number of seven as Jacob asserts that God has "seen" his "affliction" ('oni; 31:42).[24]

As he breaks away from Laban, Jacob looks back at his treatment in Aram and describes it in language of the covenant—"affliction" ('oni). And, as he begins his journey home to the land of his fathers, he recalls his experience of exile and utters the remaining key word—"I have sojourned" (garti; 32:4).[25] Like Abraham, Jacob was not aware when he left the promised land, suffered in exile, and accumulated wealth that he was fulfilling the terms of the covenant. Indeed, the actions of both of these patriarchs in their respective lands of exile comment negatively on their morality as well as on their awareness of destiny. But, just as characters can change and grow, past experiences can be transformed through reinterpretation. And Jacob demonstrates the beginning of the process of his personal transformation as he transforms his past through an awareness of his role in the fulfillment of the covenant.[26]

But this is not all. As I mentioned earlier, Jacob's sons can be seen as the fourth generation referred to by God in his covenant with Abraham: "And you shall come (tavo') to your fathers in peace (beshalom) . . . And the fourth generation shall return (yashuvu) here, for the iniquity of the Amorite is not complete (shalem) until then" (15:15-16). When Jacob returns to the land of Canaan, he returns "whole" (shalem; 33:18).[27] He buys a field, expressing, as did Abraham before him (ch. 23), his intention ultimately to possess the land.

But in the very next episode there is another acquisition of land, this time through conquest, and this time by Jacob's sons. Shechem rapes Dinah and, in revenge, the sons of Jacob conquer the city of Shechem "by sword" (34:25-26). If Dinah earlier represented God's judgment as a response to the oppression of Laban's house, here Dinah is the instrument of God's judgment against those who undeservedly possess the land of Canaan. Jacob's sons, the fourth generation, can begin to conquer the land, because at this moment the sin of the inhabitants of the land becomes complete. Shechem's sin is identical to the past sins of the family of Canaan, seeing a person and committing a sexual offense (34:2).[28] Through Dinah, the "iniquity of the Amorite" becomes "complete" (*shalem*)[29] and the fourth generation can return to the land.

Now of course it is not really yet time for the land of Canaan to be conquered by the descendants of Abraham, any more than it was time for the conquest of the land when Abraham defeated the four kings. That is why both Abraham and Jacob make a purchase of the land as well. But, nevertheless, while the land of Canaan will not truly be conquered until the nation of Israel returns from Egypt, both Abraham and Jacob's sons prefigure that conquest in the book of Genesis. Each element of the national covenant is lived out in the lives of the patriarchs before it is fulfilled in the history of the nation.

The conquest of Shechem is alluded to by Jacob at the end of his life as he speaks of God's eventual return of the people to the land of their fathers (*veheshiv 'etkem 'el 'erets 'avotekem*; 48:21-22). The "you" (*'etkem*, plural) who will return is ambiguous; Jacob is speaking to Joseph, and so would seem to be referring to his sons, but it is the nation that will ultimately return to possess the land. But then Jacob's twelve sons are the nation. The living out of the covenant by Jacob's family bridges the experience of individual and nation.

Now, as on his journey home from Aram, Jacob seems able to look back and understand that his family has been participating in the fulfillment of the covenant all along. Granting to Joseph an extra portion (*shekem*) he reinterprets the manner in which Shechem was acquired by his family: "which I took from the hand of the Amorites with my sword and with my bow" (48:22).[30] Jacob now affirms the conquest of his sons which he had criticized earlier (34:30); indeed he now claims their conquest "by sword" (34:25-26) as his own. And he calls the people from whom the land was conquered "Amorites," as in the covenant between God and Abraham (15:16). Aware of the covenantal meaning of his family's past, Jacob portrays the future of his descendants as a continuation of a destiny already in progress. When God returns the nation from exile and they inherit the land of Canaan, they will be completing the process begun by Jacob's family when they returned from exile to the land of their forefathers.

The covenant that God made with Abraham, then, is the focal point for the story of how the patriarchal family becomes the nation of Israel. This covenant came as a response to Abraham's battle with the kings, at the moment that the patriarch had completed his own enactment of the future nation's destiny. The enigmatic story of the battle with the kings thus inaugurates the process of the history of the nation. I would like to suggest, in addition, that it culminates the process of the primeval history of the world.

Family and world

I have, throughout this study, focused on the narrative of the patriarchal family, chapters 12 through 50, almost to the exclusion of the first eleven chapters of the book of Genesis. I have done so in what I describe as a study of kinship in the book of Genesis because, even though there is conflict between brothers earlier in the book, it is only once there is a cultural heritage to be preserved that father-son conflict emerges and that the need for a particular kind of resolution, one that will allow for cultural continuity, becomes urgent. And the cultural heritage to be passed down from father to son is first introduced in chapter 12.

I have, however, noted in passing that certain elements of the patriarchal narratives play off patterns established in the primeval history. The most important pattern for this study, discussed briefly in Chapter Four, is the selection among brothers, the migration "eastward" (*qedma*) of the ones who are not chosen, and the parallel "generations" (*toledot*) of the unchosen and chosen brothers: the unchosen branching out immediately into nationhood but dropping out of significance in the narrative, the chosen begetting a single child who is able to continue the chosen line.

Banishment eastward begins early in the book of Genesis, with Adam and Eve and then with Cain, and so does the selection between brothers and the parallel genealogies, with Cain's family disappearing from the narrative and Adam's *toledot* ("generations") continuing through Seth and onward, after ten generations, to Noah. Seth, as we saw, is really a new beginning after Cain's family self-destructs, and Noah is a second new beginning as God destroys the rest of humankind.

After Noah there can be no more true new beginnings, because God has sworn never again to destroy the world. But people still sin, and evil still results in a process of selection. The difference is that now, instead of destruction and a new creation, the process of selection is enacted through a blessing and a curse.[31]

No sooner does God forswear universal destruction (9:8-17) than Ham, "the father of Canaan," sins (9:18-22). His sin, and his brothers' refusal to sin,[32] result in the first curse and blessing imposed by men, rather than by God, and the first time that a father gives a curse or blessing to his son. Noah establishes a hierarchy among his children: Canaan is cursed as a slave to his brothers, Shem is associated with blessing and with the name of God, Yapheth is associated with neither curse nor blessing; he is to be subordinate to Shem but master of Canaan.

What follow are two sets of *toledot* ("generations"), both of which include the genealogy of Shem (ch. 10; 11:10-26). But the two are of different types. The first is a branched genealogy, with a number of descendants listed in each generation, and with Shem's family included among his brothers' families. The second is a linear genealogy, with only one child listed in each generation, and with Shem's family alone included. What comes in between these two sets of *toledot*, what makes necessary a further focusing of the process of selection, is the story of the Tower of Babel (11:1-9).[33]

This episode takes place in the land of Shinar, in a location to be named Babel (11:2, 9). Both of these place names are associated in the preceding genealogy with Nimrod, a descendant of Ham (10:10).[34] And the plot begins as the people travel *miqedem* (11:2). In essence, all the peoples of the world, in this story, become assimilated to the brother who is rejected, Ham, and enact their exclusion by going to the land of banished brothers, *miqedem*.[35] So, while before this episode the narrative could still focus on all of Noah's descendants, now there is a need for further selection among the brothers and further selection among the descendants. The second set of *toledot* is the *toledot* of Shem alone, and only one child will be chosen in each generation.

The family of Eber, Shem's great-grandson, illustrates this process nicely. Eber has two sons, Peleg and Yoktan (10:25). Yoktan's many children are listed in the first genealogy, while about Peleg we are told here only that his name reflects the division of the earth which occurred in his day (10:25-29). Not until the second genealogy are we told of Peleg's son—that is, of the one grandson of Eber in whom the narrative retains interest (11:18). Yoktan is a member of the group of people whom the narrative, after Babel, will disregard. Like Ishmael and Esau (25:12-18 and ch. 36), Yoktan becomes a nation right away and, like them, he disappears from the narrative immediately thereafter. The last we hear of him is that his family dwells at the mountain of *Qedem* ("the east"; 10:30), the place of excluded brothers and the place of the final sin in which all of humanity participates, the Tower of Babel (11:2). As for Peleg, once humankind is divided at Babel, only he of all the sons of Noah and, indeed, of all the sons of Shem remains at the center of the narrative's concern.[36]

And so, while no longer can all of humanity be destroyed and begun anew from a single individual, the genealogy of Shem suggests that, in a way, humankind is now beginning anew from a single, blessed person. From this perspective, when the genealogy gives way again to narrative after ten generations, the narrative is of the world's new beginning. And the narrative to which the genealogy gives way is the history of Abraham and his family.[37]

Thus Abraham is both the beginning of the new family and nation and the culmination of the process of creation.[38] He is the repository of the blessing inherent in creation, and he will be the source of blessing to the rest of "the families of the earth" (12:3). But, while he is born in the tenth generation of the blessed line of Shem, it is only in the episode of the battle with the kings that Abraham actually comes into the blessing of Shem.

This episode has two parts, a long section before Abraham enters the action (14:1-12) and an equally long section with Abraham as a participant (14:13-24). While the whole chapter is puzzling in many ways, scholars have had an especially difficult time accounting for the first half, which seems in no way to be relevant to the Abraham narrative in which it is embedded.[39] But the two parts together constitute a working-out of the blessing and curse of Noah's sons, and, I believe, the two halves parallel the two visions of the relationship between Noah's descendants, one prior to Babel and one after it.

The relationship established by Noah defined Canaan specifically as a slave ('eved) to his brothers, and stated that Yapheth would "dwell in the tents of Shem" (9:25-27). This is precisely the situation at the beginning of chapter 14. The five kings of Canaanite cities (14:2; 10:19) are enslaved ('avdu) to Kedarlaomer, the king of Elam, the nation which bears the name of Shem's first son (14:1, 4; 10:22). Kedarlaomer's confederates include the king of Goyim and the king of Shinar, names associated with Yapheth and with Ham, respectively (14:1; 10:5, 10).[40] And, so, at the beginning of this story we find the protagonists of the primeval narrative exactly where we expect them. As in the genealogy of chapter 10, all of the sons of Noah are represented, and they assume the hierarchical relationship that Noah described in chapter 9. The first half of this story tells of the subjugation of Canaan to his brothers and of the successful battle of Shem, Yapheth, and Ham against their accursed kinsman.

When Abraham enters the story, the relationship shifts to that described in chapter 11. Abraham, the descendant of the chosen line of Shem, conquers the rest of the descendants of Noah. He asserts his ascendancy over Canaan, of course, by conquering their conquerors.[41] But he goes beyond that, subordinating all of Ham and all of Yapheth and all of the non-chosen descendants of Shem.[42]

At this moment, Abraham manifests his significance as the end-point of the genealogy of Shem in chapter 11. Abraham acts out the blessing of Shem. In him is focused the promise of creation, the promise which had to be narrowed from all of humankind to Seth, to Noah, to Shem, and finally to Shem's chosen descendants. And, at this moment, when Abraham demonstrates himself to be the possessor of Shem's blessing, Abraham in fact receives a blessing.[43] The blessing, transmitted by the mysterious Melchizedek, contains a single element, the linking of Abraham to the God of creation (14:19).[44] Noah had given a blessing to his son, Abraham ultimately receives that blessing, and, in the very next episode, Abraham will ask God to grant him a son who will inherit and pass on both God's special blessing to Abraham and the universal blessing inherent in creation.[45]

And so the story of Abraham's battle with the kings is crucially linked to the forging of God's covenant with Abraham immediately following.[46] We read the terms of the covenant and come to see that the future of Abraham's descendants will have the shape of Abraham's own past. And, looking back at the battle with the kings, we realize that, at the precise moment that Abraham had enacted the primeval blessing, he had enacted the destiny of the future nation of Israel—indeed, that the destiny of the patriarchal family and of the nation is a fulfillment of the promise of creation.[47] In the book of Genesis, national and world history, future and past are encapsulated in the patriarchs' quest for the blessing and for a way to pass on that blessing to their sons.

Conclusions

The typological view of the patriarchal narrative discussed in this chapter has a number of implications. I would like to mention three which I think are especially fruitful for an understanding of the book of Genesis and which bear directly on the present study: first, the connection between the family narrative and the history of the world and of the nation of Israel; second, the role of the person in shaping his experience and his future; and third, the significance of interpretation as an act of self-definition. I will discuss briefly how each emerges from this chapter and how each relates to the larger study.

In this chapter, I have suggested that the patriarchal narrative is intimately connected to the larger biblical narrative. First of all, it constitutes the narrative link between the primeval history and the history of the nation.[48] And the link is by no means a weak one. If the biblical narrative is seen as a book of "generations" (*toledot*), as a process of selection, a search for the way to realize the promise of creation, then the patriarchal narrative flows directly from the primeval history and into the history of the nation poised to enter the promised land.

In addition to this linear relationship, I have suggested a typological relationship in which, at certain crucial moments, the patriarchal narrative stands above itself, at once describing the experiences of individuals and transcending individual experience to talk of the distant future and the primeval past. At such moments the narrative is at once saga, history, and myth. The patriarchal narrative, then, is a meta-narrative; it goes beyond linking the narrative of the past to the narrative of the future— rather, it *is* a narrative of the past and of the future. The quest of the individual, in this narrative, is the quest of the nation and of all humanity for redemption, for the fulfillment of the promise of creation.[49]

This typological reading supports and enhances the symbolic understanding of kinship which underlies this study. I proposed in Chapter One that the family narrative constitutes a search for a stable foundation for the future nation and, further, that the family narrative, in a broad sense, represents the self-perception of an emerging culture. Kinship, I suggested, is a symbolic structure which represents the ability of the society to survive and to continue to transmit its cultural heritage. As a reflection of the society's self-perception, the family narrative also can be seen as a reflection of the society's world-view. This is true of many early narratives, but it is especially true of the family narrative in Genesis, sandwiched as it is between the history of the world and the story of the emerging nation. Whether a particular family narrative ultimately resolves the conflict which threatens the family and, if it does, whether the particular kind of resolution is one that allows for cultural continuity tells much about the society's vision of its own future and of the future of humanity. Is it a vision which culminates in destruction and decay, or which moves toward perfection? The family narrative in Genesis ends with a cautious, muted, yet unambiguous affirmation of promise, promise for the family, the nation, and the world.

Further, I have noted in this chapter that the typological relationship between the family narrative and the national history suggests that the individual actually shapes the destiny of future generations.[50] This is not a necessary corollary of the typological relationship, for such a relationship can be interpreted in many ways. And I am not suggesting that this is a simple cause-and-effect relationship. I am suggesting, though, that the typologies in Genesis imply that history is shaped primarily by human actors.

Such a view, I think, is one implication of the multivalence of the covenant between the pieces. The covenant refers to Abraham's past as well as to the future of the family and of the nation. God's prescription for the future, then, is not a destiny simply chosen and imposed by the divine will; it is a destiny which takes its shape from Abraham's own experiences. Through God's covenant, these experiences become resignified as destiny, a point to which I will return momentarily, but the course of that destiny is shaped by human participants.

The idea that the individuals in Genesis choose their own destiny is one which I have stressed throughout this study. Whether these individuals receive the blessing or find themselves in exile, apart from the patriarchal heritage, depends finally on their own choices. The destiny of the individual is not shaped ultimately by the acts of others, or by nationality, or by lineage, or by divine choice.

Thus, for example, Lot is excluded from Abraham's destiny not simply because Abraham fails to include him but because Lot consistently makes the wrong choices when given an opportunity to choose. Hagar is not excluded simply because she is an Egyptian; rather, her behavior confirms her Egyptian nature and shows her to be unsuited to participate in the covenant. Ishmael is not banished simply because he is Hagar's son; he is sent away from Abraham's home only when he acts in a way that shows him to be the same as Hagar. And Esau does not lose the blessing because of an arbitrary choice by God or because of his father's blindness or his mother's and brother's wiliness; he loses it because he is incapable of understanding a life of destiny.

The same, of course, can be said for those who receive the blessing. God's blessing is earned, not granted; though it may be promised, early on, to an individual who seems hardly to deserve it, the blessing is truly realized only when that person has earned it. This, I have suggested, is an important function of the narrative doubling: the doubling allows us to measure a character's growth or degeneration, and it gives the narrative the shape of a quest.

Thus the Abraham whose blessing is confirmed in chapter 22 as he finds the land and finds his son is not the same Abraham who was promised the blessing in chapter 12, as he set out on his quest. And the Jacob whose blessing is confirmed at Yabok and Beth El as he returns with his family to the land of his fathers is not the same Jacob who tricked his father and stole his brother's blessing. Yet Abram and Jacob were able to transform themselves into Abraham and Israel. The narrative doubling allows us to follow that transformation; it allows the characters to embark on their quest and to return. And it makes it clear that it is the characters themselves who bear responsibility for their fates.

Finally, I have suggested that the typology, and especially the specific ways in which it is expressed in this narrative, emphasizes the importance of interpretation. Not only is there a narrative modeling of events on one another, which by itself would leave it up to the reader alone to undertake the act of typological interpretation. There are also moments within the narrative when individuals come to understand and describe their own experiences in terms of God's covenant with the nation. And those moments transform the nature of the experience; through the act of interpretation, these individuals redefine their experiences and themselves.

Jacob in particular—the patriarch who is both individual and nation—is capable of this transformation-through-interpretation. He redefines as covenantal his experiences in the house of Laban, experiences which were nearly destructive of self and of national destiny. He redefines his loss of Rachel and his near loss of Joseph and of Joseph's sons. And he redefines his sons' dubious massacre and conquest of Shechem.

In the book of Genesis, individuals must understand the significance of their experiences if they are to be participants in the covenant. Indeed, experiences become significant only through this understanding, through the interpretation that the individual ultimately offers.

The notion that individuals interpret experience and thus define themselves in relation to the covenantal destiny of family and nation is closely connected to the idea of vision, which I have suggested is crucial to the patriarchal narrative. Participants in the covenant, I have emphasized, must have a vision for the future. If they are embedded in the present, they will not have the capacity to endure the suffering which accompanies the delay in covenantal fulfillment. Hagar and Esau, concerned only with the present moment, relinquish their opportunities to share in the patriarchal destiny. Lack of vision for the future makes present suffering unbearable, and thus rejection of that suffering is tantamount to, and indeed accompanies, rejection of the promise for the future. But the notion of interpretation of experience carries this one step further. The individual with vision tolerates present suffering and delay in anticipation of covenantal fulfillment in the future; the individual who is an interpreter of experience understands present suffering as a part of the fulfillment of the covenant.

It is especially significant, then, that the book of Genesis ends with the family in exile. The book ends with the promise not yet fulfilled, at the beginning of a long period of suffering, and this lack of resolution demands a response. The book's ending, rather than achieving closure, remains open to interpretation.

Indeed, it incorporates its own interpretation, in the words of Joseph. Joseph's vision of the future as well as his understanding of the present transforms the meaning of the narrative's conclusion and, I think, offers a model for the ongoing interpretation of experience. "And Joseph died . . . and they embalmed him, and he was put in a coffin in Egypt" (50:26).

The brothers' protector, the father's favorite, dies in Egypt; the entire family is in exile. For the first time in Genesis return to the land is impossible; for the first time no member of the patriarchal family remains in the land. Yet Joseph, the master interpreter, has already offered an interpretation of these events. Recalling God's covenant with the patriarchs, Joseph understands that his family is beginning a long exile, and knows too that God will eventually redeem them from this exile and bring them to the promised land (50:24).

Joseph understands also, as Jacob has taught him, that he must be reunited with his family, and that the family ultimately will become a unified nation when they return to the land of their fathers (50:25). Joseph recalls God's oath to redeem his brothers and bring them up into the land, and he asks his brothers to take an oath to bring his bones up into the land (50:24-25). Joseph's vision for the future is interwoven with his understanding of the present. He alone recognizes the significance of the exile and he alone speaks of the redemption and future birth of the nation. His death in Egypt, then, does not end the book on a note of despair, but on a note of promise. Joseph's bones lying in a coffin in Egypt are a symbol of temporary exile and a guarantee of future redemption. And both the exile and the redemption are parts of the covenant between God and his people.

The book of Genesis ends in exile rather than in the land, with promise rather that with fulfillment, and its ending is interpreted within the narrative itself by a member of the family-becoming-nation. As such, the book speaks powerfully to all who would be interpreters of their own experience, to all who choose to recognize that exile and suffering do not signify the rupture of the covenant but instead attest to the endurance of the covenant. Events alone do not speak; they are interpreted, and through the act of interpretation the interpreters define themselves.

The exile with which the book ends holds forth the promise of future return, but also demands a reevaluation of the meanings of exile and the land. For it is in exile that the family, for the first and only time in this book, is reunited without conflict; never in Genesis are brothers able to live together in the land. The land, as we have seen, is never large enough to be shared among brothers; neither Lot and Abraham nor Esau and Jacob find the land capable of sustaining both brothers. As a physical reality, the land cannot be shared; any sharing diminishes one's own inheritance.

But the land has another meaning in this book. It is the spiritual heritage of the patriarchal family, the embodiment of the blessing of Abraham. And this spiritual heritage, by the end of the patriarchal narrative, can be shared. Only in exile can Jacob bless his twelve sons, only in exile can the nation emerge, because only in exile can there be no confusion between the material inheritance, which engenders conflict, and the spiritual inheritance, which can, finally, be shared. Exile, then, is a formative experience for the family, as it was for the individual patriarchs in Genesis, as it will be for the children of Israel in the rest of the Pentateuch, and as it can be for the future nation when it once more finds itself outside of the promised land.[51]

And so, while Genesis ends with a promise of redemption and reunification, it stops short of portraying the reality of brothers living together in the land. So, too, does the Pentateuch as a whole, ending as it does with a glimpse of the promised land, but not with the reality of nationhood in the land. Brothers dwelling together in the land—or nation living as one in the land—is not an impossibility, but neither is it a reality. Both Genesis and Deuteronomy end one step before that; family and nationhood at last are achieved, but the sharing of the patriarchal heritage in its fullness has yet to realized. The promise of brothers living together in the land remains always a promise.

NOTES

BIBLIOGRAPHY

INDEXES

NOTES

NOTES TO CHAPTER 1
CONFLICT AND CONTINUITY

1. Freud (1923:21-22).
2. Freud (1921:37).
3. René Girard (1979:169-192) acutely discusses these two versions of the Oedipus complex but over-emphasizes the difference between them. He concludes that, by the time he wrote *The Ego and the Id*, Freud had all but abandoned the concept of identification with the father, even though Freud explicitly declares the anteriority of this identification in his 1923 monograph. It is true, of course, that the familiar formulation of the Oedipus complex virtually ignores the issue of identification in favor of the child's mother-cathexis, but Girard seems to be at pains to show that Freud actually rejected his earlier formulation in order to stress the difference between Girard's own theory of mimetic desire and Freud's theory.
4. Freud (1923:24).
5. Freud (1923:22).
6. Malinowski (1929:3-7).
7. Malinowski (1929:179-186).
8. Malinowski (1929:204-208).
9. Malinowski (1929:20-21; 194-195; 200-202). Note also the traditional view of the causal relationship between the roles of mother's husband and of nurturer, discussed below.
10. Malinowski (1929:201-202; 209-210).
11. Malinowski (1927:2-5).
12. Malinowski (1927:28-31; 44-47).
13. Malinowski (1927:77-79).
14. Malinowski (1927:80-81).
15. Malinowski (1953:79).
16. It is interesting to note, however, that in certain parts of the Trobriands conception is said to occur while the woman bathes, and the spirit-child enters through the vagina. When a woman is not able to conceive, a barrel of water is left in her hut overnight in the hope that a spirit-child may enter the woman's abdomen. This barrel of water must always be brought by either the woman's brother or her maternal uncle, the two men who, together with the woman, form Malinowski's complex.
17. Jones (1925:109-130).

18. Jones (1925:120).

19. Jones (1925:122). Jones seems to disregard Malinowski's observation that the *baloma* which impregnates the mother is usually the spirit of a maternal kinsman, while the spirit-child itself is always from the mother's clan (Malinowski 1929:171-174). This is not, then, a clear example of the "grandfather complex" which Jones develops elsewhere and appears to suggest here.

20. Jones (1925:123) uses the term "decomposition" to describe the process through which elements of the father-relationship are displaced toward a person other than the father.

21. Jones (1925:123-128).

22. Malinowski (1927:136-143).

23. Compare Freud's description of the primal horde whose violent deed of patricide leads to incest taboos and the formation of society. See Freud (1918:183-189).

24. Malinowski (1927:258-262).

25. Spiro (1968:242).

26. Leach (1969:85-112). See Spiro (1968:242). Leach's analysis of the conception beliefs of the Trobrianders and others resembles Claude Lévi-Strauss' structural analysis of myth. Like Lévi-Strauss, Leach is interested in the elements common to all these myths, including the virgin birth of Christ; his denial of the natives' ignorance of physiological paternity is partly an attempt to put the beliefs studied by anthropologists in the same category as Christian and Jewish beliefs, and to allow the student of myth to subject all of these to the same kind of structural analysis (Leach 1969:95-110). Lévi-Strauss (1965:81-106) had denied even more vehemently the significance of the differences between versions of a single myth and consequently ignored certain important features of the myths which he studied. In his analysis of the Oedipus myth, for example, he disregards the narrative interplay of the elements of the story, which implies such themes as the conflict between father and son, in his attempt to rearrange the details into a configuration which mediates between autochthony and generation from a mother and a father (89-92). Leach, though not quite as extreme as Lévi-Strauss in his insistence that all variants of a myth be studied as a single structure, was nevertheless denying the uniqueness of the conception beliefs of natives such as the Trobrianders.

27. The debate between Leach and Spiro had begun in the early 1960s, but Leach's address became an invitation for all interested scholars to respond. See especially Spiro (1968) and Kaberry et al. (1968).

28. Powell and Dixon in Kaberry et al. (1968:651, 653).

29. Kaberry (1968:311-313).

30. Spiro (1982:67). Spiro had already suggested this as one of two possible explanations in his 1968 article (256-258).

31. Spiro (1982:70 n. 11).

32. Spiro (1982:5-6; 71-73; 107-109; 167-170).
33. Spiro (1982:144-146; 163-164).
34. Spiro (1982:172-173).
35. Paul (1980:287-288).
36. While Paul feels that a fourth figure is necessary to make the myth symmetrical and sees the predicted figure of Pilate as a corroboration of his theory, this elaboration of the symbolism really seems unnecessary according to Paul's analysis. Decomposition and enactment of both impulses are alternative resolutions and, if both appear in a single myth, they would require only three figures. There is no reason for the father who both kills and preserves to be decomposed, because decomposition only serves to allow two different people to perform contradictory acts; if a single person can perform both, no antithetical double is required. In fact, Paul's analysis of the Isaac story does postulate a double for Abraham, God, but this doubling is not a decomposition as in the Oedipus story because God, just like Abraham, both kills and preserves. There is no reason, then, for God, in the crucifixion, to have a double. But if, for the sake of symmetry, he must be doubled, then that fourth figure should, like God, both kill and preserve.
37. Paul (1980:292).
38. Girard (1979:57-59).
39. Incest, for Freud (1918:183-189), not only would lead to conflict with the father, but threatened to engender violence between the brothers in the primal horde, necessitating the institution of incest taboos and exogamy. Conflict with the father gives way to fraternal conflict for Freud; for Girard (1979:74), patricide "represents . . . the reduction of the paternal relationship to 'fraternal' revenge."
40. Girard (1979:74-75).
41. Girard (1979:143-145).
42. Girard (1979:63).
43. Girard (1979:181).
44. Girard (1979:169-175).
45. Girard (1979:74-75; 143-144).
46. Malinowski (1927:260-261).
47. Girard (1979:186-189).
48. Girard (1979:59-61).
49. Jones (1925:120-123) and Spiro (1968:257; 1982:164) consider physiological paternity crucial to the Oedipus complex, but only as it implies a sexual relationship between the child's mother and the child's rival, his father. The desire to beget oneself is nothing more than the desire to replace the father in relation to the mother. Physiological paternity as indicative of a biological link between father and son is irrelevant to Jones and Spiro.
50. Paul (1980:288-289); Spiro (1982:5-6). For an elaborate psychoanalytic study of the complementary Oedipus complex, see

Devereux (1953). Girard (1974:146-147; 174-175), while focusing on the son's, or disciple's, "double bind," sees this as originating with the father's, or model's, contradictory messages. Freud (1962:24) had also discussed the double message which the child receives from his father and ultimately from his superego.

51. Otto Rank (1964b:78) goes even further, seeing the mythical hostility of the father as projection: "The projection mechanism . . . necessitates the uniform characterization of the myth as a *paranoid* structure, in view of its resemblance to peculiar processes in the mechanism of certain psychic disturbances."

52. Craig (1979:94-96).

53. Craig (1979:95).

54. Rank (1964a:296-315).

55. Rank (1964a:299-301).

56. Rank (1964a:304).

57. Rank (1964a:306).

58. Rank (1964a:309-313). Rank sees Oedipus' incest with his mother as an attempt to resolve the contradictory "wish to have no children at all (Laius) and . . . necessity to renounce one's own immortality in favor of children" by "beget[ting] oneself as the mother's son" (306). Compare this with the Freudian interpretation by Jones and Spiro of the desire to beget oneself as the desire to replace the father as the mother's sexual partner. Jones and Spiro see father-son conflict as rivalry for the sexual object; Rank sees incest with the mother in terms of the son's potential conflict with his own son. The difference between the two formulations lies in Jones' and Spiro's emphasis on the sexual relationship and on the son, as opposed to Rank's focus on the problem of immortality and on the father.

59. Rank (1964a:309). Note that Rank, like Freud, implies that fraternal conflict results from father-son conflict.

Rank is not alone in emphasizing that the different versions of the Oedipus myth reflect different historical periods. Vladimir Propp (1983:76-121), accepting, like Rank, a universal evolution from matriarchal to patriarchal society, suggests that the Oedipus story reflects the transition from matriarchal succession, in which the son-in-law kills the king and takes his place, to patriarchal succession, in which the son, in accord with his father's wishes, takes over the king's throne. Patricide is a crime only in the patriarchal stage, according to Propp, when the king, secure in his new patriarchal authority, need no longer fear being killed by his successor; the warning oracle substitutes in the later narrative for the king's original fear, and the son's marriage to his father's wife is merely a narrative relic of the regicidal successor who marries the king's daughter (87-88, 112).

Erich Fromm (1957:204-205), too, sees the Oedipus story as emerging from "the ancient fight between the patriarchal and matriarchal systems of society." His interpretation is closer to Rank's than to Propp's, although he focuses on the son's rebellion against patriarchal authority rather than on the father's rebellion against patriarchal ideology (202). Both Propp and Fromm find that variants of the Oedipus story grow out of different stages of society. Propp (1983:86-88), for example, discusses a Zulu tale in which the son is feared by the father whom he will deliberately kill, a story which, for Propp, represents an early patriarchal stage, when the son has just recently taken the place of the son-in-law and, unlike Oedipus, is consciously feared and consciously commits patricide. And Fromm (1957:210-211) discusses earlier versions of the Oedipus myth which explicitly link Oedipus to goddesses of a matriarchal religion and which, Fromm suggests, reflect a period before the era of conflict between the patriarchal and matriarchal systems.

60. Rank (1964a:309).

61. Rank (1964a:313).

62. Girard (1979:1-4).

63. Rosenberg (1986:91) notes that the Genesis narrative is "firmly grounded in an awareness of human mortality, and sees in generational continuity alone a kind of qualified immortality."

64. Meir Weiss discusses this kind of "test" of an interpretation and quotes I. A. Richards: "When an interpretation hangs together . . . we call it correct . . ." (1984:21).

NOTES TO CHAPTER 2
THE GENESIS OF THE FAMILY

1. Westermann distinguishes between different types of promises in the patriarchal stories and discusses the different strata of composition to which each belongs. Specifically, he distinguishes between the "promise of a son" and the "promise of increase" and separates the "promise of land" from the "promise of descendants" (1980:11). But, while these may have originated as separate promises, it seems clear, by the end of the Abraham stories, that the different elements combine to form a single complex, a blessing which must be handed down as a unit.

2. Speiser (1982:85-86) rejects the Masoretic pointing which would translate "and you shall be a blessing" (12:2) as "syntactically unacceptable" and prefers the third person "that it may be a blessing." I read the Masoretic pointing as yielding an imperative; see Cassuto (1964:313-314). The imperative, perhaps, emphasizes the relationship between the command and the promise, since both can be read as commands. Abraham must seek both, he must define them for himself and respond to them. For a further discussion of the relationship between the command and promise within the blessing of Abraham, see the analysis of Isaac's second blessing of Jacob, in Chapter Four. Verse 3 suggests that Abraham will actually *become* a source of

blessing for others (Cassuto 1964:315); both Isaac and Jacob use Abraham's name to invoke a blessing for their descendants (28:4 and 48:16). For a discussion of Abraham as bringing blessing to the world, see Chapter Five.

3. See Helyer's discussion of the crisis precipitated by Lot's departure (1983:77-88).

4. Leibovitz (1954:100-101) discusses the various ways in which Ishmael is described in this episode as reflecting the viewpoints of each of the characters. See also Bar-Efrat (1989:43).

5. Bereshit Rabbah 39:9 dramatizes the moment of recognition through an elaboration of God's command to sacrifice Isaac which accounts for the progressively specific identification of the one who is to be sacrificed. God tells Abraham to sacrifice his "son," and Abraham replies that he has two sons. "Your only son." "Each is an only son to his mother." "Whom you love." "I love both." God finally spells it out—"Isaac." Abraham has shown concern for his son Ishmael whenever it has been suggested that Isaac would succeed him (17:18; 21:11). The choice now of Isaac as a sacrifice means that Isaac, not Ishmael, will be Abraham's heir.

6. Commentary on Genesis 22:12.

7. See the discussion of Abraham's circumcision and Jacob's thigh-wound at the end of Chapter Four. Both accompany a change in name that signals the wounded person's transformation into a patriarch; both symbolize a limitation of the individual in favor of immortality through his descendants. Note that God's command to Abraham to circumcise himself and his son comes at a point in the narrative parallel to the occurrence of God's command to Abraham to sacrifice Isaac (chs. 17 and 22). Preceding each command is the story of Hagar's departure from Abraham's house and the ruling out of Ishmael as Abraham's successor (chs. 16 and 21). Thus, each time that Abraham faces the designation of his true successor, the realization is coupled with a moment of danger, either real (ch. 22) or symbolic (ch. 17).

8. See, for example, Nachmanides' commentary on Leviticus 1:9 and Girard's discussion in the first chapter of *Violence and the Sacred* (1979). Girard sees sacrifice as a preventive measure, often taken by a community before its collective violence finds a victim; sacrificial substitutes are chosen from a class both similar to and distinct from the members of the sacrificing community. The similarity allows the victim to act as a surrogate, while the distinction insures that the violence enacted against the surrogate victim will not spread to members of the community.

The mechanism of sacrifice requires that the victim be both self and other; the son, I am suggesting, is both self and other to the father, hence the most appropriate sacrificial substitute for the father. This is not Girard's interpretation of the binding of Isaac. Girard does not see Isaac as a sacrificial victim at all; he discusses only the ram as the surrogate for the real victim, Isaac (1979:2-4).

9. ". . . only he who draws the knife gets Isaac" (Kierkegaard 1974:38). Kierkegaard sees the contradiction inherent in this episode as the tension between the ethical and religious demands: "The ethical expression for what Abraham did is, that he would murder Isaac; the religious expression is, that he would sacrifice Isaac; but precisely in this contradiction consists the dread which can well make a man sleepless, and yet Abraham is not what he is without this dread" (41).

10. David Silber first called to my attention that Abraham's sacrifice of the ram constitutes the father's reclamation of his son.

11. Bakan (1979:14-15) discusses "biological immortality" through children and notes that a "large part of the Bible's moral burden is to prevent infanticide from actually taking place." Bakan connects "the shift to animal sacrifice" to "the establishment of patriarchy," but does not note the relationship between the idea of sacrifice and fatherhood. For Bakan, human sacrifice originally was possible because of the belief in divine impregnation. With the acceptance of biological paternity, the father wanted to protect his child, and animal sacrifice allowed him to do that. "It allowed the maintenance of the institution of sacrifice, but without the killing of offspring" (148-9). Sacrifice itself, then, has nothing to do with paternity, according to Bakan. Furthermore, Bakan sees the father as simply trying to protect his son.

12. Fokkelman (1975:89) notes that, when Rebecca seeks the oracle because she feels the children struggling inside her, she is told that her twins will be competitors.

13. If we picture Jacob dressed up in the skins of the slaughtered animals and carrying their flesh, the correspondence between chapters 27 and 22 becomes even more striking. In chapter 22, Isaac presumably is to be the sacrificial victim to be brought by his father (22:7-8). Ultimately, what "God provides" is a surrogate victim, the ram which Abraham sees and sacrifices (22:13-14). In chapter 27, the surrogate victim is prepared in advance; nevertheless, when Jacob appears to take his father's blessing, he appears dressed as the sacrificial victim. Seen in this way, the danger of the moment of transfer emerges as shockingly real, as does the identity between the son, the true object of the violence, and the surrogate victim.

14. Girard (1979:4-5) notes the sacrificial nature of Jacob dressing in his brother's garments and so "slipping into" his role.

15. Even Joseph's dreams of power have nothing to do with succession. Jacob understands that Joseph dreams of his entire family bowing to him, including his father and mother; this is a dream of power within the family, which of course comes true, but not of replacing the father, which Joseph never does.

16. See Chapter Four and notes to Chapter Five for a discussion of the children as participants in the competition between their

mothers. 37:2 implies a schism within the family, based on the relationship between Jacob's wives.

17. When Reuven, the eldest son, sleeps with his father's concubine, Jacob does not react. The passive "and Israel heard" (35:22) is typical of Jacob's response to problems within his family—to Rachel's childlessness, to the rape of Dinah and, to a lesser extent, to the ambitions of Joseph. Jacob stands back and lets his wives and sons work out their conflicts.

18. Joseph's wife is not explicitly connected to Rachel, although there may be a link between them. David Silber has suggested that 'on (41:45) is connected to Ben 'Oni (35:18) and that both evoke idolatry in addition to the commonly accepted meaning of "virility." Rachel has an affinity for idolatry, as evidenced by her theft of the teraphim, and Joseph marries the daughter of an idolatrous priest. Compare also the divination that characterizes Rachel's father (30:27) and in which Joseph claims to engage (44:5,15). Both the word 'on and the divination, as well as the theft of an object used for such practices, are linked to Benjamin, Silber points out, in Rachel's naming of her son (whose birth she may link to the teraphim; see 31:35) and in Joseph's accusation that Benjamin has stolen the divining cup. These connections are crucial to an understanding of the dynamic of the reclamation of Rachel and Joseph through Benjamin, discussed below. The significance of the name of Tamar's second husband, Onan, needs to be investigated further in this context.

19. Judah's refusal to allow Shelah to enter into levirate marriage with Tamar is thematically connected to the brothers' abdication of fraternal responsibility for Joseph in the previous episode. This theme seems to be reflected in an early tradition that the brothers bought shoes with the money acquired through the sale of Joseph. The tradition apparently is alluding to the practice of halitsa, the removal of the shoe of a man who refuses to redeem his dead brother through levirate marriage. The Testament of Zebulun, in fact, explicitly links this tradition with halitsa, though the interpretation offered there for the symbolism of the shoe is hardly convincing; see Carmichael (1977:322 n. 2). It is the burden of the Tamar episode to reverse the disregard for a brother's life that the selling of Joseph represents.

20. Speiser (1982:298) discusses the significance of these objects, especially the signet. The "seal . . . served as the religious and legal surrogate for the person who wore it, and its impression on a document signalized the wearer's readiness to accept all consequences in the case of non-compliance . . . . The possessor of such a seal was thereby marked as a responsible person." See also Jacob (1974:259).

21. Alter (1981:10-11) connects this kid with the goat in the previous chapter, noting that the kid is used to trick Judah, and the goat to deceive Jacob. See Cassuto (1929:30-31) for this and other

connections between the two stories and for some references to these connections in rabbinic midrashim.

22. The very act of sending implies distancing, as we shall see in Chapter Three.

23. Andriolo (1973:1661-2) notes the similarity between the two sets of twins. Significantly, while Jacob is born trying to hold Esau back, Perez is born first by managing to break forward. Thus, the very manner of their birth suggests that Jacob and Esau are in conflict and Perez and Zerah are not. Here, furthermore, the one that will ultimately be the leader is actually the elder, while Jacob, as the younger, must engage in conflict in order to become ascendant over his brother. Note that Tamar's two sons serve as replacements for both dead husbands. See Cassuto (1929:36). This strengthens the parallel between Judah's and Jacob's quandaries, discussed below, because Judah can redeem two sons through offering Shelah, while Jacob must redeem both Simeon and Joseph through sending Benjamin to Egypt.

24. Ackerman (1982:104-105) notes the parallel between Judah's dilemma with respect to Shelah and Jacob's with respect to Benjamin.

25. David Silber has pointed out that Tamar's name can be seen as a play on the word meaning "to substitute." The noun *temura*, "substitution," is used in the book of Ruth (4:7), which is related to the story of Judah and Tamar. The story of Judah and Tamar, in fact, involves a series of substitutions and reverse-substitutions, as noted above. Tamar reverses now-obsolete sacrificial substitution by holding on to the symbols of Judah's identity, which Judah initially offered as substitutes for the animal which is a substitute for himself. Thus, of course, Tamar gets Judah, rather than any substitute. In the same process, Tamar reverses the tendency for fraternal responsibility to substitute for paternal responsibility by claiming Judah as a substitute for the son through whom Judah was expected to discharge his responsibility. Both the progressive distancing through sacrificial substitution and the progressive relinquishing of paternal responsibility are reversed in this chapter through the actions of Tamar.

NOTES TO CHAPTER 3
THE QUEST FOR A SUCCESSOR

1. Ultimately, it is Judah who is singled out for leadership of the family and, in retrospect, his ascension to leadership begins in chapter 37. Both Reuven and Judah attempt to modify their brothers' plot to kill Joseph, but Reuven's plan is eventually discarded in favor of Judah's. Reuven, in fact, does not try to lead his brothers; his plan is simply to save Joseph behind their backs and, finally, he fails. Judah, in contrast, attempts to lead his brothers, and he succeeds in influencing them to spare Joseph's life. Note, too, that Judah combines a pragmatic appeal to profit with an ethical appeal to brotherhood; Reuven

offers only a dubious distinction between active and passive murder. Much the same pattern occurs later, when Reuven and Judah each tries to convince Jacob to send Benjamin to Egypt. See Goldin (1977: 40-43) and Ackerman (1982:101-102). Thus, the story of the selling of Joseph signals the emergence of Judah as leader of the family. Note that the next episode concerns Judah, suggesting that he will now be the focus of the patriarchal narrative.

2. Fokkelman (1987:49-50) notes the "triple distribution of narrative data" in this episode. He divides the story into the same three segments that I have outlined, subdividing each into speech (verses 1-2, 7-8, 11-12) and action (verses 3-6, 9-10, 13).

3. Fokkelman (1975:106-7) points out that the narrative always uses *qatan* and *gadol*, "small" and "big," to describe Jacob and Esau, never *tsa'ir* and *bekor*, "younger" and "firstborn." Only the boys themselves use the word *bekor*.

4. Jacob, of course, does not object on moral grounds; he objects because he is afraid that the plan won't work and that, in approaching his father, he will be harmed. See Bar-Efrat (1989:73-74).

5. In fact, Jacob claims to have said *hineni* in response to a divine call much earlier, before he leaves Laban's house (31:11). For a discussion of some of the ironic elements of Jacob's purported dream in Padan Aram, see the notes to Chapter Five. Jacob seems to know all the right words, but he has not yet come fully to understand his mission.

6. Leibovitz (1954:96) notes that the response *hineni* is common to this story and the binding of Isaac.

7. Speiser (1982: 288-90) translates "look" and adds the following note: "Heb. *halo'* 'is it not?' which is merely another way of saying *hinne* 'here, behold.' " Note that Speiser defines *halo'* with its equivalent, *hine*, precisely the word which we would expect to find here.

8. David Silber has pointed out the theme of missed opportunity throughout this narrative, suggesting that the brothers' move from Shechem represents their movement away from the possibility of reconciliation—Shechem is where the brothers had asserted the fraternal bond in avenging Dinah. See the discussion of Shechem and its connection to the stories of Dinah and Joseph in the notes to Chapter Five.

9. There is a series of puns on the words *shlh*, "to send," and *shlk*, "to throw." Jacob tells Joseph that he will send him on a mission, *ve'eshlahaka*, and he does so, *vayishlahenu* (37:13-14). The brothers plot to kill Joseph and throw him into the pit, *venashlikehu* (37:20), planning to explain to their father that a wild beast killed him. Reuven warns the brothers against murder, using the idiomatic "do not send a hand upon him," *tishlehu vo*, and suggests instead that they simply throw Joseph into the pit, *hashliku* (37:22). Ultimately, not knowing what happened to Joseph, the brothers send his bloodied

cloak to their father after all, *vayeshalehu* (37:32), reinforcing the idea discussed in Chapter Two that, in terms of the family, Joseph has indeed been killed.

The word *lishloah*, "to send," is one step further in the progression of verbs: *laqahat/laleket* (go/take), *lehavi'/lavo'* (come/bring), *lehagish/lageshet* (approach/ present). The brothers send the cloak to their father before they dare to come to him. Similarly, Jacob had sent the gift of animals to Esau before meeting him, and the brothers will send a message to Joseph, after Jacob's death, before they plead their cause in person. Judah, too, offers to send a lamb as payment to Tamar, but Tamar refuses, forcing Judah to give her his signet and staff.

Lishloah, however, is one step too far. Something is sent when the sender is too fearful, or simply too distant, to bring the object himself. That is why, of all the verbs mentioned, *lishloah* is the only one that is not part of a pair; there is no coming near that accompanies the bringing. Because there is no coming near, because sending, as opposed to bringing, is a way of remaining distant, it is a wholly inadequate means of reconciliation.

10. The "take" (*qah*) has always been what allowed the person to approach while protecting him. Here, it seems, the mechanism still functions. The brothers must come to Joseph with their father and, it turns out, after their father's death, when Jacob can no longer mediate between the brothers and Joseph, the brothers are afraid that Joseph will harm them. Invoking what they claim was their father's command, they approach Joseph on their own with a fearful "here we are" (*hinenu*; 50:18). Compare the brothers' expectation of fraternal conflict after the death of the father with Esau's plan to kill his brother when Isaac will die; see the discussion below.

11. Jacob's hesitation on his way to Joseph becomes more poignant in this context. God reassures him, telling him not to be afraid to "go down" to Egypt, promising to "go down" with him, and informing him that Joseph will close his eyes on his deathbed. While Jacob had anticipated a reunion with his son in death, God tells him that he will be reunited with Joseph in life.

Ackerman (1982:107) notes the comparison between Sheol and Egypt; Ackerman (1982:92) and Sternberg (1985:299) note that Jacob anticipated going down to Sheol as a mourner should Benjamin die (42:38), reinforcing the parallel between Joseph and Benjamin, and doubling the power of the reversal when Jacob goes down to Egypt to meet Joseph.

12. For discussions of the doubling in the Joseph story see Ackerman (1982:85-113) and Sternberg (1985:294-308).

13. Abraham is mentioned before chapter 12 and he engages in important affairs after chapter 22, but the cycle which stretches from chapter 12 to chapter 22 is clearly the main part of the Abraham

narrative. The two outermost episodes represent the first and last times that God speaks to Abraham; these speech acts define the limits of Abraham's mission. The other passages in which Abraham appears serve as bridges between the Abraham narrative and the genealogy of Shem, on the one side, and the Isaac narrative, on the other. Gros Louis notes that the mention of Nahor's family, at the end of chapter 11 and at the end of chapter 22, serves as a frame for the Abraham narrative (1982c:76). Chapters 12 and 22 are marked by the phrase for "go," *lek leka*, which appears in both but nowhere else. For this and other parallels between chapters 12 and 22, and for the symmetry of the entire Abraham cycle, see Cassuto (1964:296 ff.), Sarna (1970: 160-161), Jacob (1974:143), Buber (1982:41), Fox (1983:83), Rendsburg (1986:28 ff.), Rosenberg (1986:73 ff.), and Bar-Efrat (1989:212-213, 217). I am suggesting that the symmetry is more than just a structural phenomenon, that it conveys narrative meaning.

14. Speiser (1982:27) notes that a change of name marks a turning point in the person's life.

15. Speiser explains the verb *tshq* very differently and maintains that the meaning changes in different contexts, the occurrences simply constituting "wordplay" on Isaac's name (1982:125, 155). I am suggesting that all occurrences of a word must be taken into account when analyzing the connotations of the word in any given context.

16. See Speiser (1982:150-2) for an example of this kind of explanation.

17. See Bakan (1979:68) and Sarna (1970:102-3) for a discussion of Hurrian marriage. Speiser (1982:91-94) analyzes the wife-sister motif and concludes that Abraham's, and later Isaac's, claim raised the patriarch's status in the eyes of his foreign hosts, while the endogamous marriage was "an implicit guarantee of the purity of the wife's descendants."

The claim that Sarah is Abraham's sister may be reflected in another passage which lends the relationship additional significance. The verse which describes their marriage states: "And Abram and Nahor took wives for themselves; the name of Abram's wife was Sarai, and the name of Nahor's wife was Yiska, the daughter of Haran, the father of Milka and Yiska" (11:29). Two verses later, we read: "And Terah took Abram, his son, and Lot, his son's son, and Sarai, his daughter-in-law, the wife of Abram, his son . . ." (11:31). Haran apparently had three children: Lot, Milka, and Yiska. After his death (11:28), one brother married his daughter Milka, and the other married a woman named Sarai. Milka is related to *melek*, "king," and Sarai is related to *sar*, "officer." Yiska, moreover, may be related to the word *nesek*, "libation" or "anointing" (Cassuto 1964:277; others disagree—see, for example, Sarna 1989:87), and hence may also be related to the idea of royalty. Abram's marriage to Sarai is parallel to Nahor's marriage to Milka (11:29), and the wives of the two brothers have similar names. The text may be hinting that Abram, like Nahor, married his niece, Yiska, and that Sarai and Yiska are the same person. The notion that each brother incorporates one of Haran's children into his family gains additional support through Terah's fostering of the third child, Lot, whom Abraham later will foster. The similarities between Abraham's later treatment of Lot and of Sarah become more pointed if Sarah can be seen as identical to Yiska. They are, in a sense, both his protegées, Sarah as wife and Lot as son. Each could offer Abraham the possibility of a successor, but Abraham treats them as sister and brother for whom he has little concern, as we will see below.

A number of early retellings of the biblical narrative identify Sarai with Yiska; see Vermes (1961:75) for some of the sources for this idea which also occurs in rabbinic midrashim. This identification is usually seen as an apologetic for Abraham's claim in chapter 20. I think it is more than that. Like many of the early identifications of lesser known with more central biblical figures, such as those discussed in the notes of Chapter Five, I think this is either a very early interpretation of the narrative, in this case of chapters 11, 12, and 13, or possibly an ancient, pre-canonical tradition.

18. The use of the word *hesed* is particularly interesting here, because elsewhere it refers to brother-sister incest (Lev 20:17). The repeated use of the word in chapter 24 may reflect the close kin relationship between Isaac's family and Rebecca's; Isaac, like Abraham, will later say that his wife is his sister (26:7).

19. Eisen (1986:9-10, 196 n. 13) notes Abraham's stammering response to Abimelek and his casting blame on God.

20. This word, as will be discussed below, has the connotation of being lost to one's destiny. See its occurrences in 21:14; 27:12; 37:15, each at a moment when a person is in danger of precisely such a fate. As we will see later, chapter 22 represents a reversal of the directionless wandering described in chapters 20 and 21. The occurrences of this word—or, in chapter 22, the marked non-occurrence—point to the three transfer stories on which we are focusing. The particular ways in which the word is used also reflect the degree of resolution in each of these narratives: in chapter 22, Abraham is not "lost"; in chapter 27, Jacob is in danger of being "lost" (27:12); in chapter 37, Joseph is indeed "lost" (37:15).

21. Rosenberg (1986:78) points out that the as yet unborn Isaac is the hidden focus of the wife-sister stories. Fokkelman (1987:48) notes the emphasis on fertility throughout the Abimelek story.

22. Speiser (1982:148) translates: "Let that serve you as a blind to everyone who is with you; you have been publicly vindicated." He notes that the literal translation is "a covering for the eyes," which implies the "diverting or forestalling [of] suspicion," but adds that "Whether the phrase carries special overtones cannot, of course, be

determined" (150). I hope to show that the term *kesut 'enayim* has overtones which echo throughout the Abraham stories. Speiser suggests that the verb which he translates "to vindicate" means "to decree," "to set right," or "to give judgment" and notes the "legal or disciplinary connotations" which will appear again in Gen 21:25 (150). The occurrence of this word in these two episodes, both involving Abimelek, will be discussed below.

The pronoun *hu'*, as I have indicated in my translation, can mean either "it" or "he." "It" would refer to the money, but "he" would imply "your brother," that is, Abraham. If *hu'* is to be read as "he," Abimelek is suggesting that Sarah's relationship to Abraham would vindicate her honor—possibly, should she give birth soon after leaving Gerar. The implication is that people might suspect that Sarah's child was begotten by Abimelek, exactly what the narrative strives to negate. See Sarna (1989:144, 361 n. 10).

23. Helyer (1983:84) and Fokkelman (1987:48) note the ambiguity of Isaac's paternity which results from the sojourn in Gerar. Abimelek's name, of course, is similar to Abraham's, both incorporating the word for "father," *'av*.

24. See Rosenberg (1986:76-77, 83) for a discussion of the gradual separation of Lot and its connection to the succession of Isaac. Gros Louis (1982b:55-58, 64, 76-77) notes the inappropriateness of Lot's choice of place both here and in chapter 13.

25. Jacob (1974:132) notes the similarity between these two questions.

26. The names Gerar and Hagar seem to play on each other and on the word *lagur*, "to sojourn," hence "to be a stranger." See Eisen (1986:9) for the connection between Gerar and *ger*. The impotence of the sojourner is implied in the Sodomites' challenge to Lot: "One has come to sojourn [*lagur*] and he has dared to judge" (19:9). To "sojourn" (*lagur*) is to be in a land where one does not belong; thus, Abraham "sojourned [*vayagar*] in the land of the Philistines" (21:34) but "dwelt [*vayeshev*] in Be'er Sheba" (22:19). The parallel between Hagar's blindness and Abraham's blindness in Gerar is reinforced by the place names Qadesh and Shur which appear both in the Gerar episode (20:1) and in the first Hagar episode (16:7, 14).

27. Sarah says, ". . . perhaps *'ibane* from her" (16:2). The word means "I will be built" but may also be a play on the word *ben*, meaning "son": ". . . perhaps I will be sonned through her." See Rosenberg (1986:89), who suggests the translation "enchilded."

28. While many scholars interpret *Shur* as referring to a wall or walled city, the word can also denote "seeing," and thus constitutes an additional element in the wordplay. See, for example, Num 23:9 and 24:17 for the verb *'ashurenu*, meaning "I see him." See Sarna (1989:120, 360 n. 7) for a discussion of both meanings of the word and of the play on the word *'ayin*.

29. Note the midrashim which, in attempting to solve the contradictions concerning the duration of the nation's enslavement in Egypt, see the "four hundred years" as beginning with the birth of Isaac or the "four hundred thirty years" mentioned in Exod 12:40-41 as beginning with the covenant between the pieces. (See Bereshit Rabbah 44:18 and the parallels cited in the commentary, 1965:440-441; see also Nachmanides' commentary on Gen 15:13 and Exod 12:40.) These midrashim understand the lives of the patriarchs as a life of sojourning, even while the patriarchs dwell in the land of Canaan, since the land is not yet theirs. Thus, the patriarchs are already living out the covenantal experiences of the future nation.

30. Brevard S. Childs (1974:50-60) rejects the possibility that the sign refers to the later revelation at Sinai, suggesting instead that the sign is the burning bush.

31. For the occurrence of *'oni* in chapters 15 and 16 see Buber (1982:39) and Rosenberg (1986:89-90, 237 n. 70). Rosenberg also notes that the letters of the word appear in the word *'ayin.* David Silber first called to my attention that the three key terms of the covenant appear in the Hagar story.

32. See Shiloah (1964) for a discussion of the functions of the repetition of "and he said." Shiloah interprets the repetition in this episode differently (257-258), but notes that such repetition elsewhere suggests a pause for an anticipated response that does not come (251-253). See also Bar-Efrat (1989:217).

33. That Hagar's servitude and affliction are alleviated is clear from the conclusion of the story. Hagar no longer has any relationship to Sarah, although initially she was to function not only as slave but as surrogate mother for her mistress (16:2). Hagar never again is depicted as being under Sarah's control, and the son whom she bears is hers and Abraham's, not Sarah's (16:15-16). In chapter 21 Hagar is called by the angel simply "Hagar" (21:17), while in chapter 16 the angel addressed her as "Hagar, slave of Sarah" (16:8). Even Sarah changes the way she refers to Hagar, in chapter 16 using *shifha* (16:2, 5), the female counterpart to *'eved*, "slave," and in chapter 21 using *'ama* (21:10). An *'ama*, while also paired with *'eved*, is described in the book of Exodus as having different rights (Exod 21:1-11). Most significantly, an *'eved*'s children belong to his master (Exod 21:4), but an *'ama* is treated more as a member of the family (Exod 21:7-11). If we may draw a parallel to Hagar, while she is a *shifha* she is expected to bear a child for her mistress; after she refuses, she becomes defined as an *'ama*, and the child remains hers. See, however, Genesis 25:12.

34. See Jacob (1974:137). That Ishmael's laughter be seen as a mocking of Isaac and his special status as Sarah's son is suggested also by Sarah's expectation that all who "hear" (*hashome'a*) will laugh (21:6). While many translations suggest that the laughter will be joyous—"will laugh with me"—laughter until this point has been

mocking or disbelieving. Ishmael, whose name includes the word "to hear," is the one who now laughs, and it seems reasonable to conclude that, like Hagar and as Sarah anticipates, he laughs at Sarah and Isaac.

Ishmael's laughter can also be seen as a usurpation. Sarah sees "the son of Hagar the Egyptian, whom she had borne to Abraham, laughing [metsaheq]" (21:9), but it is Sarah's son whose name signifies laughter and whose characteristic it is to laugh; Isaac, we read later, is metsaheq with his wife (26:8).

35. That Egypt is a place of evil is not an idea which first appears in the narrative at this point. It is important to note that Abraham is aware of Egypt's sinful nature before he arrives there (12:12). The particular crime of which Abraham correctly suspects Egypt is the crime of Ham: sexual misconduct consequent upon seeing (9:22). Egypt and Canaan, the borders of whose land are Sodom and Gerar (10:19), are brothers, both sons of Ham (10:6); Egypt, Sodom and Gerar all participate in the crime of Ham within the Abraham narrative, and this is to be expected of them. For connections between Sodom and Gerar, see Cassuto (1964:213-216).

36. Many early and later biblical interpretations see Hagar as part of the property that Abraham takes with him out of Egypt. See Vermes (1961:102, 123). In a sense, Abraham has left Egypt, but Egypt has not left him. He has not rid himself of the blindness which brought him to Egypt; in fact, Egypt and Egypt's sin is even more with him now.

37. See Leibovitz (1954:100-101), Jacob (1974:137), Bar-Efrat (1989:36-37, 73).

38. Buber (1982:37-43) discusses the theme of seeing throughout the Abraham narrative and especially in chapter 22.

39. Speiser (1982:87, 163) suggests the meaning "guiding, oracular" for More and notes the connection between Moria and the verb "to see." For a juxtaposition of the verbs ra'o and 'amor, note ki 'amera 'al 'er'e ("for she said: 'Let me not see' "; 21:16) and YHWH yir'e 'asher ye'amer hayom behar YHWH yera'e ("God will see, as it is said today, in the mountain of God will be seen"; 22:14).

One more verb plays on Hagar's inability, and Abraham's ability, to see. Both the angel who calls to Hagar and the angel who calls to Abraham use the verb yr', "to fear." Hagar is told not to be afraid ('al tire'i), for God has heard her son's voice (21:17), and Abraham is told that God now knows that Abraham fears him (yere'; 22:12). While the two incidences of the verb differ in object and connotation, their associations with the other verbs in the word play, ra'o, yaro and 'amor, allows them to function outside their syntactic contexts to underscore the point—Abraham does recognize (fear/see) God, but Hagar does not. See Amit (1989:108-109) for a discussion of some of these words and for the idea of seeing as crucial to chapter 22.

40. Rosenberg (1986:80, 85) notes that the two Hagar episodes are similar to the story of the binding of Isaac, but offers a different interpretation.

41. The angel says: ". . . God has heard the voice of the lad where he is," suggesting a criticism of Hagar for leaving Ishmael. See Jacob (1974:139).

42. Fox (1983:79) notes the parallel between Hagar's and Abraham's predicaments; both need to find a way to save their sons.

43. See Fox (1983:83).

44. The meaning is obscure. I translate according to the Masoretic parsing, which separates between YHWH and the verb, and vocalization, which gives a passive form of the verb. The most likely alternative would translate "in the mountain God will be seen," which still has man as the one who sees and, indeed, affords a more striking parallel with Be'er Lahai Ro'i; Abraham would be claiming that God sees and that man sees God, much like Hagar's claim "I have seen him who sees me" (16:13). See Buber (1982:42). The vocalization *yir'e*, though, would give "in the mountain God sees." See Speiser (1982:163-4).

45. Isaac is blessed by God after Abraham dies (25:11); though never blessed by his father, he comes into his father's blessing at his father's death. See Jacob (1974:174-5).

46. Fokkelman (1987:50) notes the triple occurrences of the words *yahid*, "only" or "alone," and *yahdav*, "together" and concludes: "by showing his willingness to give up his only son, Abraham gets him back, and a much deepened togetherness begins, both between father and son and between the Lord and his obedient follower." See Amit (1989:107-8).

NOTES TO CHAPTER 4
MOTHERS, BROTHERS, AND THE LAND

1. See especially Fokkelman (1975) and Fishbane (1979) on the structure of the Jacob narrative and Sternberg's (1985) analysis of the significance of Joseph's manipulation of events in Egypt to mirror his family's earlier experiences in Canaan.

2. Rosenberg (1986:81) notes that chapters 23 and 24 concern the two parts of Abraham's blessing, land and progeny.

3. Rebecca also, unlike Isaac, receives a blessing from her family (24:60). Her blessing, as Sarna (1989:60) notes, is similar to the blessing given to Abraham in 22:17, the blessing which Isaac will receive automatically through his father's quest. Significantly, it is from her brother and mother (24:55) rather than from her father that Rebecca receives the blessing; the emphasis in this episode on maternal kin will be discussed below.

4. Similarly, Abimelek seeing Isaac through the window when Isaac is "laughing" (*metsaheq*) emphasizes Isaac's lack of awareness

(26:8). The connection between Isaac's inability to seek a wife and his inability to transfer the blessing to his son will be discussed later. We can note now that the words "take and go" (*qah velek*), as mentioned in Chapter Three, appear as a pair when Pharaoh sends away Sarah and when Laban sends away Rebecca. But, while Pharaoh speaks to Abraham (12:19), Laban does not speak to Isaac; he sends Rebecca with Abraham's servant (24:51). Thus "take and go" seems to represent one's ability to seek a wife as well as one's ability to seek the blessing. Jacob will be able to seek the blessing only if he is able to seek a wife. Isaac, as we shall see, will send Jacob on this double quest with "take and go." Esau, however, like his father, will not be capable of finding an appropriate wife or of getting his father's blessing.

5. Speiser (1982:141, 143) points out the play on the name *Tso'ar* and discusses Lot's weakness in this episode. See also Gros Louis (1982b:57-58).

6. Von Rad (1972:172) notes the comparison of Sodom "with Paradise and with Egypt" and the connection between Lot's choice in this episode and his fate later on.

7. See Von Rad (1972:107).

8. While Eve speaks of Seth as replacing Abel, Seth is as much a replacement for the lost Cain—"she called his name Seth [*Shet*], because the Lord has given [*shat*] me another son, instead of Abel, for Cain slew him" (4:25). See Cassuto (1961:190-191). The names of Cain's descendants had incorporated both Cain and Abel, and only after the destruction of both lines does the narrative tell of the birth of Seth.

Eve had not given a reason for Abel's name, although the word *hevel* means "breath" or "nothingness" and suggests the transitory nature of Abel. See Cassuto (1961:202) and Sarna (1989:32). Eve had, however, explained Cain's name, at the end of a verse which closely parallels the description of Seth's birth: "I have acquired [*qaniti*] a man together with God" (4:1). The word *qaniti* signifies not only acquisition, but creation. See Cassuto (1978:197-201); Cassuto translates "I have created a man equally with the Lord." Eve presents herself as God's partner in the creation of her first son, but gives God alone credit for giving her the last son. See Cassuto (1961:245-246). The element of creativity implied by Cain's name characterizes Cain's occupation as well as the accomplishments of his descendants, particularly the occupation of smith, which may also be related to Cain's name. Even Abel's name, "nothingness," becomes reinterpreted in the names of Cain's descendants *Yaval*, *Yuval*, and *Tuval-Cain* as "fruitfulness" or "productivity," corresponding to the innovations of these people. See Cassuto (1961:235). That same quality of presumptuous creativity, though, is what leads to Cain's demise and to his replacement by Seth, whose name suggests an acknowledgement of the limitedness of human creativity vis-à-vis God. God's unfavorable judgment of Cain's offering seems to be related to this same issue. Cain, unlike Abel, is a producer; he offers God "*of the fruit of the ground*" (4:3), rather than the choice fruit, because, like Eve, he sees himself as God's partner in the bringing forth of the earth's produce. Abel, merely a watchman of God's creation, offers God the firstlings and the fat (4:4), as biblical law will dictate, a recognition that the animals really belong to God.

Wilson (1977:155) discusses the framing of Cain's genealogy by Cain's and Lemek's crimes: "The overall effect of placing the Cainite genealogy in this context is to give a negative interpretation to Cain's line. By virtue of being Cain's descendants, the people named in the genealogy all inherit his curse." Wilson suggests that Seth's line contrasts with Cain's, and he notes the similarities between the two genealogies (155-166). It is important to point out, though, that Cain's crime is repeated by his descendants; they do not undeservedly inherit Cain's curse. The same is true of figures such as Ham's descendants and Ishmael. The narrative's negative evaluation of the ancestors will be repeated for the descendants, but only once the descendants behave in such a way as to merit that evaluation.

9. Edmund Leach (1969:21) notes that the fate of the concubines' sons resembles Cain's fate. For further discussion of *qedem*, see Chapter Five.

10. Twelve sons signify nationhood; Jacob will have twelve sons, and Nahor, Abraham's brother, has twelve sons as well (22:20-24). Benno Jacob (1974:147-148) and others note that Nahor has eight children from his wife and four from his concubine, corresponding to Jacob's eight sons from Leah and Rachel and four sons from Bilhah and Zilpah. See Bereshit Rabbah 57:3. Professor Uriel Simon has pointed out that the news of Nahor's family reaches Abraham immediately after the binding of Isaac, emphasizing the contrast between Abraham's striving for a single son to carry on his mission and the growth of his brother's family into a nation.

11. Sarna (1989:176) interprets *le'umotam* as referring to tribal units within a single nation. In this context, though, it seems to indicate separate nations, since immediately following, in the episode introduced as the *toledot* of Isaac, Rebecca's two children are described both as two *goyim* ("nations") and two *le'umim* (25:23); Jacob and Esau certainly become separate nations. Indeed, God had promised Abraham that Ishmael, through giving rise to twelve *nesi'im* ("princes"), would constitute a single *goy* ("nation"; 17:20). But, as the details of Ishmael's growth to nationhood suggest, Ishmael's descendants are more fragmented—the *nesi'im* are leaders of separate *le'umim*.

12. Sarna (1989:177) notes the predatory connotation of *nafal*.

13. Sarna (1989:176) notes that nowhere else does *Qedma* appear as the name of a tribe and that "the word usually means 'eastward.' "

Unlike Cain, Lot, and the concubines' sons, Ishmael cannot actually go east, because he must dwell in the south, near Egypt, his mother's birthplace. But the inclusion of the word *Qedma* within his genealogy makes the point that, figuratively, Ishmael has gone east, to the place of exiled brothers.

14. See Bereshit Rabbah 24:5 on 5:1 and 63:6 on 25:22. Both the *toledot* of Adam and the *toledot* of Isaac contain the word "this," the letters of which, though *gematria*, add up to twelve. The midrash makes the point that both Adam and Rebecca were worthy of having twelve sons. Since Adam had two sons, one of whom murdered the other, he was not granted twelve sons. Rebecca, similarly, feeling the struggle of the children inside her, exclaimed that she did not want to give birth to twelve sons. Both midrashim suggest that the delay in the formation of the chosen nation is necessary if that nation is not to destroy itself through fraternal conflict.

15. Fokkelman (1975:87) designates the *toledot* of chapters 25 and 36 as the boundaries of the Jacob story. He notes that the unusual *toledot* of chapter 25 alert the reader that "with this 'generation' something special is the matter."

Steinberg (1989:44) notes the parallel contrasting genealogies of Isaac/Ishmael and Jacob/Esau and adds the genealogies of Terah and Shem. For a discussion of the contrast between the *toledot* of the sons of Noah and the *toledot* of Shem, see Chapter Five. Steinberg aptly states that "Genesis is a book whose plot is genealogy" (41) and summarizes the relationship between narrative and genealogy accurately: "narrative represents a state of disequilibrium designed to return family life back to the state of equilibrium found in genealogy" (43). This is especially true of Cain's narrative and Seth's genealogy. But it is important to notice that the "state of equilibrium" may be a false equilibrium, as is the case with the *toledot* of Ishmael; if genealogy comes instead of narrative, it often is because it is of no interest to Genesis to have that family achieve "equilibrium." When narrative comes instead of genealogy, though, it is because, as Steinberg and Fokkelman note, some problem must be resolved before nationhood is achieved. Thus the structuring motif of *toledot* highlights the covenantal idea of the delayed fulfillment of destiny.

16. Joseph and his brothers do return temporarily to the land of Canaan, on a mission to bury their father (50:7-14). The promise of ultimate return, although unfulfilled at the end of the book, is nevertheless certain to be fulfilled. Joseph, imitating his father this one time, makes the children of Israel swear that they will bring his bones out of Egypt at the time of their redemption. Thus, the family's temporary journey to Canaan to bury Jacob is the model for their final journey to Canaan when they will take Joseph's bones back to the land. The last words of Genesis, then, are strangely but unambiguously optimistic: "And Joseph died. . . and they embalmed him, and he was placed in

a coffin in Egypt" (50:26). The bones of Joseph, lying in a coffin and awaiting burial, are the guarantee that God will redeem Israel; God will "bring up" the children of Israel, and they will "bring up" Joseph's bones (50:24-25; cf. Exod 13:19). See the discussion of the ending of Genesis in Chapter Five. Ultimately, redemption and unification of the family are simultaneous.

Two midrashic traditions about the mysterious Serah, daughter of Asher, highlight this point. One explains that, when the brothers wanted to tell Jacob that Joseph was alive, they were afraid that the shock might be too great for their father, and so they asked Serah to break the news gently to Jacob. The other tells that, when the time came for the Israelites to leave Egypt, Moses was delayed because he could not find the coffin in which lay Joseph's bones; Serah, though, knew how to find it, and thus were the Israelites able to leave Egypt with the bones of Joseph. Midrashic tradition links together these two moments by connecting Serah with each of them. In each, Joseph is reunited with the family/nation, and the nation's redemption is dependent on this reunification. Note that a third tradition, which identifies Serah with the wise woman of II Samuel 20 who prevents civil war between the Judahites and the Israelites, supports the characterization of Serah as unifier of the nation.

17. Gerar, Like Sodom, is a border land. When Abraham goes to Gerar, he leaves Canaan proper, just as Lot does when he goes to Sodom. When Isaac goes to Gerar, Gerar seems to be considered more a part of Canaan, as God's words suggest. God's definition of Gerar and his contrast of Gerar with Egypt, though, do not appear until after we are told that Isaac goes to Gerar, and it is this which creates the expectation that this episode will be another instance of a patriarch leaving the land, an expectation immediately undercut by God's words to Isaac. The redefinition of Gerar seems to have occurred through Abraham's covenant with Abimelek and his continued dwelling in "the land of the Philistines" (21:34).

There are many other important differences between Isaac's behavior and Abraham's in the parallel episodes. Isaac leaves the land because of a famine (26:1), he claims that his wife is his sister only when he is asked and because he is afraid (26:7), he responds to Abimelek straightforwardly and honestly (26:9). Significantly, just as Isaac never leaves the land, even though he goes to Gerar, he also never loses his wife (26:8), even though he claims that she is his sister.

18. David Silber points out that Isaac's chosenness is confirmed by Abimelek as well (26:28).

God's statement is introduced with the words "do not fear" (26:24), the same words which God spoke to Abraham after Lot's departure and the battle against the four kings and before Abraham asks for a son (16:1) and which he will speak to Jacob on his way to Egypt to meet his son, Joseph (46:3). The words "do not fear," then, seem to respond to the fear of imminent danger by referring to future survival through one's children. This contrasts sharply with Esau's lack of concern for the future at a moment of vulnerability (25:32).

19. Bereshit Rabbah 65:1 suggests that Esau is imitating his father in marrying at the age of forty, but portrays Esau as an evil person attempting to appear righteous.

20. See Fokkelman (1975:107, 118). The verb *lasuah*, which describes Isaac's purpose in going to the field, recalls the word *siah*, "shrub," a frequent partner to the word *sade*, "field" (see Gen 2:5).

21. Jacob (1974:182) notes the connection between Isaac's affinity for the *sade* ("field") and the aroma of Esau's garments, and links this affinity to the content of the blessing that Isaac offers when he smells the garments.

22. Fokkelman (1975:106) describes Esau's marriage to the Canaanite women as indicating that he "has no sense of the special task of his family under the sign of the blessing." See also Jacob (1974:186). For a statement of this same point in anthropological terms, see Prewitt (1981:87-98).

23. Speiser (1982:210) notes the wordplay in 27:36, and Fokkelman (1975:98-101) traces it throughout the narrative. See also Jacob (1974:183).

24. See Alter (1981:45). "His selling of the birthright . . . is in itself proof that he is not worthy to retain the birthright." Esau's explanation of why he doesn't care to retain the birthright is telling—"Behold, I am going to die, so of what use to me is the birthright?" (25:32). The birthright, rather, is necessary precisely because one is destined to die; it is individual mortality which necessitates the passing down of one's heritage to one's children, an opportunity afforded by possession of the birthright.

25. Rebecca's seeking of divine counsel contrasts with Isaac's prayer for a child; the contrast supports the characterization of Rebecca as a person of vision who is able to undertake a quest and of Isaac who, while not a seeker, has a special relationship with God. David Silber has pointed out that Isaac's prayer and God's immediate response, both expressed by the same word, vocalized differently, suggest Isaac's closeness to God (25:21). Rebecca, unlike Isaac, has to seek God and is capable of seeking God and of achieving understanding (25:22-24). Similarly, Isaac possesses God's blessing and it is he who must transmit the blessing to his son, but it is Rebecca who can understand the nature of the blessing and who understands the nature of her sons.

26. Speiser (1982:215) suggests the translation "greeted" for the literal "blessed" because the blessing does not begin until verse 3, and Speiser sees no connection between the command to marry and the blessing. "The intervening passage [28.1-2] deals, instead, with strictly mundane matters. It is not improbable that *P* had a particular purpose

in mind in employing the stem *brk* repeatedly in this context (cf. 4,6—*bis*), namely, to emphasize that Isaac had nothing but the friendliest feelings toward Jacob . . . ."

27. Note that Esau responds to his father's sending of Jacob (28:6) and to his father's disapproval of Canaanite women (28:8); Jacob, though, is sent by both parents (27:43; 28:2, 6) and obeys both his father and his mother (28:7). The contrast between Esau's relationship with his father alone and Jacob's relationship with his mother as well as, for the first time, with his father is highlighted by the sandwiching of verse 7, Jacob's obedience to his parents, between verses 6 and 8, Esau's response to his father. This same sequence of verses highlights Esau's reaction as an outsider (*vayar'* . . . *vayar'* [28:6, 8]; "he saw . . . he saw") in contrast to Jacob's interaction with his parents (*vayishma'* [28:7], "he heard," occurring here in the sense of "he obeyed"). Thus, while Esau "goes" and "takes" (*vayelek . . . vayiqah*; 28:9), he is not fulfilling his father's command.

28. See Bereshit Rabbah 67:13 for a discussion between two rabbis about the merit of Esau's second marriage. The second rabbi, in response to the first rabbi's positive evaluation of the marriage, points out that the fact that Esau keeps his first wives indicates that such an evaluation is impossible; rather, he says, as the first marriage was bad so too was the second marriage.

29. Fokkelman (1975:101). Eisen (1986:197 n. 22) points out that Esau marries his cousin, just as do Isaac and Jacob, and is not able to understand that Ishmael's daughter is an unacceptable wife.

30. Jacob, of course, marries his cross-cousin. Such a marriage is, in many societies, the ideal, and Oden (1974:197-199) suggests that the occurrence here of "the union which is a key to elementary structures of kinship generally is the same alliance which is recapitulated in the marriages of the man Israel." Oden, however, does not bring biblical evidence for the preference for cross-cousin marriage. I believe that we must examine the relative merit of Jacob's and Esau's marriages to their cousins in the context of the information about kinship which the narrative provides.

31. Leach (1969:20-21) discusses "the overriding virtue of close kin endogamy" in Genesis, but does not note the distinction between different types of kin, specifically the distinction between paternal and maternal kin which is emphasized in this text. Thus, he notes that "Isaac's wife Rebekah is his father's brother's son's daughter," but he does not note that she may also be described as his mother's brother's son's daughter, through Sarah's kinship to Abraham, or as his father's brother's daughter's son's daughter, through Milka's kinship to Abraham. In other words, the relationships can be defined in more ways than one, and the way the narrative defines them is significant. Rebecca, it is true, is defined as Isaac's paternal kin, but Jacob's wife, from the very same family, is defined as from his maternal kin, while

Ishmael marries from his paternal kin. The way the narrative defines the relationship is what requires an explanation, especially since the definition is a matter of choice.

32. The first notice of this separation comes at the announcement of Nahor's incipient nationhood with the birth of his twelve sons (22:20-24), starkly contrasting with Abraham's near loss of his one successor. Oddly, this coincides with the announcement of the birth of Rebecca (22:23), who will link Nahor's family to Abraham's. Nahor's family in Padam Aram, then, is delicately balanced between constituting a separate people and being a part of Abraham's family.

The episode in which Abraham sends his servant to find a wife for Isaac from his paternal kin has a striking alternation of the terms *bet 'av* and *bet 'em*, "father's house" and "mother's house." The servant asks Rebecca about her "father's house" (*bet 'av*; 24:23), and she speaks of her father as the son of Milcah and Nahor (24:24). Both her grandfather and grandmother are related to Isaac, just as Rebecca is related to both Abraham and Sarah. The servant goes on to speak of "the house of the brother of my master" (*bet 'ahe 'adoni*; 24:27), but Rebecca runs to "the house of her mother" (*bet 'imah*; 24:28). The servant continues, throughout the episode, to speak in terms of the paternal line (24:48-49), while Rebecca's mother joins Rebecca's brother in the negotiations (24:53-55), replacing Rebecca's father (24:50). This story, then, suggests the progressive transformation of Padan Aram into a maternal home and thus reflects the beginning of the progressive separation of the people of Padan Aram from Abraham's kin. Already Padan Aram offers an alternate lineage, although Isaac is not threatened, as Jacob later will be, by absorption into this lineage. Now, as later, Laban claims to be unable to "speak good or bad" (24:50), but is unwilling to send the woman to Canaan (24:55). Abraham's refusal to send Isaac to Padan Aram becomes more significant when chapter 24 is compared with Jacob's experiences in the house of Laban, who tries to incorporate his kinsman into his own family.

When Isaac finally sends Jacob to Padan Aram, he speaks of Rebecca's "father's house" (*bet 'av*; 28:2). Rebecca, though, does not speak of her paternal home; she sends Jacob to her brother, without mentioning her father (27:43). Thus, Jacob's departure to Padan Aram constitutes both a brother's exile to maternal kin and a son's fulfillment of his paternal mission. It is the tension between these two perspectives, both of which are suggested by the narrative, that must subsequently be resolved. Jacob must unambiguously become his father's successor. The two meanings of Jacob's departure, it should be noted, correspond to the different reasons his mother and father give for sending Jacob to Padan Aram: he must leave the land of Canaan both because he cannot live together with his brother, much like the other exiled brothers in Genesis, and because he must find a wife in order to inherit the blessing of descendants who will possess the land.

33. The connection between Isaac's death and Esau's plan to kill Jacob is underscored by the word *mitnahem*, "consoling himself" (27:42). Esau's intention to kill his brother is described as a consolation; his plan will be realized during the "days of mourning ['*evel*]" for his father (27:41).

34. Fishbane (1979:51) emphasizes the fraternal relationship between Jacob and Laban. The contrasting names '*Edom* and *Lavan*, meaning "red" and "white," support the parallel between Laban and Jacob's brother, Esau, as Fokkelman notes (1975:150). Jacob's experiences with Laban seem to parallel both his relationships with Esau and with Isaac. Laban, however, seems more a surrogate father than a surrogate brother. Since fraternal and paternal conflict are related, Jacob will have to resolve both through his experiences in Laban's house, and he will have to encounter both his true brother and his true father after he leaves Padan Aram.

35. Oden (1983:200-203) discusses the avunculate relationship between Laban and Jacob. He notes the generally benevolent nature of such relationships, but this unfortunately causes him to wave away Laban's and Jacob's thefts as "highly conventionalized freedoms." Oden concludes that the complex system of kinship in Jacob's family, manifested in avunculate residence as well as in cross-cousin marriage, is what defines Jacob as Israel, the eponymous ancestor of the nation. I, in contrast, am suggesting that Padan Aram is an alternative which must be rejected in the formation of the nation.

36. The use of the verb *shuv*, "return," is significant. God's statement contrasts with Rebecca's assertion that she will "send" for her son and "take" him back home (27:45). The verb *shuv* might have been expected there: Rebecca speaks of Esau's anger "returning" or "turning away" from Jacob, using the verb *shuv* twice, and she has just told Jacob to "dwell" in Padan Aram, using a similar sounding word, *veyashavta* (27:44-45). But the verbs which she uses to describe Jacob's return, "send" and "take," once again emphasize her own manipulation of events. God replaces these with *shuv*, "return," and changes the subject of the verb from Rebecca to the God of Jacob's fathers. Jacob then casts the verb in its simple, active form; he is leaving now, but he plans to "return" to his father's home. In fact, the process of Jacob's return to his father will be gradual and difficult, and Jacob will not return without God's intervention (31:3). Significantly, even when Jacob decides to return, he does not mention his father (30:25), and the omission persists even after God tells Jacob to return "to the land of your fathers and to your birthplace" (31:3); Jacob tells his wives that God has told him to return only "to your birthplace" (31:13).

37. Many scholars have noted this parallel; see Cassuto (1961:64), Alter (1981:45), Fokkelman (1975:128-129), Fishbane (1979:45, 55), Andriolo (1973:1667).

38. Here, as throughout, Laban resembles Abimelek; compare this statement with Abimelek's at 20:9. Compare also the establishment of a covenant and the calling of God as witness in 21:30, 32, in 26:26, and in 31:44, 50. Like Abraham, Jacob meets a character similar to himself, and the change in the patriarch can be traced to the break with his foil, when the two establish a covenant. When Jacob first meets Laban, the uncle is a deceiver (rimitani) like the nephew (29:25). When he last meets Laban and establishes a covenant at Gal'ed, paralleling Abraham's covenant with Abimelek at Be'er Sheba, Jacob sets up a pillar (vayerimeha; 31:45). Jacob's behavior here represents both a break with his uncle and a relinquishing of his past of deception. Laban, though, is still the 'Arami (31:24), perhaps a play on the relationship between Padan Aram and the quality of deceitfulness which Laban embodies.

39. Andriolo (1973:1667) analyzes this story as "a symmetrical inversion of the Jacob-Esau story," noting the parallel between the sisters, Leah and Rachel, and their father, Laban, and the brothers, Esau and Jacob, and their mother, Rebecca.

40. Fokkelman (1975:133-136) notes the passivity of Jacob and the similarity between the words of Rachel and of Sarah.

41. See Rachel's rationale for Naphtali's name (30:8); Rachel talks of a struggle with her sister in language similar to that describing Jacob's struggle as he is about to meet Esau (32:29). See the discussion in the notes to Chapter Five of the children as emerging from the competition between siblings, indeed serving as pawns in that competition, and hence as inevitably in fraternal competition with each other. Reuven, especially, takes part in his mother's rivalry with her sister. He brings Leah mandrakes, which themselves become a focus of competition between the sisters; compare Leah's complaint in 30:15 that Rachel is doubly taking what is hers to Esau's complaint in 27:36 of Jacob's double usurpation. Reuven also sleeps with Bilhah after Rachel's death (35:22), which, among other things, ensures that Jacob now will have no remnant of his connection to Rachel.

42. In the context of Isaac's combined blessing and command, Fokkelman comments: "The fulfillment of the charge, Isaac says, will lead to the realization of the blessing which is given you in farewell" (1975:112 and n. 38). Fokkelman (138) and Fishbane (1979:57-58) note the connection between the birth of Rachel's son and Jacob's departure. Indeed, Jacob was to have remained in Padan Aram, according to Rebecca, for only a short while (yamim 'ahadim; 27:44). This period, as Fokkelman (128) points out, corresponds to Jacob's perception of his period of waiting for Rachel (yamim 'ahadim; 29:20). Jacob, then, was to remain only as long as it would take to marry

Rachel, his chosen wife, so that he could begin building his family. While he remains much longer, his belated decision to return home is motivated by the birth of a child to the wife whom he was sent to marry. We will discuss further the connection between Joseph's birth and Jacob's decision to leave in Chapter Five.

43. Fokkelman (1975:127, 137) discusses the emphasis in Laban's family on business relationships rather than family relationships. Leah, for example, speaks of "hiring" Jacob for the night (30:16). This detail is particularly interesting, I think, in the context of its inversion in chapter 38, when Judah hires Tamar but Tamar refuses to accept his payment and forces Judah to take responsibility for his action as well as for his previous inaction toward the members of his family. The significance of these business dealings and of Jacob's request to be released by Laban will be discussed further in Chapter Five.

44. See the midrash on Deuteronomy 26:5, included in the Passover Haggadah, which portrays Laban as attempting to destroy Jacob and which compares Laban, unfavorably, with Pharaoh. The Jacob/Israel and Laban/Pharaoh typology will be discussed further in Chapter Five.

45. Neither, as noted above, does Laban's sister, Rebecca, "send" for him, as she had anticipated doing (27:45). Jacob's fate is no longer to be controlled by his mother or her family.

46. Fokkelman (1975:163) notes that these two verses imply that Rachel is "related by nature to Jacob."

47. That possession of the gods determines inheritance has been suggested by many scholars, on the basis of Nuzi legal practices. See, for example, Speiser (1982:250). The issue, of course, is not so much material inheritance as title of "paterfamilias," which Greenberg (1982:239-248) suggests is the only title contingent on possession of the gods. Greenberg, in fact, rejects the possibility that the aim of Rachel's theft was to bestow title on Jacob and suggests that Rachel simply was following a custom of taking along family gods when moving to a new home. Nevertheless, in our narrative, as I discuss, the issues of material inheritance, of "paterfamilias," and of paternal gods cannot be separated from one another. Furthermore, whatever the significance of the idols, Rachel is bringing with her something that is of her father's house; this in itself links her to Laban.

Rachel's secrecy about the theft suggests that this may be another strategy to gain ascendancy over her sister. David Silber has suggested that Rachel takes the *teraphim* in an attempt to become pregnant again. Her excuse for not rising for Laban—"for the way of women is upon me" (31:35)—is relevant in this context. Attribution of the birth of Benjamin to the power of the *teraphim*, Silber notes, may explain Rachel's name for Benjamin and also why Jacob changes the baby's name; see the discussion of '-*v*-*n*, above. Indeed the word is juxtaposed with *teraphim* in I Samuel 15:23 and Zechariah 10:2. This link between the *teraphim* and childbirth also explains why Rachel's death occurs specifically at the birth of Benjamin; she must, as noted, leave Jacob's family before his return to his father in Canaan, but Benjamin's birth as the cause of her death underscores why Rachel cannot be a part of Jacob's family—she has never left behind her kinship with Laban.

48. The expectation that the word *vayignov* ("and he stole") will have as its object the word *tso'n*, referring to Laban's sheep, is set up not only by the fact that Jacob has indeed just taken these sheep, but also by the phrase which precedes the notice of Rachel's and Jacob's acts of theft: "And Laban went to shear his sheep" (*ligzoz 'et tso'no*; 31:19). The verb *ligzoz*, followed by *vatignov* and *vayignov*, suggests a pattern to the ear, and this pattern further prepares the reader to hear the word *tso'no* mentioned again after the word *vayignov*. The unexpected object, "Laban's heart," thus comes as a surprise to the reader, and the effect enhances the realization that Jacob is doing something new and unexpected—he is breaking away from Laban.

49. Fokkelman (1975:170); Fishbane (1979:51, 56).

50. Fokkelman (1975:174-183) notes that the progression from "our brothers" to "my brothers and your brothers" suggest Jacob's separation from Laban. He discusses the possibility that Laban had intended Jacob's marriage to his daughters to be a *tsadiqa* marriage, in which the man becomes part of his wife's clan.

51. Fishbane (1979:52).

52. Fokkelman (1975:227); Fishbane (1979:52).

53. Fokkelman (1975:234) notes that the blessing which God confirms is Isaac's second blessing, not the blessing which Isaac had planned for his *bekor*. See the notes to Chapter Five for a somewhat different way of understanding the significance of Jacob receiving both types of blessing from his father.

54. The description of Esau's departure omits the name of his destination in a way which calls attention to the omission: ". . . he went to land ['*erets*] because of his brother Jacob" (36:6). The word "land" cannot stand alone, without either an article or a modifier. Speiser (1982:279) summarizes the attempts at emendation. The omission has the effect of generalizing the narrative and recalling its parallels, when brothers departed to '*erets qedem* ("the land of the east," 25:6), '*artsa bene qedem* ("to the land of the sons of the east," 29:1), and '*erets Nod qidmat 'Eden* ("the land of Nod east of Eden," 4:16). Esau cannot actually go to the land of *qedem* because, like Ishmael, his land is not in the east. See further the discussion in Chapter Five and notes concerning the omission of the word *qedem* here and the use of the word in describing Jacob's earlier departure from Canaan.

55. Berlin (1983:77-78) notes, among other differences between Hamor's promises to Jacob's sons and his statements to the Shechem-

ites, that Hamor tells Jacob's sons that they will be able to take possession of the land (34:10) but omits this important detail in his discussion with the townspeople (34:21). Possession of the land is central to this story; in fact, despite the Shechemites' intentions, Shechem becomes, in this episode, the first part of the land of Canaan to be conquered by the Israelites. See Chapter Five for a discussion of the significance of this episode for the fulfillment of God's covenant with Abraham.

56. Oden (1983:195-196) notes that through Jacob the patriarchal genealogy is "linear" and after Jacob it is "segmented," and he relates this to the "external" and "internal" definition of Israel as a nation.

57. I have periodically noted the places where particular events occur. Locations are significant, and they make the narrative patterns more conspicuous. An event which occurs in Shechem relates to siblings—see Jacob's statement about brothers in 48:22. Hebron implies a link with one's father; Abraham bought the burial plot in Hebron, concretizing the link between the land and the paternal heritage. And Be'er Sheba, the place where Abraham established a covenant with Abimelek, implies responsibility toward one's son. As examples of how these names can serve as signposts in a reading of the narrative, note the following: the episode of Dinah's rape and her brothers' revenge occurs in Shechem, but Jacob returns to his father in Hebron, "where Abraham and Isaac sojourned" (35:27); when Joseph leaves his father to seek his brothers, he travels from "the valley of Hebron" to Shechem (37:14); finally, when Jacob begins his trip to Egypt to find his son, he stops at Be'er Sheba, where God assures the success of his quest (46:1).

58. Deborah's death seems to serve much the same function; see Sarna (1989:214). Deborah's death, though, may signify Jacob's break with Rebecca, as well. We never hear of Rebecca's death, nor, as I have noted, does she ever send for Jacob to bring him home. Jacob, in returning to his father, must sever all ties to his mother's kin, and that includes both Rachel and Rebecca. Rebecca has no further role in the patriarchal mission, and so we never hear of her again. The notice of Deborah's death suggests that Jacob has severed his tie to Rebecca without giving Rebecca significance in the narrative; at the same time, though, the loss of that link to Rebecca is duly noted and mourned (35:8). See Bereshit Rabbah 81:5 for the tradition that Jacob hears of the death of Rebecca while he is mourning Deborah. David Silber points out that Rebecca's nurse was sent with Rebecca to Canaan by Laban and his mother (24:59), and thus she represents specifically Rebecca's connection to her family in Padan Aram.

59. As we have noted, the father has the power both to bless and to curse his son. Rebecca offers to accept the curse (*qelala*) of Jacob's father, leaving only the blessing to her son. Rachel, too, is cursed by

her husband, although the word *qelala* is not used, while her son receives his father's blessing. Interestingly, when Hagar is pregnant with the future competitor of Sarah's son, the text describes her attitude toward Sarah with the word *vateqal*—Sarah "became light" in her eyes. This word is related to the word *qelala*; Sarah too seems to absorb the negative side of the paternal blessing which her son is to receive. Rendsburg (1986:73) relates Rebecca's death in Jacob's absence to her acceptance of her son's curse.

60. Rosenberg (1986:89-90, 95) suggests another significance of the Ishmaelites' appearance here: the descendants of Hagar, who was enslaved by the ancestors of Joseph and his brothers, bring about the enslavement of Joseph, first, and then of the entire family. Compare this idea of a causal relationship between the behavior of the patriarchs and the Egyptian enslavement with Joseph's consolidation of Pharaoh's power to a degree that allows Pharaoh to enslave his subjects (47:13-26).

61. The root *kzv* signifies deception, particularly a disappointment of expectations, and is especially appropriate here, for Judah deceives Tamar by sustaining and then disappointing her expectation that he will give Shelah to her as a husband. Sarna (1989:266) points out that the root *shlh* has the same meaning as *kzv*.

62. Most scholars assume that Tamar is a Canaanite, primarily because the text does not say otherwise. See, for example, Emerton (1976:90-91). In my view, we must account for the information or lack of information which the narrative offers. That the narrative does not identify Tamar with the Canaanites, nor with any other nation, is the significant point. Jacob (1974:262) notes that, while in his opinion Tamar must have been a Canaanite, Tamar is not linked to any nation, while Judah's wife is explicitly linked to the Canaanites. Thus, Jacob points out, Tamar has a sense of mission which Judah's wife's sons are incapable of possessing; in contrast, a "genuine son of Abraham begets children for his people and for eternity" (263).

63. See Cassuto (1929:30-31) and Sarna (1989:263). The word *haker* appears numerous times throughout the Joseph narrative, and many puns on the word appear as well. When Joseph sees his brothers, "he recognized them [*vayakirem*] and made himself a stranger [*vayitnaker*] to them" (42:7). See Alter (1981:163). His reaction may echo the brothers' reaction to seeing him from afar back in Canaan: "they plotted [*vayitnakelu*] against him to kill him" (37:18). See Ackerman (1982:89-90) and Sternberg (1985:288). Two other unrelated verbs with which the text plays and which it sets against the backdrop of recognition and estrangement are *kmr* and *mkr*: Joseph is overcome with compassion (*nikmeru rahamav*; 43:30), and Joseph identifies himself to his brothers as the one "whom you sold" (*mekartem*; 45:4).

64. See Bereshit Rabbah 85:7 for the comparison between Rebecca and Tamar: "Two covered themselves with veils and gave birth to twins." That the women are veiled emphasizes the idea that they cannot be seen—in other words, that Isaac and Judah both lack the ability to perceive. Rebecca and Tamar, on the other hand, are capable of seeing.

65. Both uncle and grandfather are safe surrogate fathers, but kinship with the uncle takes the nephew away from the patriarchal family, while kinship with the grandfather allows the grandson to remain within the patriarchal family. For a discussion of the comparison of nephew and grandson on the basis of Indo-European kinship terms, see Benveniste (1973:188-190). Benveniste goes on to discuss the similarity between the reciprocal terms for grandfather and grandson which, he says, implies "the belief that a newly born child is always the reincarnation of an ancestor, going back a certain number of generations. They even believe that, strictly speaking, there is no birth, because the ancestor has not disappeared, he has only been hidden away. In general, the process of reappearance is from grandfather to grandson. When a son is born to somebody, it is the grandfather of the child who 'reappears', and this is why they have the same name. The young child is, as it were, a diminutive representation of the ancestor which it incarnates: it is a 'little grandfather', who is born again after an interval of a generation (191).

66. Interestingly, while the Genesis narrative generally links the death of the father to the ascendancy of the son, suggesting that the unit of succession is father-son, some midrashim portray the father as living on after the biblical notice of his death and as dying at the moment his grandson assumes a position of leadership, suggesting that the unit of succession is grandfather-grandson. Thus, for example, according to midrashic tradition, Jacob's acquisition of the birthright occurs during the period of mourning for Abraham, whose death is mentioned in the biblical narrative before the *toledot* of Ishmael and Isaac, and Isaac dies at the moment that Joseph stands before Pharaoh, though his death is mentioned in the biblical narrative before the *toledot* of Esau and Jacob. Indeed, the ages of Abraham and Isaac at their deaths suggest that their lifetimes extended beyond the narrative moment in which the notices of their deaths are imbedded. Nevertheless, for the biblical narrative their deaths are relevant as their sons succeed them, while the midrashim highlight the link between these patriarchs and their grandsons. See Bereshit Rabbah 61:11 and 84:22 and the related midrashim cited in the commentary on the latter passage (1965:1028).

67. See Ackerman (1982:105) and Sarna (1989:263-264); Ackerman connects the word's appearance here and in chapter 38 with the parallel between Jacob and Benjamin, in this episode, and Judah and Shelah, in the earlier episode. Note that Jacob, in taking responsibility

for Laban's property, begins: *terepha lo' heve'ti 'eleka*—"I have not brought to you an animal which was torn up . . ." (31:39). Judah, taking responsibility for Jacob's son, says: *'im lo' havi'otiv 'eleka*—'If I do not bring him to you . . ." (43:9). The statements of Jacob and Judah are extremely similar, then, and it is especially striking that Jacob expresses his dutifulness in terms of a *terepha*. A *terepha* is exactly what Joseph becomes in chapter 37—*taroph taraph Yoseph* (37:33). Judah's promise that Jacob's youngest son will not now be lost is appropriately modeled on a statement which guarantees that a *terepha* was not brought—the fate that befell Joseph will not befall Benjamin. At the same time it highlights the connection between Rachel, Joseph, and Benjamin, each of whom is lost, or almost lost, to the family and each of whom ultimately must be reclaimed.

68. See Alter (1981:172), Ackerman (1982:92).

69. The contrast between chapter 37, in which the brothers do not identify with Joseph and in which sacrifice comes too late to save Joseph, and this episode, in which are the beginnings of identification between brothers and in which there is a mediating sacrifice, is reinforced by the "eating of bread" which occurs in each episode. In 37:24-25 the brothers eat bread together while Joseph is alone in a waterless pit; in 43:31-32, Joseph and his brothers all eat bread, though Joseph still does not eat together with his brothers.

70. Ackerman (1982:90) points out that, earlier, Joseph spoke harshly to his brothers (42:30), much as they could not speak to him peaceably (*leshalom*) when he lived among them (37:4). Now, when Jacob sends the brothers to Joseph with Benjamin and with the gift (*minha*), the brothers are able to speak to one another in peace.

71. See Alter (1981:173). Sternberg (1985:304) notes the similarity between the brothers' condemnation of the thief and Jacob's in 31:32. Bereshit Rabbah 92:8 links the two narratives by having the brothers, when the cup is found in Benjamin's sack, exclaim "thief son of a thief!" Note, too, that both Joseph (44:5) and Laban (30:27) are said to practice divination. Joseph's "stolen" cup is used for divination, and so Benjamin's alleged theft closely resembles Rachel's theft of the *teraphim*. The roles of Benjamin, the brothers, and Joseph, in this story, parallel those of Rachel, Jacob, and Laban, in the earlier episode, and thus this episode presents an opportunity for the brothers to reverse, through their behavior toward Benjamin, not only their earlier treatment of Joseph but also the family's treatment of Rachel.

72. Joseph's words echo conversations between the patriarchs and Laban and Abimelek. Compare his accusation, "What is this deed which you have done?" (44:15), with Jacob's quarrels with Laban (29:25-26; 31:26) and with Abraham's and Isaac's quarrels with Abimelek (20:9; 26:10).

73. Sternberg (1985:306) notes that Joseph's suggestion that the individual alone, rather than the group, is responsible for his misdeed is the ultimate test of the brothers.

74. Sternberg (1985:307-308) notes that this speech, like so much of the brothers' conversation, "reveals even more [to Joseph] than the speaker intended."

75. The word *stm*, "hate," and *nhm*, "comfort," appear both in the context of Esau's plan to kill Jacob (27:41-42) and in this episode (50:15, 21).

76. See Ackerman (1982:109) for a discussion of the blind Jacob's vision.

77. See Jacob (1974:326). The blessing is introduced in the Massoretic text with the words "He blessed Joseph." Speiser (1982:357) finds these words "obviously in disorder" and adopts the Septuagint reading, "He blessed them [Joseph's sons]."

David Silber offers an explanation of the detailed description of the placement of Menasheh and Ephraim which supports the idea that, through Jacob's blessing of his grandsons, he reclaims Joseph, the father of these children, as his son. The narrative explains that Joseph places Ephraim at his own right, which is Jacob's left, and places Menasheh at his own left, which is Jacob's right (48:13). Rather than switching the boys, Jacob switches his hands (48:14). The sons' placement with respect to Joseph would seem to be irrelevant, but Silber points out that, by leaving the boys where they are, Jacob is defining them with respect to their father. While Joseph does not understand that Ephraim must come before Menasheh, Jacob demonstrates that, in fact, Ephraim is and ought be at his father's right side, and Menasheh must remain at his left. Thus, though it is Jacob who blesses them, the children are in a stance which suggests that they are being blessed by Joseph. And so, by blessing Menasheh and Ephraim, Jacob is blessing Joseph as the father of these blessed children.

The word used to describe Jacob's switching of his hands (*sikel*; 48:14) also emphasizes, according to Silber, the idea that Joseph becomes his father's son when his own sons receive Jacob's blessing. This puzzling word has the same consonants as the word *shkl*, to be bereaved of children. Jacob uses this word earlier, when he agrees to send Benjamin to Egypt in order to redeem his brothers: "And may God Almighty give you mercy before the man that he may send to you your other brother and Benjamin; and I, if I am bereaved, I am bereaved [*ka'asher shakolti shakalti*]" (43:14). Jacob does not lose Benjamin and, in fact, he regains both Simeon and the "other brother" whom he thought was certainly lost, Joseph. At the moment when Joseph truly is restored to him, when Jacob blesses Joseph's sons, the narrative signals the reversal of Jacob's expected bereavement by using the word *sikel*; reversing his hands to bless Menasheh and Ephraim, Jacob gains two sons, rather than losing two sons as feared, and also gains the son of whom he was bereaved long ago.

78. Eisen (1986:10) notes that this field and the field in which Abraham buries Sarah are the only two purchases of land in Genesis. Jacob (1974:328), identifying this field with the portion which Jacob gives to Joseph at the end of his life (48:22) and noting that Joseph, eventually, is buried in Shechem, suggests that Jacob is giving his son a burial place. Jacob is indicating to Joseph that, just as Jacob demands to be buried in the field purchased by Abraham, Joseph too, when God redeems the nation of Israel, must be buried in the land of Canaan, in the field purchased by Jacob.

79. Significantly, the only two laws which are mentioned in Genesis are circumcision (17:9-14) and the prohibition against eating the *gid hanashe* (32:33). It is at the circumcision of Abraham and the wounding of Jacob that the narrative of the patriarchs intersects with the history of the nation, and it is at these two moments that the narrative offers a glimpse of the future practices of the nation.

80. Abraham, of course, is commanded both to be circumcised and to circumcise his sons. The commandment to circumcise the son appears as well in the book of Leviticus: "When a woman conceives and bears a male, she shall be impure seven days . . . . And on the eighth day the flesh of his foreskin shall be circumcised" (12:2-3). Another ritual law in Leviticus is stated in similar terms: "When a bull or sheep or goat is born, it shall be beneath its mother for seven days, and from the eighth day on it shall be accepted as a sacrifice . . ." (22:27). A comparison of these two laws suggests that circumcision is a sacrificial act and that, like the sacrifice of a young animal, it occurs at the moment when the infant ceases to be linked to his mother. If we can assume that circumcision has these same connotations in Genesis, it is particularly significant that Isaac is the first child to be circumcised at eight days of age (21:4). The mother at first defines her son's relationship to her husband; by circumcising his son, the father then acknowledges his paternity. And, of course, as many scholars have noted, circumcision is infanticide-in-miniature, a ritualized, harmless form of Abraham's near-sacrifice of Isaac, at which Abraham confirms that Isaac is the son who will succeed him. In a strange episode in the book of Exodus, Moses' wife Zipora circumcises their son, since Moses, apparently, has not done it himself (4:24-26). The account has a definite sacrificial connotation, and Moses' negligence is especially interesting since Moses seems never to become a true father to his sons; indeed, he is not succeeded by his son.

The idea that circumcision marks the beginning of the father's relationship to his son, and the end of the son's exclusive relationship to his mother, is important for an understanding of midrashic traditions about what led up to the binding of Isaac, the episode during which Abraham finally and conclusively claims Isaac as his chosen son. The need for Abraham and Isaac to prove themselves is linked frequently in midrashic tradition either to a dispute between Isaac and Ishmael about whose circumcision was more meritorious or to events surrounding Isaac's weaning party. See Bereshit Rabbah 55:4 and the parallels noted in the commentary (1965:587). Weaning, of course, has significance parallel to what I am arguing is one of the significances of circumcision—the son, at that moment, no longer is dependant on the mother; he can now become his father's son. The son assumes his cultural role at the moment he becomes his father's successor; thus, in this narrative, dedication to God and filiation with the father occur simultaneously through the act of sacrifice. Questions about the dedication of Abraham or Isaac which are raised concerning the circumcision or weaning of Isaac can be resolved through the test of the binding of Isaac, when Abraham proves his and his son's devotion to God and also proves that Isaac is his son.

In the biblical narrative, Ishmael's laughter is mentioned immediately after Isaac's weaning party, and in response Sarah insists that Ishmael not share in Isaac's inheritance (21:8-10). By reading into Ishmael's exchange with Isaac a discussion about circumcision and by seeing this discussion as the prelude to the binding of Isaac, the midrash is relating the ideas of weaning and circumcision and suggesting that these events raise the question that is answered conclusively at the binding of Isaac—who is Abraham's true son?

81. Speiser (1982:178), noting that this oath entails placing the hand on the genitals, suggests that the act may imply the threat of infertility to the one who may fail to carry out his oath. Freedman (1976:3-4), citing the Babylonian practice of taking an oath on a divine symbol, posits that the biblical oath required the one swearing to hold a ritual object; hence Abraham and Jacob require "the circumcised membrum . . . [to be] held in hand."

82. Placing a child on one's knees is, of course, a demonstration of parenthood. Rachel, giving Bilhah to Jacob, hopes that the maidservant "will give birth on my knees [birkai]" (30:3). The word beraka is linked in this narrative to the word berek, with its connotation of acceptance of paternity. When Jacob blesses Joseph and his sons (vayivarek, 48:15; vayivarakem, 48:20) he becomes their father.

Later, just before Joseph asks his brothers to swear that they will bring his bones out of Egypt, we are told that Joseph's great-grandchildren "were born on the knees of Joseph" (50:23). The information is significant for a number of reasons. First, Joseph, like Jacob, has become a patriarch. In addition, as Benno Jacob (1974:343) noted, the fourth generation is that which, according to God's covenant with Abraham (15:16), will return to the land. The mention of Makhir, Menasheh's son, is particularly significant, because he pioneers the conquest of the land, dispossessing the Amorites from Gil'ad (Num 32:39). Thus, this brief notice is an appropriate introduction to the last verses of the book of Genesis, verses which hold the promise of redemption, national unity, and continuity of the patriarchal destiny.

NOTES TO CHAPTER 5
THE FAMILY IN CONTEXT

1. I use the word typology for want of a better term. By its use I mean only the modeling of later events on earlier ones; what the implications of such modeling might be is open to interpretation. For Nachmanides, "the deeds of the fathers are a sign for the children" in a very real way; like prophets who by their actions cause future events to come to pass, the patriarchs shape the future of their descendants. (In his commentary on 12:10, he describes a different kind of causal relationship: the exile of the Israelites in Egypt is a punishment for Abraham's sin in going there.) For the Passover Haggadah, I think, the typology implicit in the biblical passages cited and in the midrashim on the "wandering Aramean" passage (Deut 26:5ff.) suggests a cyclical view of history which allows the Passover *seder* celebrants to identify their experiences with their past history and to be confident that they, like the patriarchs and the nation of Israel, will be redeemed. See Fishbane (1989:350ff.) for a recent discussion of inner-biblical typologies.

2. See Buber (1982:38-39). Buber notes that "God took him [Abram] out of Ur, without Abram's realizing it, to bring him into the land." See also Jacob (1974:100) and Fishbane (1989:376); Van Seters (1975:264-5) notes the connection to the exodus from Egypt but offers a different interpretation.

3. Daube (1963) discusses this specific meaning of the term '*oni* (65-66) and the technical meaning of the term *shlh* (29-30). Cassuto (1964:334-7; 1974:14) lists more ways in which Abraham's experiences in Egypt parallel the nation's. See also Bereshit Rabbah 40:6; see Jacob (1974:90) and Fishbane (1989:375-6). I am focusing specifically on those elements which relate to the terms of the covenant. For parallels between other elements in the Abraham narrative and the later history of Jacob's family and of the nation, especially the trip to Shechem, see Cassuto (1964:304-5, 328) and Nachmanides' commentary to Genesis 12:6.

4. The situation of Lot and the Sodomites here is in some ways comparable to the situation of a people enslaved. See 14:4, where the Sodomites and their allies are indeed said to have served ('*avdu*) the enemy kings. I will discuss this relationship further below.

5. Probably '*Eyn Mishpat* (14:7), with its connotation of judgment, is related to this idea as well. This place name occurs nowhere else in the Bible; see Sarna (1989:106).

6. The word *rekush* appears a number of times in this narrative, but it is in verse 16 that the *rekush* is obtained by the freed person, as

it is within the terms of the covenant. The word return (*shuv*) also appears in this story and in the covenant; see 14:16 and 15:16.

7. The people who are judged, in this story, are the ones who must be dispossessed from the land, corresponding to the Amorites in verse 16 of the covenant, rather than the oppressing nation whom God promises to judge in verse 14 of the covenant. In a sense, the four kings are both the possessors and the oppressors, as I mentioned in note 4. Later on, in the Jacob story, the root *dyn*, "to judge," will be significant both in the escape from the oppressor and in the wresting of the land from the possessor. Perhaps in juxtaposing the sin and judgment of the oppressors of the people and of the possessors of the land, who ultimately will be the Egyptians and Canaanites respectively, the text is once more underscoring the fundamental equivalence of these two peoples.

8. The names of some of the nations conquered by the four kings recall the nations mentioned at the beginning of Deuteronomy as having previously inhabited the land; note the mention of the Horites and Zamzumim in chapter 2 and the repeated mention of the Amorites, 'Emim, and Rephaim in chapters 2 and 3. This point was called to my attention by David Silber. Cassuto and, following him, Astour have pointed out the correspondence of the national names as well as a correspondence in the routes travelled in Genesis 14 and Deuteronomy 1-3: the four kings travel in a circular route which is the reverse of the route taken by the Israelites (M.D. Cassuto 1954:328-9; Astour 1966:69-73). The 'Emim and Rephaim are mentioned as previously having possessed the land of Ammon and Moab, the descendants of Lot, which links chapter 2 of Deuteronomy to chapter 14 of Genesis. Of course it is Kedarlaomer and his allies, not Abraham or Lot, who conquer these peoples but, as Cassuto has claimed and as we will discuss later, in conquering the four kings, Abraham conquers as well the nations whom they have conquered (U. Cassuto 1964:215-216; M.D. Cassuto 1954:329; Astour 1966:73-74).

9. M.D. Cassuto (1954:330); Buber (1982:38).

10. The first of these verses (Exod 2:24) is followed by the verbs *vayar'* ("he saw") and *vayeda'* ("he knew") two words linked to covenantal fulfillment—see the discussion of "seeing" as a covenantal response in Chapter Three and compare the occurrence of "knowing" in the introduction to the covenant between the pieces (Gen 15:8, 13). The second of these verses (Exod 6:5) follows God's statement that he has already fulfilled his covenant with the patriarchs by giving them the land of Canaan. Note that here too the verbs "see" and "know" are used, but the implication is that God has only *begun* to reveal himself to and fulfill his covenant with Abraham, Isaac, and Jacob; the true revelation and fulfillment will take place in the experience of the nation. Cassuto (1974:29-30) notes the covenantal connotations of the words *vayizkor*, *vayishma'*, and *vayar'* in Genesis and Exodus.

11. This is especially clear in Exod 2:23: the Israelites sigh and cry out because of the "labor" (*'avoda*), and their cry caused by the enslavement goes up to God—God, that is, takes notice of their pain caused by the *'avoda*, but there is no suggestion here that the Israelites actually cry out to God. Compare Deut 26:7, in which, after the covenantal terms for sojourning, affliction, and enslavement appear (26:5-6), the Israelites are said to have cried out to God. Note that the Passover Haggadah, in its extended midrash on the "wandering Aramean" passage, juxtaposes this verse with Exod 2:23-24.

12. Cassuto (1974:12) notes the sevenfold mention of *'vd* before the end of chapter 2. The root appears seven times again in chapter 5. Strikingly it does not appear at all in between these chapters; it is noticeably absent from God's speech to Moses in chapters 3 and 4. God will not utter the word *'vd* until he introduces to Moses the idea of covenant in chapter 6 (I owe this explanation of the absence of the word in God's speech until this point and its presence in chapter 6 to David Silber). At that point God presents his remembering of the covenant as a response to the cry caused by the covenantal *'avoda*.

13. Cassuto throughout his works notes the sevenfold repetition of important words. Seven appears as a covenantal number in a number of contexts, including the Sabbath, the renewal of the covenant of Sinai every seven years (Deut 31:10), and Abraham's gift of seven ewes to Abimelek at Be'er *Sheva*. Note the occurrences of the number in the story of King Yoash, in whose day a covenant is made between God, the king and the people (II Kings 11:4, 17): Yehosheva protects him (11:2); the covenant is made in the seventh year (11:4); Yoash is seven years old when his reign begins, corresponding to the seventh year of Yehu's rule (12:1-2); his mother is from Be'er *Sheva*.

14. Fokkelman notes the sevenfold mention of *'vd* in this part of the Jacob narrative and suggests that the patriarch endures the later experience of the nation (1975:130).

15. Dinah's name is the only one for which the text offers no etymology, and her birth is in no way explicitly connected to its narrative context. In a way, her birth and naming stand outside the main narrative, informing us how to read that narrative in a manner that transcends the surface plot.

16. For this and other parallels between the story of Jacob and the enslavement in Egypt, see Daube (1963:62-72). Daube notes that both Jacob and the Israelites begin as welcome guests and only later become subjugated. Daube (29, 64) and Sarna (1989:211) discuss the special meaning of *shalheni* in the Jacob story.

17. In Laban's house, in fact, everyone is treated as property to be traded: Rachel and Leah are Jacob's wages (*skr*; 29:15) and Jacob is rented (*skr*; 30:16) by Leah from Rachel. Compare 30:28 and 31:7-8, where *skr* is used to refer presumably to wages paid in livestock, but in the context of the word *nqvh* ("designate"; the same consonants

can read "female") and of the idea of trickery and switching would seem to allude to women as wages again. The confusion between person and property is hinted at by the names of Laban's two daughters, both words for livestock, and of the parallel treatment by the newcomer Jacob of Laban's *Rachel*, his "ewe," and Laban's sheep: Jacob sees "Rachel the daughter of Laban his mother's brother and the sheep of Laban his mother's brother," he gives the sheep water (*vayashq*) and he gives Rachel a kiss (*vayishaq*; 29:10-11).

Of course, the bulk of the story of Jacob in Laban's house is concerned with his wives and livestock bearing children for Jacob. The absurdity is nowhere more apparent than when Jacob calls Rachel and Leah to come to his flocks in the field (31:4). Here Jacob tells them of a dream he claims to have had, paralleling his dream in Beth El. But now, instead of angels ascending and descending (28:12), he-goats are ascending onto his flock to impregnate them (31:10). And instead of God promising Jacob children who will inherit the land of his fathers (28:13-14), now an angel calls Jacob's attention to the fecundity of his flock (31:12). This last verse begins with the words "lift up your eyes and see," a phrase used in 13:14 to refer to God's grant of land to Abraham "north, south, east, and west." In 28:14, Jacob's seed is to spread in these four directions. But now the concern is neither with land nor with children, the elements of the promise, but with livestock.

The equivalence of people and property is surely an indication of how antithetical membership in Laban's family is to a consciousness of promise, and of how desperately Jacob needs to break away from this family before he becomes fully a part of it. But, to my mind, it is also the clearest demonstration that Jacob, and indeed his wives as well, are slaves in Padam Aram—they are no more than human property, both in the eyes of Laban and in each other's eyes.

18. Daube (1963:68, 70) notes the verb *ntsl* used in reference to the gaining of wealth by a slave from his master both here (31:9, 16) and in the exodus story (Exod 12:36).

19. This corresponds to the idea discussed above that Rachel and Leah are, like Jacob, treated as property in the house of Laban.

20. The occurrences of this combination are discussed above, in Chapter Three, in the context of Hagar, whose *'oni* is merely "heard," as she rejects the offer to participate in the experience of covenant.

21. The association of Dan with the covenant may explain why Jacob makes reference to God's salvation as the end of his blessing of Dan (49:18). I am indebted to David Silber for this point.

22. More work needs to be done on the names of Jacob's children and their relationships to the narrative. Noteworthy is the fact that the names of both of Rachel's surrogate children reflect the struggle between the sisters, paralleling Jacob's struggles with his family and especially his encounter at Yabok (compare Naphtali's etymology at 30:8 with Israel's at 32:28), while the names of Leah's surrogate

children reflect Leah's contentment (although Gad's etymology is ambiguous). See Fokkelman (1975:135, 140; 1987:44) for the parallel struggles and the significance of Naphtali's name. We noted above that Rachel, through her theft of the idols, demonstrates her tie to Laban's house and to that part of Jacob which he must leave behind. Perhaps her competition with her sister ought to be seen as another reason that Rachel must be left behind as Jacob is transformed. When Jacob meets Esau on the way back, he is more Leah-like than Rachel-like; he is happy with his lot and is content to let Esau have his own share. Earlier, of course, Jacob's behavior toward Esau was Rachel-like, both because of the theft and because of the attempt to gain ascendancy over the sibling.

Dinah's birth marks the third occurrence of the root *dyn* ("to judge") in this story; the evocation of God's judgment is highlighted at this point. Dinah is the seventh child born to Rachel's competitor, a point underscored by Leah's repetition of the fact that she has borne six sons (30:19-20), and so her birth is the moment at which Rachel's suffering becomes sevenfold. And Joseph, whose birth expresses God's response to the suffering and to the covenant, is the seventh son born to Jacob's main wives, Rachel and Leah. The connection between the birth of Dinah and the birth of Joseph is made by the midrash, versions of which appear in numerous sources, that Leah was pregnant with a son but the matriarchs begged God to change him into a daughter so that Rachel might bear a son instead. See Bereshit Rabbah 72:6 and the parallels cited there (1965:844-845). Other midrashim identify Joseph's wife, Asnat, as the daughter of Dinah through Shechem. And, as noted earlier, the family's relationships to Dinah and to Joseph are contrasted by the biblical narrative with respect to Shechem. This contrast is underscored by a midrash in which Joseph subtly suggests to his brothers that they ought to have behaved toward him as they did toward Dinah; see Bereshit Rabbah 91:6.

23. David Silber pointed out to me that at the seventh mention of the word in each series in the Jacob story the text offers a clue: the fourteenth occurrence of the word is followed by the word "fourteen" (31:41), while the seventh occurrence is linked to the word "seven" (29:30).

Oddly, while all seven occurrences in the first series in both Genesis and Exodus refer to Jacob/Israel, one occurrence in each of the second series refers to other *'avadim* (Gen 30:43 and Exod 5:21). I do not know whether or how this is significant.

24. The combination of "see" and *'oni* occurs twice in the Jacob narrative and twice in the exodus story (Exod 3:7 and 4:31).

25. Daube (1963:67) notes that Jacob's affliction parallels the nation's experience in the book of Exodus.

In Exodus, God responds to the covenant only after all three words appear. David Silber has pointed out that sojourning appears in the naming of Moses' son, *Gershom* (Exod 2:22; cp. *ger*, "sojourner"). In both stories, the word for sojourning is used by the sufferer himself, not by the narrator. Silber suggests that sojourning, more than enslavement and affliction, is a subjective experience and one that can only be articulated once the sojourner has left the "land which is not his." While he remains in exile he feels to some degree at home there; only when he leaves does he realize that was not his place.

26. Fokkelman describes Jacob as "the master-interpreter of his own history . . . a story of deliverance by God" (1975:192).

27. As noted above, his first stop is Shechem, which parallels Abraham's arrival in Canaan as well as the nation's. In 35:27 Jacob finally returns to Hebron, in a sense coming (*vayavo'*) to his fathers in peace; the verse makes explicit reference to Hebron as the place of Abraham and Isaac. This verse immediately follows the listing of Jacob's twelve sons (35:23-26). It is the fourth generation which takes possession of the land.

28. Ham with Noah, Pharaoh with Sarah, the Sodomites with the visitors, and eventually the wife of Potiphar with Joseph all commit or attempt to commit such an offense. Canaan and Egypt are both sons of Ham; a third brother is Put, which David Silber has suggested should be seen as linked with Potiphar and his wife. See Sarna (1989:64) for a catalogue of the sexual crimes of Ham; see Cassuto (1964:168) for a comparison of the Sodomites' sin with Ham's offence. Sexual mistreatment is frequently connected to the word *'oni*, as in our verse.

29. The word is used ironically in 34:21; in 33:18 it is both ironic and not, for Jacob physically is not *shalem*, but he has rid himself of the trickery (*mirma*; cf. 27:35) which now characterizes his sons (34:13).

30. For a discussion of the many problems presented by the verse and especially for the association of the word *shekem* with the city of Shechem, see Sarna (1989:330). The word *laqahti* can be translated "I took" or "I shall take." Here it means both at once; what happened in the past anticipates what will happen in the future. Bereshit Rabbah 80:10, 12 connects this verse with the conquest of Shechem by Jacob's sons and suggests that Jacob was opposed to his sons' actions because it was not yet time for the covenantal promise of conquest to be fulfilled, but that, once his sons had anticipated the fulfillment, Jacob felt compelled to defend them with his "sword and bow."

31. Until this point the blessing has been given to all creation; thus, God blesses Noah's family, his new creation, as he blessed his first creation—compare 9:1 with 1:28. But now the blessing will be focused in on the chosen line.

32. For our purposes, it makes no difference what was the precise nature of Ham's crime. It is simply the primordial "seeing of nakedness," a term used later for assorted sexual offenses. Ham's brothers

refuse to "see their father's nakedness"; in fact, they "cover their father's nakedness," in a sense doing the opposite of what Ham had done (9:22-23). See Sarna (1989:66).

33. The emergence after Babel of a linear genealogy of Shem which culminates with Abraham may be reinforced by a play on the word *shem*, "name." The tower-builders want to make for themselves a *shem* (11:4), but their plan is frustrated and their story gives way to the ascendancy of *Shem* (11:10 ff.). God promises Shem's chosen descendant, Abram, that he will make his *shem* great (12:2). This last occurrence of the word, pointed out to me by David Silber, underscores the contrast between Abraham and the tower-builders: the latter see themselves as without limit, building a tower which reaches to heaven and creating a name for themselves, while Abraham will get a great name through subordinating himself to the will of God. See Fishbane (1979:37-39) for a discussion of the plays on the word *shem* in this narrative. For Abraham as the one who stands up against the people who build the Tower of Babel, see the next note.

34. Nimrod is associated with the Tower of Babel in a number of early sources. See especially Pseudo-Philo, Josephus, and numerous rabbinic sources listed in Ginzburg (1925:201). Nimrod is seen midrashically as epitomizing Ham, in a sense as Anti-Shem. See below on his midrashic identification with Amraphel, who must be conquered by Abraham. The midrashim portraying Nimrod as Abraham's arch-enemy are many and varied. See, for some examples, Vermes (1961:67-90). Pseudo-Philo makes much of Abraham's refusal to participate in the building of the Tower of Babel.

35. Arnold M. Eisen sees the tower-builders as "on the way back from the wrong direction," translating *miqedem* as "from the east," hence westward (1986:7). But *miqedem* places the traveller in the east; see Gen 13:11, where Lot travels *miqedem* to go to Sodom, which is to the east. See Cassuto (1964:240) and Sarna (1989:81); while translating differently, both situate the tower-builders in the east. Fishbane (1979:36) notes that the term *qedem* here links the tower-builders to Adam and Eve and to Cain.

36. In Pseudo-Philo, Yoktan is the leader of those who build the Tower of Babel; indeed, it is he, rather than Nimrod, who casts Abraham into the furnace for refusing to participate in the construction.

Sarna (1989:79) questions whether the division referred to in connection with Peleg's name is the dispersement of peoples at Babel. The interruption of the genealogy by the Babel story at the generation of Peleg and Yoktan as well as the occurrence of *qedem* in the context of both the Babel story and Yoktan's family suggests that indeed the division does refer to Babel. According to the interpretation which I am offering, the division consequent to Babel is not only the scattering of humankind referred to in that story but also the further subdivision of humanity in God's plan.

37. One might expect, given the facts that the genealogy branches out again after Terah (11:26), that Terah's family is introduced with another *toledot* (11:27), and that what follows is a brief account of the doings of Terah's whole family (11:28-31), that Terah should be considered the beginning of this new history. In fact, in the Book of Jubilees, as well as in the Septuagint, there is one extra generation within Shem's genealogy, placing Terah in the tenth generation from Shem and, I think, suggesting that Terah is a significant figure in this new history. See Cassuto (1964:250-251). This corresponds to Jubilees' portrait of Terah as basically a good person and a monotheist who deals with idols purely out of cowardice; he is metaphorically, as the Bible tells us he is literally, "on the way" to the land of Canaan (11:31), but he cannot quite make it. (Compare Jubilees' casting of the dialogue between Terah and Abram in chapter 12 in language based on biblical conversations between patriarchs and their sons. Jubilees, in general, is explicitly concerned with the transmission of knowledge across the generations; this is especially striking within the primeval history as well as in the framing of the book as the transmission of ancient knowledge to Moses.) Rabbinic midrash tends to take a dimmer view of Terah and to portray Abraham as *sui generis*. I think the biblical text presents Terah as an in-between figure, an appropriate conduit for the legacy of Shem, but hardly the father of the new history about to unfold.

It is interesting to note in this context, as Cassuto has pointed out (1964:199, 219-221), that a number of Terah's descendants recall descendants of Noah from the lines that were not chosen. This recurrence of names, I think, may serve the same function here as does the repetition of names from Cain's genealogy in Seth's genealogy, discussed above. That repetition suggested that Seth is a new beginning, a doing over of the humankind that did not work. This repetition supports the idea that the second, linear genealogy of Shem is a new beginning, a doing over of the humanity listed in the branched genealogy of chapter 10, which also did not work. The repeated names are Uz and Aram, from the family of Nahor (22:21), and Yokshan, Sheva, and Dedan from the family of Abraham through Keturah (25:2-3)—compare 10:7, 23-25, 28.

Cassuto (1929:36) notes as well that the seventy descendants of Jacob parallel the seventy nations listed in the genealogy of chapter 10; thus Jacob, in becoming a nation, in a sense begins world history anew. Abraham too is a "father of many nations" (17:5); if my count of Esau's family is correct, Abraham too has 70 descendants: Ishmael {1}, Isaac {1}, the sons of Keturah {16}; the sons of Ishmael {12}, Esau {1}, Jacob {1}; the sons (36:10-14) and *'aluphim* (36:40-43) of Esau {15+11}, the sons of Jacob {12}. Both patriarchs whose lives prefigure the nation's history become, as well, a new world, replacing —or redeeming—the corrupted world of the primeval history.

38. Buber (1982:25-29) discusses the processes of selection and the emergence of Abraham as carrying forth the mission of creation. See also Gros Louis (1982a:37-52). Numerous midrashim portray Abraham as a new creation; see, for example, Bereshit Rabbah 12:9, which links Abraham with the *toledot* of heaven and earth (2:4). A striking exposition of the ongoing process of selection and the focusing in of the potential for perfection inherent in creation can be found in the liturgical poem for the Day of Atonement, *'Amits Koah*.

39. See, most recently, Sarna (1989:102). The notable exception is Cassuto, on whose work much of the following analysis depends, although I depart from his conclusions in some important ways. See his *Commentary on Genesis* (1964:168-70) for his linking of this chapter to the blessing and curse of Noah's sons. Cassuto did not live to write his commentary on Genesis 14, and one can only imagine how much more Cassuto might have illuminated this episode.

40. See Cassuto (1964:169) for the connection between Goyim and Yapheth. While the word *goyehem* appears in the genealogy of each of the brothers, the form *goyim* receives additional mention in Yapheth's genealogy, suggesting that it refers to a specific people or peoples (10:5). Cassuto sees the alliance between the king of Goyim and the king of Elam as fulfilling the words "and he shall dwell in the tents of Shem." He does not account for the presence of the king of Shinar within Kedarlaomer's confederacy, interpreting the episode more simply as Shem and Yapheth subordinating Ham. The land of Shinar is associated with Nimrod, the son of Ham's first son, and thus occupies a place in Ham's family parallel to that of Elam in Shem's family. Genesis Apocryphon, Onkelos, and Neofiti all have Babel here instead of Shinar, an interchangeable pair as we saw above. See Vermes (1961:105, 118). Perhaps the alliance of Shem and Yapheth with Shinar/Babel, paralleling the assimilation of all of humankind to Shinar/Babel at the beginning of chapter 11, paves the way for the displacement of all three families by the chosen line of Shem. The listing first of Shinar in 14:1, even though Elam seems to be at the head of the confederacy, may function to call attention to this parallel. Much early biblical interpretation, in fact, identifies Amraphel King of Shinar with Nimrod; see Bereshit Rabbah 41:4 and the parallels listed in Ginsburg (1925:223). And, as noted above, the idea of Nimrod's involvement in the Babel episode is commonplace as well.

41. Cassuto (1964:215-216).

42. This is the significance of Ham and Shem being represented here by their first-named sons; victory over the leader of the family signifies victory over the entire family.

43. Sarna (1989:110) describes this blessing as "an acknowledgment or affirmation of a reality exemplified by the victory." That

Abraham here manifests the blessing of Shem may account for the strange appearance of the term *ha'ivri* (14:13), used in this episode but nowhere else in the Abraham narrative. If we are to understand this term as referring to Eber, we can see why this description of Abraham may be relevant here.

44. The language of the following verse, in which God himself is blessed, is similar to Noah's blessing of Shem (14:20; 9:26). That Melchizedek blesses Abraham as Abraham manifests the blessing of Shem is crucial for an understanding of early biblical interpretations which identify Melchizedek with Shem.

45. Isaac, Abraham's son, does transmit two different blessings to Jacob, one of which was to have gone to Esau. This blessing, as noted above, is not the blessing of Abraham; it is, rather, a blessing which evokes creation. Jacob, then, receives the patriarchal blessing and also the blessing of creation.

Intriguing in this context are the midrashim which link Esau to Nimrod (both are hunters—25:27; 10:9) and see Esau's garments as having belonged to Nimrod, who got them from Ham, who took them illegitimately from Noah. They were the garments which God had made for Adam, and which Adam took with him when he left the Garden of Eden. It is these garments which Rebecca took from Esau and in which she clad Jacob, so that he might receive the blessing from his father. See Bereshit Rabbah 63:13 and 65:16 and the parallels to each cited in the commentary (1965:697, 727-728). According to these midrashim, the promise of creation was misappropriated by Ham and Nimrod and then by Esau, his spiritual descendant. Only in Jacob's time is that original promise redeemed through Shem's descendant.

This idea of the misappropriation or perversion of creation and its subsequent redemption and fulfillment goes a long way toward explaining a troubling aspect of the *qedma* motif: why is it *qedem*, the location of Eden, that signifies the place of banishment, the place of people who are excluded from the promise? Indeed, when *qedem* is mentioned in the context of Sodom and Egypt, the most sinful places, it is linked to the "garden of God" (13:11-12). This is troubling because it in no way seems that Eden has been redefined as a place of evil. But perhaps, as these midrashim suggest, we are to see Eden, symbolic of the possibility of perfection within creation, as having fallen into evil hands, as indeed the whole world continually falls to doing evil. If the mission of Shem's descendants is to bring blessing to the world, then they, symbolically, reappropriate Eden and restore its promise. Thus, when Isaac is about to give the blessing of creation to the son whom he thinks is Esau, he gives it in response to smelling Esau's special garments and noticing that they smell "like the smell of a field which was blessed by God" (27:27), a description similar to that of Sodom mentioned above. The blessing evoked by these Eden-like clothes is received by Jacob, and henceforth it shall be up to him and his descendants to recreate Eden.

Jacob, as I noted in Chapter Four, goes *qedma* when he leaves his father's house, and at that point in the narrative there surely is the suggestion that he is in danger of being lost to his family. But, of course, he ultimately is not lost. Jacob is the first who goes *qedma* and returns, and perhaps this is because *qedem* has now been redefined. Can it be that this accounts for the impossible phrase "and he went to land" in 36:6? Esau is, finally, the brother who leaves. Like Ishmael, he cannot actually go *qedma*, because his land is not eastward. But the *toledot* of Ishmael do include the word *qedma* as the name of one of Ishmael's sons, while the word is entirely absent from the *toledot* of Esau. Perhaps this is because exiled brothers no longer go *qedma* once Jacob receives the blessing of creation, goes *qedma*, and returns. When Esau leaves, we expect to hear "to the land of *qedem*" (*'el 'erets qedem*) but instead hear only "to land" (*'el 'erets*). *Qedem* now belongs to Jacob's family; there are similarities between Eden and the land of Canaan, which Israel will inhabit, as well as the Tabernacle, which will rest in Israel's midst (Cassuto 1974:335, 375-376; Fishbane 1989:370).

46. There are many verbal links between these two chapters, besides the ones mentioned above. The name Damascus appears in both (14:15; 15:2). Abraham eschews the property of Sodom (14:16-24), is assured of reward by God (15:1), and requests a son rather than any other sort of reward (15:2)—the word for reward, *skr*, is the word for property, *rksh*, spelled backward. The word "righteousness" appears in the name Melchizedeq (14:18) as well as in 15:6. David Silber pointed out this last connection to me. See Buber (1982:38) for Melchizedek's description of God as "creator of heaven and earth" (14:19) as a link between the similes of 13:16 and 15:5.

47. Astour, analyzing chapter 14 from the perspective of ancient Babylonian texts, arrives at a similar evaluation of the significance of this narrative. He identifies the four kings as monarchs of four powerful nations that represent the four quadrants of the earth; these, in the Babylonian conception, have their counterpart in heaven. Astour concludes: "Thus, the symbolism of Genesis 14 is not limited to Palestine. Through the introduction of the Kings of the four world quadrants, the author widens his symbolism to the universal, even cosmic dimensions" (1966:76-81). I do not mean to suggest that Astour's interpretation of this narrative is the same as mine, but simply that his comparative analysis of the four kings and an internal analysis based on Noah's genealogy both result in a multi-level reading of chapter 14.

48. See Steinberg (1989:47-48) for a discussion of the functions of the genealogical framework of Genesis, one of which is the linking of the primeval history and the history of Israel.

49. Fishbane (1989:357) points out that, with what he terms "cosmological-historical" typologies, "historical redemption becomes a species of world restoration" and unique events have a "metahistorical dimension."

50. Fishbane (1989:378), discussing "biographical" typologies, notes that, according to Hosea 12, Jacob's "behavior has to some degree *determined* the behavior of his descendants"; he sees this as a retrospective interpretation of the Genesis narrative.

51. Eisen (1986:33) discusses "home" and "homelessness" as other than "possession of" or "displacement from" the land. Both exile and return have meanings other than their literal meanings in biblical texts as well as throughout Jewish history, and these conceptions are the subject of Eisen's book. Deuteronomy suggests that exile is an experience which can allow the nation to return to God; this idea is articulated explicitly and frequently in the prophetic writings. See, for example, Hosea 2, where removal of the physical bounty of the land and return to wilderness, both a place and a state of being (2:16, 5), allow a renewal of the relationship between God and Israel.

BIBLIOGRAPHY

Ackerman, James S. 1982. "Joseph, Judah, and Jacob." Pp. 85-113 in *Literary Interpretations of Biblical Narratives II*. Ed. Kenneth R. R. Gros Louis and James S. Ackerman. Nashville: Abingdon.

Alter, Robert. 1981. *The Art of Biblical Narrative*. New York: Basic Books.

Amit, Yairah. 1989. "The Multi-Purpose 'Leading Word' and the Problems of its Usage." *Prooftexts* 9:99-114.

Andriolo, Karin R. 1973. "A Structural Analysis of Genealogy and Worldview in the Old Testament." *American Anthropologist* 75:1657-69.

Bakan, David. 1979. *And They Took Themselves Wives: The Emergence of Patriarchy in Western Civilization*. New York: Harper and Row.

Bar-Efrat, Shimon. 1989. *Narrative Art in the Bible*. Trans. Dorothea Shefer-Vanson. Sheffield: Almond Press.

Benveniste, Émile. 1973. *Indo-European Language and Society*. Trans. Elizabeth Palmer. Coral Gables: University of Miami Press.

Berlin, Adele. 1983. *Poetics and Interpretation of Bibilical Narrative*. Sheffield: Almond Press.

Buber, Martin. 1986. "Abraham the Seer." Pp. 22-43 in *On the Bible: Eighteen Studies*. Ed. Nahum N. Glatzer. New York: Schocken Books.

Carmichael, Calum M. 1977. "A Ceremonial Crux: Removing a Man's Sandal as a Female Gesture of Contempt." *Journal of Biblical Literature* 96:321-336.

Cassuto, Umberto. 1929. "The Story of Judah and Tamar." Pp. 29-40 in *Biblical and Oriental Studies I (1973)*. Trans. Israel Abrahams. Jerusalem: Magnes Press.

―― 1961. *Documentary Hypothesis*. Trans. Israel Abrahams. Jerusalem: Magnes Press.

―― 1964. *A Commentary on the Book of Genesis: From Noah to Abraham*. Trans. Israel Abrahams.Jerusalem: Magnes Press.

―― 1974. *A Commentary on the Book of Exodus*. Trans. Israel Abrahams. Jerusalem: Magnes Press.

―― 1978. *A Commentary on the Book of Genesis: From Adam to Noah*. Trans. Israel Abrahams.Jerusalem: Magnes Press.

Childs, Brevard S. 1974. *The Book of Exodus: A Critical, Theological Commentary*. Philadelphia: Westminster Press.

Craig, Daniel. 1979. "Immortality through Kinship: The Vertical Transmission of Substance and Symbolic Estate." *American Anthropologist* 81:94-96.

Daube, David. 1963. *The Exodus Pattern in the Bible.* London: Faber
and Faber.

Devereux, George. 1953. "Why Oedipus Killed Laius: A Note on the
Complementary Oedipus Complex." *International Journal of
Psychoanalysis* 34:132-141.

Eisen, Arnold M. 1986. *Galut: Modern Jewish Reflection on Homelessness and Homecoming.* Bloomington, Indiana: Indiana University
Press.

Emerton, J. A. 1976. "An Examination of a Recent Structuralist Interpretation of Genesis XXXVIII." *Vetus Testamentum* 26:79-98.

Fishbane, Michael. 1979. *Text and Texture: Close Readings of Selected
Biblical Texts.* Schocken: New York.

—— 1989. *Biblical Interpretation in Ancient Israel.* Oxford: Claren-
don Press.

Fokkelman, J. P. 1975. *Narrative Art in Genesis.* Amsterdam: Van
Gorcum.

—— 1987. "Genesis." Pp. 36-55 in *The Literary Guide to the Bible.*
Ed. Robert Alter and Frank Kermode. Cambridge: Harvard
University Press.

Fox, Everett. 1983. *In the Beginning.* New York: Schocken Books

Freedman, R. David. 1976. " 'Put Your Hand Under My Thigh'—The
Patriarchal Oath." *The Biblical Archeology Review* 2:3-4.

Freud, Sigmund. 1918 (reprint 1946). *Totem and Taboo.* Trans. A. A.
Brill. New York: Random House-Vintage.

—— 1921 (reprint 1959). *Group Psychology and the Analysis of the
Ego.* Ed. and trans. James Strachey. New York: Norton.

—— 1923 (reprint 1962). *The Ego and the Id.* Trans. Joan Riviere,
ed. James Strachey. New York: Norton.

Fromm, Erich. 1957. *The Forgotten Language: An Introduction to the
Understanding of Dream, Fairy Tales, and Myths.* New York:
Grove Press.

Ginzberg, Louis. 1925. *The Legends of the Jews, V.* Philadelphia:
Jewish Publication Society.

Girard, René. 1979. *Violence and the Sacred.* Trans. Patrick Gregory.
Baltimore: Johns Hopkins University Press.

Goldin, Judah. 1977. "The Youngest Son or Where does Genesis 38
Belong." *Journal of Biblical Literature* 96:27-44.

Greenberg, Moshe. 1962. "Another Look at Rachel's Theft of the
Teraphim." *Journal of Biblical Literature* 81:239-48.

Gros Louis, Kenneth R. R. 1982a. "Genesis 3-11" Pp. 37-52 in *Literary Interpretations of Biblical Narratives, II.* Ed. Kenneth R. R.
Gros Louis and James S. Ackerman. Nashville: Abingdon.

—— 1982b. "Abraham: I" Pp. 53-70 in *Literary Interpretations of*

Biblical Narratives, II. Ed. Kenneth R. R. Gros Louis and James S. Ackerman. Nashville: Abingdon.

—— 1982c. "Abraham: II" Pp. 71-84 in Literary Interpretations of Biblical Narratives, II. Ed. Kenneth R. R. Gros Louis and James S. Ackerman. Nashville: Abingdon.

Helyer, Larry R. 1983. "The Separation of Abram and Lot: Its Significance in the Patriarchal Narratives." Journal for the Study of the Old Testament 26:77-88.

Jacob, Benno. 1974. The First Book of the Bible: Genesis. Ed. and trans. Ernest I. Jacobs and Walter Jacobs. New York: Ktav.

Jones, Ernest. 1925. "Mother-Right and the Sexual Ignorance of Savages." The International Journal of Psycho-Analysis 6, part 2:109-130.

Kaberry, Phyllis, H. A. Powell, R. M. W. Dixon, K. O. L. Burridge, Edmund Leach, and Melford Spiro. 1968. "Notes." Man 3:311-13, 651-6.

Kierkegaard, Søren. 1974. Fear and Trembling. Trans. Walter Lowrie. Princeton: Princeton University Press.

Leach, Edmund. 1969. "Virgin Birth." in Genesis as Myth and Other Essays. London: Jonathan Cape.

Leibovitz, Nehama. 1954. "Ketsad Liqro' Pereq BaTanah." In Nefesh Vashir, Iyunim 19/20: 90-204.

Lévi-Strauss, Claude. 1965. "The Structural Study of Myth." In Myth: A Symposium. Ed. Thomas A. Sebeok. Bloomington: Indiana University Press.

Malinowski, Bronislaw. 1927 (reprint 1953). Sex and Repression in Savage Society. London: Routledge and Kegan Paul.

—— 1929. The Sexual Life of Savages in North-Western Melanesia. New York: Harcourt, Brace and World.

Oden, Robert A., Jr. 1983. "Jacob as Father, Husband, and Nephew: Kinship Studies and the Patriarchal Narratives." Journal of Biblical Literature 102:189-205.

Paul, Robert. 1980. "Symbolic Interpretation in Psychoanalysis and Anthropology." Ethos 8:286-294.

Prewitt, Terry J. 1981. "Kinship Structures and the Genesis Genealogies." Journal of Near Eastern Studies 40:87-98.

Propp, Vladimir. 1983. "Oedipus in the Light of Folklore." in Oedipus: A Folklore Casebook. Ed. Lowell Edmunds and Alan Dundes. New York: Garland Press.

Rank, Otto. 1964a. "Forms of Kinship and the Individual's Role in the Family." in The Myth of the Birth of the Hero and Other Writings. Ed. Philip Freund. New York: Vintage.

—— 1964b. "The Myth of the Birth of the Hero." in The Myth of the Birth of the Hero and Other Writings. Ed. Philip Freund. New York: Vintage.

Rendsburg, Gary A. 1986. *The Redaction of Genesis.* Winona Lake: Eisenbrauns.

Rosenberg, Joel. 1986. *King and Kin: Political Allegory in the Hebrew Bible.* Bloomington: Indiana University Press.

Sarna, Nahum M. 1970. *Understanding Genesis.* New York: Schocken Books.

—— 1989. *The JPS Torah Commentary: Genesis.* Philadelphia and New York: Jewish Publication Society.

Shiloah, Meir. 1964. *"Vayomer . . . Vayomer."* Pp. 251-267 in *Sefer Korngreen.* Ed. Asher Weiser. Tel Aviv: Niv.

Speiser, A. 1982. *Genesis.* (Anchor Bible.) New York: Doubleday.

Spiro, Melford E. 1968. "Virgin Birth, Parthenogenesis and Physiological Paternity: An Essay in Cultural Interpretation." *Man* 3:242.

—— 1982. *Oedipus in the Trobriands.* Chicago: University of Chicago Press.

Steinberg, Naomi. 1989. "The Genealogical Framework of the Family Stories in Genesis." *Semeia* 46:41-50.

Sternberg, Meir. 1985. *The Poetics of Biblical Narrative.* Bloomington: Indiana University Press.

Theodor, Judah and Chanokh Albeck. 1965. *Bereshit Rabba.* Jerusalem: Wahrmann Books.

Van Seters, John. 1975. *Abraham in History and Tradition.* New Haven and London: Yale University Press.

Vermes, Geza. 1961. *Scripture and Tradition in Judaism.* Leiden: E. J. Brill.

Von Rad, Gerhard. 1972. *Genesis: A Commentary.* Philadelphia: Westminster Press.

Weiss, Meir. 1984. *The Bible From Within.* Jerusalem: Magnes Press.

Westermann, Claus. 1980. *The Promises to the Fathers.* Trans. David E. Green. Philadelphia: Fortress Press.

Wilson, Robert R. 1977. *Genealogy and History in the Biblical World.* New Haven: Yale University Press.

INDEXES

GENERAL

BIBLICAL REFERENCES